Betwixt and Between

Betwixt and Between
Explorations in an African-Caribbean Mindscape

Barry Chevannes

Ian Randle Publishers
Kingston • Miami

First published in Jamaica, 2006 by
Ian Randle Publishers
11 Cunningham Avenue
Box 686
Kingston 6
www.ianrandlepublishers.com

© Barry Chevannes

National Library of Jamaica Cataloguing in Publication Data

Chevannes, Barry
    Betwixt and between: explorations in an African-Caribbean mindscape / Barry Chevannes

    p.;   cm

    Includes index

    ISBN 976-637-233-0 (pbk)

1. Caribbean Area — Civilization — African influences 2. Acculturation – Caribbean Area 3. Caribbean Area – Culture 4. Jamaica – Social life and customs 5. Rastafari movement
I. Title

305. 89609729   dc 21

All rights reserved. No part of this publication may be reproduced, stored in a retrieval system or transmitted in any form or by any means electronic, photocopying, recording or otherwise, without the prior permission of the publisher and author.

Cover and book design by Shelly-Gail Folkes.
Printed in the United States of America.

Sabon 11/15

For Abena and Amba

Table of Contents

Acknowledgements ix
Introduction xi

PART I
THE AFRICAN PRESENCE

Chapter 1   Africa and the Caribbean:
             Reflections on an Identity 3
Chapter 2   Forward to the Past: Jamaica is Africa 31
Chapter 3   Ambiguity and the Search for Knowledge 62

PART II
THE SPIDER GOD

Chapter 4   Rastafari and the Paradox of Disorder 81
Chapter 5   Rastafari and the Critical Tradition 107
Chapter 6   Fatherhood in the African–Caribbean
             Landscape 124

PART III
THE MORAL ORDER

Chapter 7   The Evasion of Moral Responsibility:
             A View from Within 141
Chapter 8   The Values We Live By 149
Chapter 9   Cosmological Reproduction:
             Space and Identity 166

PART IV
Integration and Control

Chapter 10 Law and the African–Caribbean Family 179
Chapter 11 Criminalizing Cultural Practice:
            The Case of Ganja in Jamaica 196
Chapter 12 Those Two Jamaicas:
            The Problem of Social Integration 216

Notes 223
References 228
Index 237

Acknowledgements

The opportunity for putting together this collection of essays was provided by funding from Centre Naçional de Récherches Scientifiques (CNRS) in France through La Maison des Sciences de l'Homme d'Aquitaine (MSHA), Université de Bordeaux III, April to July 2003. I thank both for the support and hospitality, in particular Mde Anne-Marie Pasquet and other members of staff of the MSHA who made my way smooth. To Christine Chivallon of the CNRS, whose idea it was that I apply for the fellowship, and who has since become a very good friend and colleague, I owe an incalculable debt for the numerous and still on-going debates, the collegiality, and above all inclusion in her network of family and friends. Principal Kenneth Hall and Vice Chancellor Rex Nettleford were both very supportive of my leave of absence from duties as Dean of the Faculty of Social Sciences at Mona.

The Rockefeller Humanities Foundation awarded the fellowship which allowed me to research and put together the essay 'Forward to the Past' in 1993. I thank the Foundation, the Latin American Studies Department of the University of Florida, its indomitable Head at the time, Helen Safa, and other colleagues there, including Olabiyi Yai of the Centre for African Studies, and Deidre Crumley of the Department of Anthropology.

My debt to my colleagues at the University of the West Indies is incalculable for their critical remarks. Special thanks to Lorna Goodison for permission to include two poems from her collection, *Travelling Mercies*, and to Kamau Brathwaite for permission to include an excerpt from his *Rights of Passage*.

I thank the anonymous reader for the many thoughtful suggestions, Mary Morgan for her very careful proofreading, and La-Raine Carpenter of Ian Randle Publishers for her endless patience.

Finally, I acknowledge with undying gratitude the support I have received from my family in allowing me the time and space to write.

Introduction

The essays in this collection were written over the past ten years. They represent the development of a perspective formed as far back as the mid-1970s. At that time venturing for the first time among the Nyabinghi and Bobo houses of Rastafari, I was struck by clear evidence of continuities with Revivalism, a religion with a pedigree of over 200 years, and from which the Rastafari had projected themselves as having made a clean break. In spiritual empowerment through ritual singing and dance — indeed many songs were the same except for a change of key words — in certain ritual symbols, in the attitudes to health and healing, the new order that Rastafari represented had been built on the foundations of the old. In this respect the movement was very Jamaican, rooted in an outlook, an approach to reality that had been developed over the course of centuries. A contributed collection appearing in 1995 showed further similarities between Rastafari and Revival, and by comparison with Suriname religions, and raised the issue of deeper historical continuities with Africa, but at the level of worldviews.

As is now quite well known, Africa as a source of origin entered the discourse on African-Caribbean and African-American cultures mainly through the work of Melville and Frances Herskovits and their students. However they were met with a great deal of skepticism by those who failed to see continuities and instead saw cultures as rooted in the creative experiences of the Americas. Thus began what has been referred to since as the creativity versus continuity debate.

The appearance in 1976 of a stimulating and influential essay on the subject by Sidney Mintz and Richard Price, two of the most prominent Caribbeanists, failed to put an end to the debate, but the book had become such an important reference point that it was republished in 1992 under a different title. A very superficial reading would interpret the change in title from *Anthropological Approach to the Afro-American Past* to *The birth of African-American culture: an anthropological perspective*, as confirming the authors' bias towards the creativity school. But, in the new preface, Mintz denies this. Moreover, he explains, a general shift has taken place away from claims for African retentions, pure and simple, to 'the importance of focusing on *process* in the development of African-American cultures' (1992, x). Through 'process,' the African created new institutions, (here he quotes Kamau Brathwaite) 'using the available tools and memories of his traditional heritage' (p. xi).

The argument of the authors remains on the assumption that 'No group ... can transfer its way of life and the accompanying beliefs and values intact from one locale to another' (p. 1). This is so, because of the 'conditions of transfer,' and also the new physical and social environment. And as culture is 'a body of beliefs and values, socially acquired and patterned, that serve an organized group ("a society") as guides of and for behavior' (p. 8), the study of cultural transfers cannot be successfully undertaken in the abstract, without reference to the behaviour, the social relations, in which the beliefs and values are rooted. Pointing to M.G. Smith, that 'social structure is embodied in cultural process ...[and] vice versa,' adding that 'the study of African heritage [in the New World] in purely cultural terms is not adequately conceived and cannot by itself reveal the processes and conditions of acculturation' (p. 19), the authors conclude that culture therefore cannot be treated 'as a list of traits or objects or words' (p. 22). Rather, we find the authors speaking of the 'cultural content — modes of behaviour, styles of speech, beliefs and values, etiquette, cuisine, and the rest of the substance of daily conduct' (p. 32), and 'cultural materials' (p. 40) that inform social relations. The emphasis is on what they call the 'social-relational,' that is to say the institutions that were formed as 'a sort of framework in which cultural materials could be employed, standardized, and transformed into new tradition' (p. 41). Thus, whether slaves fell in love and created families, or gathered to worship, the content of their behaviour was but 'an aspect of the social relationships' (p. 41).

One of the difficulties some scholars have had with this approach may be traced, I believe, to the authors' restrictive understanding of culture, and, as a result of this understanding, the framing of their argument. Since, in their view, culture is inseparable from institutions, and since the Africans came without their institutions, ergo they came without their culture. 'What the slaves undeniably shared at the outset was their enslavement; *all- or nearly all-else* had to be *created by them*' (p. 18). By '*all- or nearly all-else*' Mintz and Price are referring to institutions, 'normative patterns of behaviour [which] could be created only on the basis of particular forms of social interaction' (p. 18).

However enslavement was not all that the slaves shared, as a careful reading of their own text shows. While not sharing normative patterns of behaviour — indeed many did not speak the same language — the slaves *did* share something more than their enslavement. Drawing on the work of Victor Turner, Mintz and Price acknowledge that 'most West and Central African religions seem to have shared certain *fundamental assumptions about the nature of specific causes, about the active role of the dead in the lives of the living, about the responsiveness of most deities to human actions, about the close relationship between social conflict and illness or misfortune*, and many others' (p. 45; *my emphasis*). However, they relegate these 'fundamental assumptions' to the unconscious level of 'cognitive orientations,' the underlying 'grammatical principles,' a term coined from Herskovits's 'grammar of culture.' These grammatical principles came into play once the new normative patterns of behaviour began to take shape, producing new cultural systems.

It is these grammatical principles I call worldview, and the following essays are devoted to an exploration of it. A worldview gives shape to a culture by informing the people's patterns of behaviour, their social relationships, their values and sensibilities. Despite the wide currency of the word in anthropology, I have yet to discover any systematic treatment of the concept. First coined by Kant, the word has come into English from German philosophy and sociology, where it had been used, according to Wolters (1989), in five ways either distinguishing it from or identifying it with philosophy. For him 'it represents a point of view on the world ...a way of looking at the cosmos.' Geertz (1957) limits worldview to the cognitive or existential relation to the world — a picture — and distinguishes it from ethos, arguing that both are expressed in the system of symbols we call religion. For Berger and Luckman (1967), worldview is a theory of ideas.

One element that everyone seems to agree on is that aspect of systematic philosophy which used to be called 'cosmology': ideas about the cosmos, its origins, its constituent parts and their interrelationships, its processes. Some authors limit worldview to cosmology, others include ethics. As is clear from my inclusion of the three essays in Part III, I tend to the latter, since, I would argue, the premises on which moral interrelations between human beings and relations between human and non-human beings are based derive ultimately from how the constituted cosmos is viewed. For example, the friendliness and kindness which many travellers to Jamaica note about the people appear on deeper inquiry to be founded upon an implicit system of mutual obligation and reciprocity. I help you in your need so that if and when I should be in need there will be someone to help me — an assumed causal relationship between human actions. Worldview includes the value system, including notions of the good, the beautiful and their opposites. In this sense, worldview would be similar to the concept of 'ideology' as used by Raymond Williams, 'an articulated system of meanings, values, and beliefs of a kind that can be abstracted as [the] "worldviews" of any social grouping' (quoted in Comaroff and Comaroff 1992, 29).

I make the following assumptions about worldview. First, worldview may be conceived of as a substrate, in somewhat the same way that linguists conceive of the structure of a language. Language structure is inferred from the patterned relationships of the words. Linguists classify languages into groups, based on the assumption that although words may be different, the structure may be similar. Noting that half the people turning to the healing cults in Kinshasa belong to a culture different from the one in which the rites are performed, René Devisch (1993) remarks that they 'easily cross cultural boundaries because the cults possess a common cultural substratum.' He is, in my view, referring to one aspect of worldview. Similarly, Mervyn Alleyne (1988), in defending the position of cultural continuity between Africa and Jamaica, speaks of 'predispositions.' I hold that he is also talking about worldview. What is the nature of this substrate? It refers to a certain level of abstraction from human practices, whether by way of rationalization or explanation.

Second, worldview influences and is influenced by behaviour. According to Marshall et al. (1989), Abraham Kuyper, the founder of the Free University of Amsterdam, used worldview in his Princeton lectures as 'a set of beliefs that underlie and shape all human action.' For Olthuis (1989), it 'functions both descriptively and normatively,' that is it tells us what is and what is not, what ought and ought not to be.

Third, a worldview is not necessarily consciously known by all the people whose behaviour expresses it. As Marcel Griaule told us, the Dogon worldview as explained to him by Ogotommeli was known in its fullness only to a certain circle of elders. But it is possible to infer a worldview from belief and behaviour, as when John Mbiti (1969) for traditional Africans and Robin Horton (1971) for premodern Europeans identify a this-worldly orientation. This-worldliness is an abstraction made after examination of what people consciously believe and do.

The first three essays form a unit, in that they treat variously with identity, considered in the light of the African past or of the African heritage. The first essay, 'Africa and the Caribbean,' written while enjoying a visiting research fellowship at the Maison des Sciences de l'Homme at the University of Bordeaux III in 2003, takes off from the recent publication of Professor Maureen Warner-Lewis's *Central*

Africa in the Caribbean, the result of very painstaking work tracing linguistic retentions. I raise the issue of identity as a central preoccupation among Caribbean intellectuals, critiquing Paul Gilroy's approach, drawing on Edward Chamberlin's discussion of the works of Anglophone Caribbean poets, but including as well two other literary luminaries, George Lamming and Rex Nettleford. In the second essay, the fruit of a Rockefeller Humanities Foundation Fellowship at the University of Florida in the Fall semester of 1993, I argue that to prove the African cultural heritage of African-American culture, one does not have to reconstruct the historical acculturative process, as Mintz and Price suggest. Since the historical origins of the African-Jamaican people, for example, are not in doubt, revealing the similarities of their worldview with those of the West Africans may serve just as well. The case is made by comparing the worldview underlying Revivalism in Jamaica with the worldview underlying the Aladura movement in Nigeria. The third essay in Part I, 'Ambiguity and the search for Knowledge,' was delivered as an inaugural professorial address in 2000. It focuses on the search by Nettleford for a language to express what he clearly sees as the ambiguity of the identity of black or African–Caribbean persons, and it turns, as Nettleford himself does, once more to the arts for answers.

The remaining essays make no attempt at a comparison with Africa or to debate the question of identity, but are expositions of various aspects of the African–Jamaican worldview. I contend that the *Two Jamaicas* that historian Philip Curtin presented in his interpretation of the 1865 Morant Bay Rebellion continue to exist but at the level of worldview, although important developments, not least the independence of the country from colonial rule and the rise of a Jamaican nationalism, have contributed to closing the gap between them.

The discussion of ambiguity segues nicely, I think, into Part II, which focuses on the Trickster-Hero, a living part of the folk culture of the African-Caribbean. In the first I present an entirely novel way of viewing Rastafari as the embodiment of a trickster deity whose trick in changing the social order is accomplished through music and song. It was first presented in July 2003 at a seminar in Paris organized by Dr Christine Chivallon of the Centre Naçional de Récherche Scientifique. The second expands on the place of Rastafari in the intellectual tradition of Jamaica and by extension the region, taking off from Lamming's essay on the role of the Caribbean intellectual in building an authentic history. It was delivered at the 2001 annual conference of the Society for Caribbean Research at the University of Vienna. In the third essay, 'Fatherhood in the African-Caribbean Landscape,' I attempt to show the importance of the trickster in making the '*jacket*' or '*ready-made*' phenomenon in African-Caribbean sexual and kinship relations work. This was first presented at a Conference in Barbados sponsored by UNICEF and organized by Professsor Christine Barrow of the University of the West Indies, Cave Hill and has since appeared in the volume, *Caribbean Children* edited by her.

The three essays in Part III are recent attempts at understanding some of the values held by the vast majority of Jamaicans. They are apropos of a growing concern with the breakdown of social order, instanced by high rates of homicides and aggression against the person, and while they do not propose an answer they suggest an approach to understanding the problem before we are in a position to write the prescription. The first two, 'The Evasion of Moral Responsibility' and 'The Values We Live By,' were presented at Conferences held at Mona in 2002, the first by the Department of Management Studies and the second by the Research and Policy Group in the Mona School of Business. 'Cosmological Reproduction,' which explores the mindscape of a corner crew of young men in a working-class community in Kingston, was delivered also at Mona as the Annual Philip Sherlock Lecture of 1994.

The final three essays that make up Part IV, Social Integration, are concerned with the interface between the state, with its legal system based on British concepts of law, property and the social order, on the one hand, and the people, with a different worldview, on the other. 'Law and the African-Caribbean Family' was delivered in 2000 at the invitation of the Sir Arthur Lewis Institute of Social and

Economic Studies at the University of the West Indies, Cave Hill. It argues that a Caribbean jurisprudence is yet to emerge, through which the family laws are more reflective of our cultural realities. The second, prepared for a volume edited by Alex Klein and Anthony Harriott (2004), argues the same point but with reference to the laws against the substance cannabis, while the third, 'Those Two Jamaicas,' brings the volume to a close with an explanation of why cultural pluralism, which was first propounded by M.G. Smith as a way of understanding the societies of the Anglophone Caribbean, failed to gain general acceptance in the academy, notwithstanding the accuracy of its depiction of the existing cultural divisions. Drawing on some of the examples discussed in earlier essays, it proposes that the Jamaican people operate in two systems of thought, between which they 'code switch' as it suits them, thus giving the *appearance* of social integration. Genuine social integration, however, first requires social recognition.

Altogether, it is my hope that these essays contribute to our understanding of the Caribbean, that unique crossroad space where, as Nettleford is wont to say, Africa, Europe and Asia meet.

PART I
The African Presence

CHAPTER ONE

Africa and the Caribbean: Reflections on an Identity

*H*er painstaking research of finding and piecing together dangling loose ends of Caribbean memory and tying them to their Central African source is finally over, the triumph of a thirty-five year quest. *Central Africa in the Caribbean* (2003) taken together with her earlier *Trinidad Yoruba, From Mother Tongue to Memory* (1996), establishes Maureen Warner-Lewis as the foremost among Caribbean scholars who are not content to assert that there are these links, but in the finest tradition of Western scholarship are prepared to go and find them. Whereas the subtitle of that 1996 publication is suggestive of a linguistic heritage soon to disappear when those elderly informants pass on and take with them the bits and pieces of a once-functioning language now relegated to memory, the subtitle of this latest *tour de force* is prepared to go further. *Transcending Time, Transforming Cultures* suggests the presence of life that has withstood rupture, and of a vitality that has given shape to living cultures within the Caribbean space.

There is nothing new here. Melville Herskovits long ago laid out many of the cultural traits that had survived the Atlantic crossing. However, while this has brought relief to the African-American minority in the United States of America, in the Caribbean race and colour, colonialism, 'and the complacency born of majority demographic status, have made the issue of Africa more subtly tortured for its peoples,' so that at academic and popular levels 'there remains resistance to the suggestion or assertion of African-Caribbean linkages' (Warner-Lewis 2003, xxiii).

So, backed by the authority of her research, she takes on the literary giant Derek Walcott, for whom the Middle Passage had dealt the enslaved Africans an 'amnesiac blow' that now becomes the starting point of 'the true history of the New World' (p. xxv). She takes on the 'formidable team of Sidney Mintz and Richard Price,' for whom, despite their acknowledgement that the slaves must have brought 'immense quantities of knowledge, information and belief,' 'cultural nakedness' was the condition of the slaves, who evinced 'a creativity which arises in response to new social conditions' (p. xxvi). In short, Maureen Warner-Lewis enters an arena which we know she would be out of her mind to enter were she not certain of the strength of her argument. And those of us without the skills but reading from the sidelines find ourselves cheering.

But, why? What is there to cheer about? After all, *Central Africa in the Caribbean* is by no means a polemic. What Maureen Warner-Lewis has done is to track lexical items back to their Kikoongo and other Central African sources, convinced that 'the use of even one African lexical item in a West Atlantic location is evidence of an integral link, at some point in time, between the particular ethno-linguistic group ... and the practice and belief to which the term relates' (2003, xxii). There are two important phrases here. 'At some point in time' is a reference to some event or process that took place sometime during the course of that long and traumatic history. There is no claim here for the names of ships, their logs, and dates. All there is instead is the trail of dust, the DNA evidence of a presence, whose paternity cannot be denied. But for me the second and more important point is 'the practice and belief' behind the lexical item. If we accept with Clifford Geertz that culture is a system of meaning with which social life is constructed, then those arbitrary sounds we call words are the first and most elemental parts of that system, for they not only embody meaning in themselves, but they function to convey other meaning. And that is what Warner-Lewis means. Behind the word is a practice, and a belief. Every word? No, not every word, for '[i]n the words of a Caribbean novelist, "Some words control large spaces. They sit over large holes. These holes might be dungeons with hairy half humans living in them. Then again they may be underground worlds"' (2003, xxii). Erna Brodber is that novelist and the novel is *Louisiana*, that complex journey into self and ancestry. So Warner-Lewis is very much aware that there are pitfalls, dungeons and prisons, but she is also aware that there is 'a treasure trove of facts and emotions and histories' (2003, xxii) waiting to be uncovered.

But why bother to uncover them? Why spend thirty-five years, working in the summer months and on weekends, a fellowship here, a fellowship there, learning a new language, just to be able to uncover an underground world which some say does not even exist? Warner-Lewis does not claim to be a historian. Her training is in literary criticism, which led her to the analysis of 'Yoruba language inventories of words, phrases, prayers and songs' for her dissertation. This is more than the quest for knowledge for its own sake, the kind of milk on which the academy nurtures its suckling. Yes, there is obviously that, too, the stuff academic careers are made of — original and creative. However, the truth is that Africa has been and remains a problem for us descendants of the enslaved Africans, personal and social, both at the same time, a matter of psychology and politics, an issue of intellectual query, but also of identity, a source of much disquiet and angst, Africa. To be correct, it is not Africa so much as Europe that is the problem — the rupture, the commodification, the contempt and humiliation, the lies, the love-hate, the patronage, the racism, the colour-ism, and now the denial, the *ego me absolvo*.[1] But just as when a murder or grave crime is committed, even when justice is served, it is the victims who are still left with the responsibility of reconstructing and readjusting their lives, which have been irrevocably altered, so in this sense our problem is Africa, that is the understanding of its place in our history of origin and defining a relation to it, and because of that history our problem is also slavery, racism and colourism.[2]

So what is there to cheer about? Every unearthing of a real, as against an imagined, link with Africa that enables Caribbean people to achieve a better understanding and begin to define that relation is worthy of celebration. The link is cultural, but the understanding and the definition encompass the realization of what it means to be black, for, as Nettleford reminds us, *Ebri John Crow t'ink im pickney white* (Every john crow thinks its child is white).[3] This is the 'subtly tortured' existence lived by many Caribbean people, who, unlike their United States counterparts are not black but everything else except white. It is an amazing experience coming from a society in which social class is papered over with the subtle variations of skin colour so skilfully that the meaning transmitted by the latter becomes an index of one's location in the former, to be confronted, as I once was, with the levelling brutality of the tar brush.

The beneficiary of high school education in pre-Independence, pre-Black Power Jamaica of the 1950s, I adjusted to the hierarchy of colour *cum* class that, while unknown to me in my deep rural background, had been the overriding ethos of the country, manifested most sharply in the capital city of Kingston and plantation communities. From half past seven in the morning a steady stream of cars would drop off children of the white and brown Lower St Andrew professionals, businessmen, and civil servants, and the more successful Chinese merchants. There was even a handful that came in chauffeur-driven cars. I can remember my own shock at seeing one of them alight from the rear seat, slam the door shut and ascend the steps of O'Hare Building without as much as a glance, let alone thanks, towards the uniform-clad, cap-and-all chauffeur, a black man old enough to have been his father. The hierarchy was visible by other indicators as well, like whether you could afford fruits from the exorbitantly expensive vendor called "Mamas" at break-time and then go on to a hot lunch at the Old Boys Club, which put you into the very top; or Mamas's fruits at break and later for lunch neatly packed ham sandwiches, the bread crusts shaved off, which put you somewhere in the middle; or a coco-bread and meat patty and a half-pint of milk, with only your bus fare left, which put you at the bottom.

A gross picture this, admittedly, for many boys from middle-class homes rode their bicycles to school, and most were part of the coco-bread and patty midday crowd. But in those days, class divisions at St George's College, and indeed at any other, could be read by divisions of colour. And with the school fees all of £7 per term, the number of students from the artisan and working class was relatively small. I should have been prepared for this, but I was not. Calabar High should have been my school, like my brother's seven years before me, but because in his view he was not brown-skinned enough to have got help from his white principal and teachers in looking for a job after Sixth Form, he advised my parents to send me to St George's, whose priests he said had a much better reputation for fairness. And so there I was, mathematics and Latin, elocution and debating, many friendships regardless, the beginner's stage of my career, but the backdrop a scenery of class and colour, taken for granted, not much a part of the plot or the dialogue, but very much part of the *mise en scène*.

This too was my frame of mind when I left Jamaica in 1959 to become a student in a Jesuit seminary deep in the Berkshire Mountains of New England, the only black person among 200 seminarians and faculty, treated, even in retrospect, without even a hint of prejudice. Then one Sunday afternoon, the Boston College Glee Club put on a concert for the seminary community, and there, as the curtain opened was a black face, the only one among the 60 choristers. My heart leapt and I was disturbed. What difference should a black face make? Why should I find in his presence there such special and evidently personal significance as to create within me this new and troubling emotion? I had never before known such feelings of affinity, and it seemed to me as unnatural as it was spontaneous. In the reception afterwards I resisted the pull for as long as I could, but it turned out that I too was not unnoticed by him, and so we met, the beginning of a lifelong and fruitful friendship, which was to usher me into the world of being black, into civil rights, Martin Luther King, and the black Boston ghetto of Roxbury. This kind of magnetic pull was, and still is to some extent, quite normal in the United States, and I recall James Baldwin making reference to it in one of his essays. However, it is quite foreign to Jamaica, where being black is the condition of the overwhelming majority, inducing that 'complacency born of majority demographic status.' Or, as George Lamming put it a long time ago, '[t]his numerical superiority has given the West Indian a certain leisure, a certain experience of relaxation among white expatriates.... Which is, precisely, his trouble' (1992 [1960], 33).

It was that complacency that defeated Marcus Garvey, who after organizing a powerful following in the United States, where 'black' cut through all the tortured subtleties of skin shades, was unable on his return to his native Jamaica to garner enough votes from eligible black and coloured franchise holders to gain a seat in the Legislative Council. Garvey's Pan-African vision made no distinction between black, brown or mulatto. African descent of whatever degree was all that mattered, since that was all that mattered to whites. His was the first broad-based, popular movement to give tangible expression to what has been felt by intellectuals before and since, namely that the descendants of the African slaves form a living whole with Africans on the continent. This is the root of the concept of diaspora, or, as Gilroy would have it, the black Atlantic, a concept I shall return to later.

But that was not all. One knew that one was black, a condition and an identity shared with millions of Americans, and the solidarity felt good. You could call that, as it was called then, a 'black nationalist' identity, forced on a group of people because of their race and common history of enslavement. What I did not know was that these people also had a culture beyond the blues and Negro spirituals. Someone thrust into my hands Herskovits's *Myth of the Negro Past*. Who, or why, I no longer recall. But what I cannot forget was the comfort and delight I found in the pages of that survey of the motor habits, religious heritage, kinship patterns, social organisation, language and recreational behaviour that had survived the trauma of slavery. It was an extraordinary revelation. The simple chore of carrying and balancing on the head the bucket of spring water every morning before running off to school was suddenly, retroactively and beautifully transformed from the burden it often was into a gesture of much elegance and pride. The drums and hand clapping of the Revival village square meetings in the night, the much taken-for-granted bankra (straw basket) lying in the corner of the house somewhere, the mortar and mortar stick used to mash fufu and corn, Son-Son's *nambu* (farmer's bag) strung over his shoulder as he set out for his field in the mornings, sometimes with his lend-a-day work partners, the money partner my mother threw, the Anansi stories at nights, the *kreng-kreng* (brambles) we were sent to look to ketch up the fire, the riddles and word games, the words of African origin, like *unu* (you) and *nyam* (eat) and word reduplications for emphasis — suddenly, within a few hours of reading, an entire life was put back in joint before realising it had been dislocated. *The Myth of the Negro Past* was like one's autobiography but written by someone else.

Herskovits, however, was the beginning of woe, for the *kalunga*, that body of water separating the world of the living from the world of the ancestors, had already been crossed. It could not be uncrossed. No rewinding the cinema reel in order to present a different sequence, leading to a different denouement. No going back. As the elation was high, so was the dejection low, the sense of loss made more acute by the emergence of the African nations and the apparent integrity of their seemingly undisturbed tradition, language, tribal dress and all. Slavery had thrown us into a new and bitter world, fuelling desires of return, or if not return, the elaboration of difference. For what is an identity if not a point of difference? But on what was that difference to be established? A black identity implies that someone else is white. In the circumstances of the Americas it signifies all those who were severed from Africa by European slavery. A white identity, on the other hand, implies a distinction from Blacks and a European or 'Middle-eastern' origin. The simplicity of this parallelism is but a mask for the complexity of the problem of a black identity based on race alone. No white American is only white and American. He or she is also a descendant of Polish or German or Italian ancestors, a fact often signified by the surname. Ronald Reagan, that most American of American Presidents, once on his way to Europe stopped off in Ireland to look up relatives. No black man or woman is able to make a similar stop anywhere on the continent of Africa. And what's more, with the European surnames that they all have, there is not a single trace of a personal connection. You know you are black, you know that some if not all of your ancestors originated in Africa, but you do not know where, and, unless you were as fortunate as Alex Haley, you would not even know where to start looking.

But the loss of personal connection, as important as that might be, would be tolerable if the roots of the rituals and cultural practices of daily life that distinguished blacks from whites could be traced to Africa. Then the heavy weight of slavery instead of being some crippling debility would become instead the triumph of what Ted Chamberlin (2000,19) calls '[t]he stubborn durability of African social and cultural traditions.' *The Myth of the Negro Past* was written to combat the racism that sought to justify itself by the 'myth' that no such traditions existed, but as a political exercise drawing upon the theory and methodology of ethnography, it was subjected to the critical scrutiny of the academy, and challenged. Where Herskovits's idea of retention was concerned, how do we know to which African people the attribution was to be made? Where was the evidence of the lineage of transmission? His demarcation of Africa into culture areas, identified by the regularity of cultural institutions and social practices, was met with similar scepticism — as a clever way of glossing over the diversity of the African peoples in the face of the impossibility of identifying the links. His idea of syncretism faced a similar difficulty of pinning down the specific African contribution to the syncretic practice. Then, too, there were those practices and beliefs that could as well be the product of transmission from the Europeans.

The long and short of it is that it would be easier to succumb to the 'amnesiac blow,' making slavery the starting point of our story, than to indulge in what Lorna Goodison (2001) in one of her poems refers to as 'quest fever.' Or, second, one could continue to look, as Maureen Warner-Lewis and others since Herskovits have done, convinced that the pre-slavery past is helpful in understanding the post-slavery present. Or still yet, third, one could ignore the need for any scientific validation of links, ignore the rupture, and make racial heritage a point of cultural difference, which is what Molefi Asante does.

AFROCENTRICITY AND THE BLACK ATLANTIC

Ignoring the rupture of slavery is what the need for adoption of African names was all about, and although that wind of change has not been completely spent, the idea of Afrocentricity introduced by Molefi Asante retains currency at the intellectual level as a perspective and way of looking at the world, if not as the complete break with European epistemological traditions it imagines itself to represent. Because '[w]e were operating ...on someone else's intellectual space and within someone else's time frame' (Asante 2002, 103), Afrocentricity grew out of the study of the work of Cheikh Anta Diop and of ancient Egyptian language and culture, at Temple University in the 1970s. But it goes further than Diopian historiography and epistemology in adding the dimension of praxis. It is in this sense not only an intellectual critique of European hegemony but also 'one way out of the impasse over social and cultural hegemony, the positioning of the *agency* of the African person as the basic unit of analysis of social situations involving African-descended people...' (Asante 2002, 102; *my emphasis*). Putting Africans at the centre of their own thought, the Afrocentric scholar grounds the unity of African thought, symbols and ritual concepts in their classical origins and delinks the study of Africa and the African Diaspora from its current position as 'a subset of the European intellectual project which maintains the study of African people...as marginal and peripheral' (Asante 1990, 56).

Such an approach leads to the rediscovery of 'the existence of an African Cultural System,' manifested in diverse ways according to particular histories, but '...respond[ing] to the same rhythms of the universe, the same cosmological sensibilities, the same general historical reality...' as shared with those on the continent. '[W]e know that Yoruba, Asante, Wolof, Ewe, Nuba, and African-Americans possess values and beliefs derived from their own particular histories yet conforming to the African Cultural System' (Asante 1980, 4-5).

If this sounds like negritude, it is because Afrocentricity borrows from it, but whereas negritude is 'a state of being,' Afrocentricity is 'a state of consciousness' (Asante 2002,113). Indeed Afrocentricity sees its own pedigree in the works and activities of the leading Pan Africanists and black nationalists, Booker T. Washington, Marcus Garvey, Martin Luther King Jr., Elijah Muhammad, W.E.B. Dubois, Malcolm X and Maulana Karenga, despite their own shortcomings. But in a development reminiscent of Garvey's attempt to build a religion to parallel his mass organization, Asante has sought to ground the 'African essence' in a collective ritual expression called Njia, whereby 'we become essentially ruled by our own values and principles' (Asante 1980, 26). Njia meetings take place on Sundays in a six-part liturgy involving libations, readings from the *Teachings of Njia*, artistic performances, and discussion, all conducted in an 'Afrocentric' (earth toned and round) meeting place, with a libation table in the middle. Putting Africans at the centre of the African's thinking radically extends even to the devising of a reckoning of time, starting with 1619, the Beginning Again. Thus, 1617 is 2 *BBA*, Before the Beginning Again, and 1621 2 *ABA*, After the Beginning Again (Asante 1980, 30).

Afrocentricity deals with the rupture of slavery as merely an unpleasant interruption which Africans in the Americas ignore by declaring the essential integrity of their culture, and thereby reaffirming their link to an 'African Cultural System.' Where race was the basis for the Pan Africanism of the nineteenth and early twentieth centuries, for Afrocentricity it is culture, even though '[a]ll cultural systems are responsive to the environment' (Asante 1980, 5), and the environments are not the same. To lay claim to this integrating Cultural System we must in effect undergo a conversion and practise a kind of secular religion. But as for overcoming European epistemology in which the thinking of blacks is embedded, Afrocentricity, according to Paul Gilroy, 'is striking both for its tacit acceptance of the idea of progress and for the easy-instrumental relationship with tradition which it suggests' (Gilroy 1993, 190).

In Gilroy's critique, slavery and the experience of slavery are critical for two reasons. First, it is important to establish that slavery is an inherent part of modernity, inherent, that is, to the Enlightenment, and not an aberration from it.

> [T]he universality and rationality of enlightened Europe and America were used to sustain and relocate rather than eradicate an order of racial difference inherited from the premodern era. The figure of Columbus does not appear to complement the standard pairing of Luther and Copernicus that is implicitly used to mark the limits of this particular understanding of modernity. Locke's colonial interests and the effect of the conquest of the Americas on Descartes and Rousseau are simply non-issues. In this setting, it is hardly surprising that if it is perceived to be relevant at all, the history of slavery is somehow assigned to blacks. It becomes our special property rather than a part of the ethical and intellectual heritage of the West as a whole. (Gilroy 1993, 49)

Second, it was through slavery that the black Atlantic was formed, critiquing the foundations of modernity, making possible 'an ethics of freedom to set alongside modernity's ethics of law' (p. 56) and connecting the rationality of modernity with the subjective. In this way the disjuncture created by the Enlightenment between art and life is restored. For Gilroy then the black Atlantic, which encompasses both Africa and the African diaspora, is very much part of the West. But it is not West because of the rationality of racism. This tension of being 'in an expanded West but not completely of it' (p. 58) yields a *double consciousness*, a phrase he picks up from Dubois, an 'ambivalence towards modernity' (p. 73) that can be verified in the writings of nineteenth and early twentieth century black intellectuals. In the face of the racism and terror of modernity, these writers and artists instead of retreating into 'tradition,' as Afrocentrists do, 'opted instead to embrace the fragmentation of self (doubling and splitting) which modernity seems to promote' (p. 188).

Gilroy comes very close to seeing slavery as the beginning. Compelled to focus on the role of expressive culture in the creation of the black Atlantic as an identifiable space in the West, he resorts to elaborating a meaning of 'tradition' that does not stand in opposition to modernity, but 'has generated specific modes of expression and some vernacular philosophical preoccupations that are absolutely antagonistic to the enlightenment assumptions with which they have had to compete for the attention of the black public' (p. 198). Central in this 'non-traditional tradition,' this 'irreducibly modern, ex-centric, unstable, and asymmetrical cultural ensemble' (p. 198) are the themes of death and suffering, the narratives of exile, loss and journeying that tell and retell the story of the group and through them 'invent, maintain, and renew identity' (p. 198). This kind of 'tradition' allows for the circulation of artistic creation and the hybridizing influences, within the black Atlantic.

But on what basis, with what language of communication, does the black Atlantic understand itself as 'the living memory of the changing same?' This is not a question Gilroy asks because his focus is the West, expanded by the critical and creative intrusion of the black Atlantic. But the black Atlantic must mean more than slavery and suffering, since the concept encompasses continental Africa as well, giving it a meaning beyond that of diaspora. Drawing on the circulation of cultural forms between Africa and the African diaspora as part of his argument in developing his concept of 'non-traditional tradition,' he cites the experience of James Brown who recognized his own musical style in the music of Fela Ransome Kuti's band in Lagos, and goes on to say that '[t]he mutation of jazz and African-American cultural style in the townships of South Africa and the syncretised evolution of Caribbean and British reggae music and Rastafari culture in Zimbabwe could be used to supply further evidence' (p. 199). Without going to the extreme of trying to limit the intelligibility or appreciation of black music to blacks, it would be disingenuous not to acknowledge a particular kind of rhythmic sensibility in African and African diaspora music which makes it more quickly understood and valued by blacks. This certainly was the case of African-American rhythm and blues in Jamaica, whose mixture with native rhythms led to the development of ska and eventually reggae. As Chivallon (2005, 100) puts it, 'the question arises whether the component that develops a "closed" identity through reference to purity and authenticity, does not in the end contradict the "intercultural" model of Gilroy.' The acknowledgement of the existence of a black Atlantic does not make inquiry into the cultural links of the diaspora with Africa less meaningful.

AN ABSENCE OF RUINS

Gilroy may not have been explicit about it, but certain Caribbean intellectuals have been very clear in their adoption of the amnesia strategy. 'History [read identity] is built around achievement and creation; and nothing was created in the West Indies,' declared Vidia Naipaul (2001 [1962], 20). Orlando Patterson captured it nicely but despairingly in the title of his novel, *An Absence of Ruins*. The novel ends with the protagonist emerging from the London tube and melting in its crowd. Were these two writers right? But if they were both wrong and there is achievement and creation here, what relationship does that achievement and that creation bear to Africa? Can one be satisfied with an origin that began in modern slavery, at the same time *fully conscious that there was a pre-modern past*?

These have been for me fundamental questions. And they have been at the root of the African-Caribbean intellectual enterprise as undertaken by most of its major artists and scholars. Commenting on George Lamming's novel, *Season of Adventure*, Kamau Brathwaite wrote that,

> what is really surprising, given the Caribbean psycho-cultural inheritance, is not really the fear/avoidance response with regard to the African presence in the New World, but the persistent attempts, at all levels, to deal with it. No writer in the plantation New World can, in fact, ignore 'Africa' for long... (1986, 228)

As Canadian literary critic Ted Chamberlin puts it, 'for West Indians, first of all it involves coming to terms with what has been taken away or taken over, in order to determine where to find it and how to get it back' (2000 [1993], 28). Africa will just not go away. Using as his motif a passage from one of Kamau Brathwaite's poems from his *Rights of Passage,*

> 'A black apostrophe to pain'
> Where then is the nigger's home?
> In Paris Brixton Kingston Rome?
> Here? Or in Heaven?

Chamberlin tracks the search for that home in the shaping of a poetry based on the language, and hence the world of experience, of the people of African descent in the West Indies. If, as Benjamin Whorf argued, 'differences in behaviour and thought ... are a function of differences in language' (Chamberlin 2000 [1993],70), and therefore language is to some extent a prison, then breaking out of the prison of the superimposed English of the enslaving white master, represents the breaking into the world of the once enslaved African, now nigger, now black. The title of Chamberlin's book, *Come Back to Me My Language* is appropriately taken from a poem of Derek Walcott, which 'marks a turning point, bringing together a mature poet's confidence in his literary inheritance with a corresponding — and newly found — confidence in his West Indian heritage' (p. 99). Achieving that kind of integration was the result of grappling with the place of Africa in the West Indian heritage, the legacy/prison of Europe already a given. Both Walcott and Brathwaite, though different in background,

> ...share a sense of the connection between the opposing elements of their heritage — African and European, slavery and freedom.... Their work has often been contrasted, with Brathwaite described as representing a radical break from the conventions of European literature by a return to his African inheritance and its translation over the past five hundred years into the traditions of the West Indian diaspora, while Walcott is said to embody a more conservative acceptance of the possibilities — perhaps indeed the inevitabilities — of his European literary inheritance, along with a deep suspicion of African nostalgia. ... In fact, both of them are

much more complex than these stereotypes would suggest, and both display an intricate and often inconsistent interaction of European and African traditions in their poetry (pp. 154-5).

Lorna Goodison, the third of the three poets Chamberlin focuses on, also 'draws on both African and European inheritances' (p. 155). 'Loose now the salt cords binding our tongues,' she invokes, as she embraces the African heritage, 'moving from the pathological invisibility of blacks in European eyes to a new visibility in the light of their African heritage' (p. 178). The opening line of her poem alludes not only to the physical shackles with which the chapter of slavery began, but also to the spiritual entrapment that became the lot of those who ingested salt. Maureen Warner-Lewis writes that '[s]everal African descendants had heard that because their ancestors had eaten salt they could not have flown back to Africa' (2003, 271), and quotes Kenneth Bilby and Fu-Kiau Bunseki (*Kumina, A Kongo-based Tradition in the New World*) for an explanation; 'In Kongo cosmology, it is believed that the ancestral dead, from whom the living derive their spiritual powers, do not eat salt. Salt repels the spirits of the dead, and thus causes weakness in the living — particularly those who are engaged in spiritual matters. ... "To eat salt," then is to lose one's power"' (Warner-Lewis 2003, 272). Loosening the 'salt cords' allows the poet to reclaim that lost power, which above all else is to be found in the *word*.

It is Brathwaite more than any other Caribbean writer who draws attention to the central importance of the *word* in Caribbean culture. In his *Development of Creole Society in Jamaica*, he introduces us to the concept of *nommo*, which grounded the attitude of the slaves to the creative as well as destructive power of a name, or the power of speech to bind the religious flock. In his later essay on 'The African Presence in Caribbean Literature, 1970/1973,' in which he defends the view 'that African culture not only crossed the Atlantic, it crossed, survived, and creatively adapted itself to its new environment' (1986, 192), he organizes that literature into four categories. There are those in which Africa is used merely as a rhetorical device; those which he calls a *'literature of survival,'* that deal quite consciously with African survivals in the Caribbean; the *'literature of African expression,'* employing, often unconsciously, elements of African and/or African-American style, content, vocabulary, custom/culture; and *'the literature of reconnection,'* by writers 'who are consciously reaching out to rebridge the gap with the spiritual heartland' (1986, 212). It is in the third category, the literature of African expression, that he discusses the word, 'the atomic core of language' (1986, 236). The use of the word as conjurer, transformer, creator

> ...is found throughout the entire black/African world. It is present in modern as well as traditional African literature. In the Americas, it reveals itself in our love of courtroom scenes (both factual and fictional), the rhetoric of yard quarrels, "word-throwings," tea-meetings and preacher/political orations. The whole living tradition of the calypso is based on it (1986, 239-241).

Discovery of this power of the word, which the turn to the African part of the heritage promises, is what loosens the "salt cords," allowing the new utterance that Brathwaite calls *nation language* to come forth, a "language that is influenced very strongly by the African model, the African aspect of our New World/Caribbean heritage" (1986, 265–266).

In his Epilogue, Chamberlin writes,

> West Indian poets have done what many others have tried, especially in the past half century. They have taken back what belongs to them — not only their own language, but the freedom to use it. And they have used this freedom to give new meaning and purpose to their lives. This achievement is not a marginal one. It recalls the great enterprises in art and literature during the Renaissance, when Europeans defined their heritage through the language of imaginative expression and in doing so both discovered and invented themselves as people for whom certain values and traditions were precious (p. 272).

In these words of the critic we understand what men and women of imagination have had to do in order to gain real freedom, a freedom of spirit. They achieved this not collectively as if by design but by each one searching to reclaim what slavery had ruptured. Until they did so, the tongue remained tied and the voice mute.

In her poem 'Natal Song,' found in her latest collection of poems (later than those discussed by Chamberlin), Lorna Goodison (2001, 45-47) makes her own personal reconnection with Africa. The title is itself a play on words, for this is indeed where, through her Guinea woman ancestor, she was born, that half that had never been told. So,

> I come to find my vital self left back here
> so that I land in Xamayca with quest fever
> and all the while Africa you had my remedy,
> my baraka in your mouth, so that even
> when they split and redirected your course
> my name remained a seed under your tongue.

By using the old Spanish name for Jamaica she indicates that the quest fever, the quest that consumes to the point of illness, has been all of five hundred years old, as old as the first slave to set foot on the islands. She is confident that Africa remembers, for as widely known and practised in Jamaica by placing a nutmeg or lime under the tongue one is able to resist the evil duppy power that in this case would cause amnesia. And so off she goes through the Natal bush 'in search of the sleeping rhino,' now become a symbol for the object of her quest, up on the high veldt, near where 'a lion ripped life from a woman's throat,' marvelling at the 'running of the wildebeests' in action older than the oldest history, passing a conference of zebras 'beneath writhing acacia trees,' and calling upon 'the elevated and figured giraffe.'

> Continent of my foremothers, to reach back I have
> crossed over seas, oceans, seven-sourced rivers.
> Under my heartbeat is where you pitched and lodged

persistent memory, rhythm box with no off-switch,
my drumbeat and monitor which never let me
settle for barracoon, barracks, camp or pagoda.

The veldt resounds with the ringing hammer
upon anvil cry of the fiery blacksmith plover.
All the time source was remedy for quest fever,
for the lion at your birth straddled your sign,
sacrificed appropriate sheep and beat back dogs
designating your song as the bleat of scapegoat.

Now the pride of even stricter lion demands
the total banishment of the captured within,
the scour and disinfection of mental barracoon,
the break and burial of old iron. Nothing less.
If you rise up full grown, assent and embrace,
will lion open your throat and silence, or lionize?

Thank you God for this day most amazing. Amen
good driver Adrian. Tomorrow I will drink bush tea
on the Island of Salt, realizing that we never
did see the rhino. But the wicked toe of the ostrich
excavated a stone with the seal of a mother and child
upon it. Kenzurida found it; and Africa, I kept it.

'All the time source was remedy for quest fever.' Finding the source is one thing; will the source accept you is another. Wademba, the African in Simone Schwarz-Bart's novel *Between Two Worlds*, who with his mystical powers returned to the village from where he was snatched and taken into slavery, was killed by his own kinsmen because slavery had severed him irrevocably from his place among them, and there was no ritual that could undo this defilement (See chapter 3 below, p. 97). So here too, Goodison comes face to face with 'the total banishment of the captured within/the scour and disinfection of mental barracoon/the break and burial of old iron.' But instead of despondency, this leads her to end on a note of optimism and possibilities in the future, 'If you rise up full grown, assent and embrace/will lion open your throat and silence, or lionize?' Maybe Africa will not speak, but then again maybe it will lionize, will roar words of adulation and praise in honour of those who were taken. And with this revelation, the quest fever is now sated, and 'I will drink bush tea,' the standard early morning hot beverage of the Jamaican country folk, 'on the Island of Salt,' from where there is no return. A 'stone with the seal of a mother and child' is unwittingly unearthed by the ostrich, no doubt the pompous strutting figure of the European, and this she keeps, the child nursing the stone-sacred indelible mark of filial identity.

'Natal Song' is not the only one in this collection in which Goodison affirms the African source of a Caribbean reality. There are several others, including one that beautifully captures what Brathwaite means when he defines the *literature of reconnection* as 'a recognition of the African presence in our society not as a static quality, but as root living, creative, and still part of the main' (Brathwaite 1986, 255), and also self-consciously identifies her role as poet, is *Crossover Griot* (Goodison 2001, 74).

> The jump-ship Irishman
> who took that Guinea girl
> would croon when rum
> anointed his tongue.
>
> And she left to mind
> first mulatta child
> would go end of day
> to ululate by the bay.
>
> 'I am O'Rahilly' he croons.
> She moans 'since them
> carry me from Guinea
> me can't go home'

> Of crossover griot
> they want to ask
> how all this come about?
> To no known answer.
>
> Still they ask her
> why you chant so?
> And why she turn poet
> not even she know.

The traditions continue even unconsciously: 'not even she know.' In describing herself as the 'crossover griot,' Goodison not only identifies her place as being within the Caribbean (crossover), but understands her role as a crossover, or different kind of griot; not the poet who is the repository of the memory of the lineage traditions of the tribe, for she is unable to recount the history of her tribe, where that Guinea girl came from, or even where 'the jump-ship Irishman' went, not that kind of griot, but poet. Our poets are our kind of griots, those that have crossed over, crossed perhaps between Europe and Africa. She is not bothered by the ambivalence that a 'mulatta' heritage bequeaths some people. Rather, she speaks "of 'the half that's never been told…and some of us going to tell it'" (Chamberlin 2000, 273).

THAT HALF THAT'S NEVER BEEN TOLD

And some of that half is what Maureen Warner-Lewis, searching for the pre-slavery links, has succeeded in telling in what must be a personally satisfying *magnum opus*. She tells how, contrary to the dismissive conclusion of Enlightenment scholarship, Central Africa survived the crossing in very remarkable ways, not as whole systemic transplants, but as influences that shaped life in the Americas lived by her informants and their ancestors, some of which may be evident up to the present. I would like to highlight some of the ways her research helps us to understand better the nature of the Caribbean, at least the Africa part of it. Beginning at the beginning Warner-Lewis digs up from the memories of her informants experiences of capture and enslavement transmitted to them in narrative and song by their ancestors. One Trinidadian tells of his grandfather arriving with other shipmates,

> They all come together in one ship and come alive. So they consider themselves brothers. If they drown, everybody drown together. They [are] in the belly of one woman — that's how they consider it — and they dying [are going to die] in their mother['s] belly if the ship sink. The sea is a mother, they say. (Nicholls 1989)

As Warner-Lewis explains,

> This vivid extended metaphor appears to derive from the semantic extension of "mother" in some Bantu languages. *Ngudi* (Ko[KiKoongo]) means not simply "mother", but also "womb", and not only the anatomical womb, but concretely 'the innermost space', the bedroom of a house, and any recessed enclosed space" .... Thus the underdeck where the slaves were crowded contained, for its occupants, these layers of meaning. Even so, the 'house' or *nzo*, a sub-division of the *kanda* or clan section inhabiting a village or village cluster, was also known as the *vumu*, or belly, which acknowledged a common tradition and was synonymous with *ngudi* in the abstract sense of 'root' or 'source' (Warner-Lewis 2003, 39).

The idea of shipmate no longer has the currency it once had in the Caribbean, since slave narratives like Nicholls's are not much part of story-telling, an art form that has declined with the rise of television and other means of entertainment. What is most interesting for me is the means by which this fictive kinship, which Warner-Lewis shows was widely practised across African societies, was made possible through the 'layers of meaning.' In contemporary Jamaica drop pan, a numbers game introduced by immigrants from Southern China and 'creolised' into the meaning-complex of the population, the number 8 may mean a pregnant woman, a bag, a hole, or any empty space. Warner-Lewis's finding substantiates an argument I have advanced elsewhere (Chevannes 1989) that many of the associations of meaning used in this game of chance are based on the popular worldview. But what is beyond any doubt is the association between the identification of the yard with the female rather than the male spouse, as Victoria Durrant-Gonzales (1976) found in her field sites in rural Jamaica, and an African worldview that identifies house with belly, with womb, with source.

In a section relating the tales of some informants that their ancestors had been soldiers in Africa prior to coming to the Caribbean, Warner-Lewis (2003, 46) draws attention to circumstances that caused war, one of them being insults to one's mother, and another 'the turning of the rump towards another, sometimes embellished by a self-administered slap,' known among the BaKoongo and also practised elsewhere in West Africa. She cites as an example Maroon leader Nanny's famous show of contempt for the British prior to launching her attacks against them. This well-known Caribbean gesture is not confined to women. Children of both sexes use it to trade insults. In a conflict you know you cannot win, you retreat a safe distance, attract your opponent's attention with a stone or a verbal insult, and when you are sure you have caught his eye you 'tear out yu batty gi' him.' And run for your life, of course.

But this meaning of the anus raises intriguing questions about contemporary Jamaican, if not West Indian, culture. One is whether the intensity of the injury done to another by the use of the bad word *raas* (for *arse*), and its combination with *hole* and *cloth,* may not be explained by how the anus is viewed. In most Western cultures excrement is used to symbolize contempt, and in a binary separation the acts of ingestion and cleaning oneself after excreting are assigned to the right and left hand, respectively, among African and Indian cultures. The anus therefore could derive added negative meaning from this association. But what is striking at least in Jamaica is the severity with which this battery of insults derived from association with the anus is regarded.

A second question is whether these associations might possibly help to explain the hostility to homosexuality, on which on the comparative scale the Caribbean would rank high with Jamaica highest of all. Elsewhere (Chevannes 2001) I raise the possibility of an explanation for Caribbean homophobia in the insecurity of achieving and maintaining masculinity within societies lacking the ritualized sanction of patriarchal family formations, and in a later publication (Chevannes 2002) explored for a possible explanation the symbolic distortion created by the intrusion into public space of an essentially private sexuality. Now with the attention drawn by Warner-Lewis to the African sources of some of the meaning given to the anus, one is left to wonder whether this may not provide another fruitful line of inquiry. To make any advance it would help to know how homosexuality is viewed in Central and West African cultures.

It would have been surprising if religion, cosmology and rituals of empowerment did not form a major focus of Warner-Lewis's book. Central African religious outlook has been responsible for the greater emphasis on manipulative, destructive power in a number of Caribbean religions and witchcraft practices. This angle of inquiry strengthens the case for a Central African origin of Pukumina in Jamaica, which is very well known for being more aggressively manipulative, and therefore feared, than Revival Zion. Edward Seaga (1969) was the first to make that case when he rejected the name 'Pocomania,' and identified its kinship with Kumina, which he had also identified with Central Africa.

Another fascinating and very original connection Warner-Lewis makes is the ritual role of fire in accessing power. Every historical or social account of Trinidad carnival gives the derivation of canboulay, the procession with torches before daylight on Shrove Monday, as *cannes brulées*, burnt canes. The slaves, so goes the common explanation, simply transformed the chore of putting out cane fires into part of the carnival celebration. Warner-Lewis disputes this.

> No reasonable connection has...been made between revelry — represented by masquerade — and work, unpleasant work at that. Why should people about to celebrate remind themselves of being awoken after twelve or more hours' work to put in further hours

amidst the heat of burning canes? Furthermore, *kambule* involved the lighting of open-flame torches, whereas *cannes brulées* or cane fires involved the extinguishing of flames (pp. 221-222).

Then she solves the puzzle, based on the motif of the fire, its corollaries in Brazil, Haiti and the Ovimbundu of Central Africa, and on the Kikoongo word for procession or parade, *kambule*, the origin of canboulay is Central African. She suggests that 'the Trinidad masqueraders may have been drawing mystic power from the fires they set, accessing superhuman strength from the flames, rather than merely trying to extinguish the flames they had set in the first place' (p. 223).

Her discussion on the role of fire in ritual immediately leads to thoughts about the origin of this important icon among the Rastafari, where there is no linguistic connection. At the entrance to every nyabinghi celebration there burns a large bonfire that is fed for as long as the ceremony lasts, as many as fourteen days. Shouts of *Fire!* or *Fire Bu'n!* are used by Rastafari to condemn or to signal disapproval of conduct, and is a favourite expression of certain Rastafari DJ artistes, who shout their disapproval of Babylon or politicians or homosexuals. I have been speculating a Bongo origin of this Rastafari iconographic practice ever since my first attendance at a Bongo dance in Bog Walk, St Catherine. Bongo, also known as Convince, is a religious fraternity of obeah men. But although Warner-Lewis does not treat it as a Central Africa derivative in the manner in which Kumina is, the possibility is quite strong, when '[t]he tangential relationship between the two religions' (Warner-Lewis 2003, 147) is taken into account.

The linkages documented by Maureen Warner-Lewis extend across the range of activities and attitudes practised in daily life, domestic affairs, sociality, respect, economic activities, rites of passage, religion, dance and recreation, and language. Some are receding into memory, while others like culinary traditions, religious beliefs and practices and the masquerade remain live expressions of the cultures of a people who look forward to the delight of funji or of gungu peas at Christmas time, who invent masks through which to access spiritual power, know and make use of the meaning of a stick, a rod or a staff, know what it means "to suck salt" and how, by tying a red ribbon on the wrist of a newborn or hanging a rosary around its neck, to give it protection from evil.

In Conclusion

The proof that the shape of many of the cultures of the region owes much to its African heritage does not negate the fact that Caribbean civilization is the result of the vigour of the people now calling that space home. Jean Besson and I (1996) have suggested that continuity and creativity should not be opposed to each other, for no serious student of history and society would deny the proof of the presence of both. Christine Chivallon is therefore right. In her excellent review of the different interpretations of black Atlantic culture she has this to say on the difference between those who, like Maureen Warner-Lewis, would make the argument for continuity and those who, like Sidney Mintz and Richard Price, would see the Caribbean as essentially something new, a creole mixture,

> The difference…might then reside simply in the point of view adopted. The point for the first would be to research the African presence in the culture systematically, and to postulate it as prior to the exchanges that follow (the importance of the process of acculturation is not refuted). The point for the second would be to bring out the new cultural complexes elaborated in the specific context of slavery, that derive in part from an African cultural base (the importance of the African presence is not refuted). In this way, a defender of continuity would see first in the Creole languages the preservation of basic African structures (morphology, syntax), whereas the defender of creolization would point out the contributions of various sources (Chivallon, 2005, 14–15).

Warner-Lewis does not refute 'the process of acculturation;' indeed she is critical of Mervyn Alleyne (1988), who seems to. The fact is all cultures undergo change, some at faster rates than others. It would be remarkable and a result of great isolation if the cultural features which the Africans practised in the eighteenth century, as witnessed and mentioned by Thomas Thistlewood (Hall 1989), for example, remained unchanged after 250 years. The same thing is therefore likely on the other side of the Atlantic, where societies that were bled of millions of their members to the European slave trade have undergone exposure to the Europeans and experienced change, if not at the same rate, without anyone daring to deny them continuity. This is why, notwithstanding Mintz and Price's line of argument in favour of the creativity-side of the debate, I believe there is much to gain from following their suggestion about exploring 'grammatical principles.' As we will see in the following chapter, comparison between the Revival religion in Jamaica and the Aladura churches in Nigeria yields remarkably close similarities, making the conclusion inescapable that both religions were given similar shapes by a shared worldview responding to a similar history of Protestant Christianity.

George Lamming, in one of his more recent publications, discusses the role of the intellectual in Caribbean society. He uses as the epigraph to one of the essays the following words of Antonio Gramsci,

> The starting point of critical elaboration is the consciousness of what one really is, and is knowing 'thyself' as a product of the historical process to date, which has deposited in you an infinity of traces, without leaving an inventory ... therefore it is imperative at the outset to compile such an inventory (Lamming 2000 [1995], 3).

My interpretation of Lamming's intent (See chapter 5 for a fuller discussion of Lamming's essay) is to argue that the task of the Caribbean intellectual is to compile out of the infinity of traces deposited by a colonial legacy our own inventory, without which we cannot begin to know ourselves, let alone know anything else. All knowledge, implies Lamming, is radically a subjective appropriation of the other. It therefore starts with self. What Maureen Warner-Lewis has done is, as she herself says, to contribute to a reorientation of Caribbean cultural history away from an exclusively public Eurocentric focus, which is the colonial heritage of the West Atlantic, and which not only imbues the thinking of the ordinary citizen, but is reinforced by the indifference, ignorance and calculated prejudices of opinion-leading elites, whether in business, bureaucracies, the media or academia. ... According to this myopic schema, the beginnings of the modern West Atlantic reside solely in the agency of European conquistadores and colonists; while the cosmological, organizational and practical contributions made by other peoples in the ethnic amalgam of the region are often neglected or treated in disparaging fashion (p. 330).

Strong words, but necessary words if the compilation of the inventory of our history is to mean anything at all to the consciousness of who we are.

In Rex Nettleford's words that compilation is not simply a scribal exercise, even if a large part of the inventory becomes the responsibility of our scribes. It is a 'battle for space.' Easily the most persistent and at times lone voice insisting on an African presence in the crossroads mix that is the Caribbean, from his role in that seminal experience of the *Report on the Rastafari Movement in Kingston, Jamaica*, through his enduring milestone essay on 'the Melody of Europe and the Rhythm of Africa,' through his creative elevation on stage of that presence in the movements of the Caribbean body, to his *Inward Stretch, Outward Reach*, and countless interstices in between and since, Nettleford wills us a Caribbean that is the site of "the battle for space between Europe and Africa on foreign soil" (1993, 85). If in this battle Europe has had control of the outer space of wealth, power and privilege, it is by the victory over the inner spaces of the mind and the imagination that Africa will first find the capacity

> to 're-integrate' self and society into an organic totality by the harmonisation of inner and outer space. We in the Caribbean have not built pyramids, pillars, cathedrals, amphitheatres, opera houses, etc. that are the wonders of the world, but we have more creative artists per square inch than is probably good for us. In addition we

have created and are creating mental structures which are intended to be the basis of that self-confidence, that sense of place, purpose and power without which there can be no integration of inner and outer space (1993, 83).

The battle over language, where 'Dutch, Spanish and French ... govern but it is sranan tonga, papiamento, patois, *etc*, that rule' (1993, 85), extends to religion, music and dance no less, in fact to every facet of life — politics, economics, culture — where we try to make sense of our existence in the Caribbean. Far from being the long, drawn-out, exhausting struggle that it could seem for all its four centuries of being waged, the battle for space is in fact 'the *force vitale* of a still groping society' (1993, 81). You could call it 'the struggle of the African presence to claim a place of centrality in the Caribbean ethos' (1993, 84).

This in the final analysis is what this discourse is all about — an on-going, seemingly never-ending, tension-filled, sometimes ambiguous African battle, in the mind and outside of it, in all walks of life including the academy, for Caribbean space.

CHAPTER TWO

Forward to the Past: Jamaica is Africa

While conducting fieldwork among his Rastafari followers in the summer of 1969, I was told by the Reverend Claudius Henry that he would no longer pursue the idea of Repatriation because on a recent trip to Africa he had been told by Emperor Haile Selassie that there was no need for Jamaicans to seek to return to Africa, for Africa was already in Jamaica. The self-styled 'Repairer of the Breach' later announced this remarkable change in a pamphlet (see Chevannes 1976). The context of this dramatic development was, quite briefly, this: In 1960, Henry, who had been preaching repatriation for at least two years previously, was arrested, charged and sentenced to ten years imprisonment for treason felony. A raid on his headquarters had revealed an arms cache and a damaging letter he had written inviting Fidel Castro, the newly installed Cuban revolutionary leader, to take over the government and country of Jamaica, since they were now about to leave for Africa. While Henry was serving his sentence, Emperor Selassie made a state visit to Jamaica in 1966 that was to contribute immeasurably to the subsequent rapid growth of the Rastafari movement, particularly among the urban youth. Released on parole the following year, Henry set about rebuilding his organization. This time, he decided to concentrate on a most impressive community development project for, and involving, his followers. It included a rather successful bakery and bread distribution network, a block factory, a dairy farm and a school, with plans for a hospital and housing. The Repairer of the Breach resolved the apparent contradiction between the praxis of sinking roots deeper and deeper in Jamaica and the ideology of repatriation with his 'Jamaica is Africa' doctrine, for which he astutely claimed divine sanction from the Emperor himself.

Repatriation is one of the fundamental cornerstones of the Rastafari belief system. Through its demand, the Rastafari not only call attention to the exigency of correcting an historic injustice done to millions of Africans, continental and diasporic, but also reject as false the identities of 'Jamaican,' 'Antiguan,' 'Brazilian,' 'American,' and so on, which they argue were imposed after the infamous Middle Passage. Consequently, the Rastafari, long before the term was (re)appropriated by the diaspora, have maintained that they are 'African.' Some of them, reasoning that the word 'Africa' is a designation of the European 'slave-masters,' prefer what they regard as Africa's original name, 'Ethiopian.'

Quite clearly, the basis on which the Rastafari and, before them, Marcus Garvey and other Pan-African thinkers were able to identify themselves as 'Africans' was their consciousness of an historical connectedness. In this sense, in the mythic conversation with Claudius Henry, the Emperor was right: there is no need to go back to Africa, because Africa is already in Jamaica.

But is the connection only historical? Might it not also be cultural? Is it possible to argue that 'Africa is already in Jamaica' in the sense that the shape, the contours and character of Jamaica's culture have already been, and are still being, shaped by the Africans? This question, framed in the context of the wider diaspora, has been one of concern in the anthropology and history of the descendants of the Africans in the Americas, as the reader would have gathered from the previous essay.

A comment on some recent contributions to the debate is useful in identifying where we have reached after three generations of scholarship beginning with Herskovits, and in defining more sharply my present essay. Most recent scholars have sought to distance themselves from the methodology and assumptions of Herskovits, the 'great ancestor' (Apter 1991, 235). Apter, with the wisdom of hindsight, calling Herskovits's syncretic paradigm 'wrong, misconceived ... simply outdated' (p. 235), 'scientistic' (p. 236), 'psychologistic' with 'racist overtones' (p. 242), faults it for its underlying assumptions of cultural purity and cultural determinism. Apter succeeds in showing that syncretism was itself a feature of Yoruba religion, though in this he was anticipated by Peel (1968). Yoruba cosmology, by creating a 'ritually safeguarded space' of deep knowledge accessed only by powerful priests and priestesses, made possible the protection of 'the hidden paramountcy' of a group's own orisas, while paying ritual obeisance to the orisas of another group exercising political dominance over them. This 'inner logic of syncretic practices as strategies of appropriation and empowerment' is what is responsible for the syncretisms identified by Herskovits as a feature of acculturation.

Fernandez (1990), according to his own account the last student supervised by Herskovits, and Scott (1991) also reveal the limitations of Herskovits's methods, but, unlike Apter, do this by placing the man and his works within their contemporary setting. If in prefacing his own masterpiece Fernandez (1982, xx) paid tribute to Herskovits, who 'initiated my interest in the 'creation of cultural realities,'" in his more recent essay he exposes the dilemma of Herskovits's cultural relativism. On the one hand he says that Herskovits affirms the equality of all cultures, while on the other hand he recoils from the ethical relativism which his critics argued was implicit. On the one hand, Herskovits pleads for tolerance of all cultures, while on the other he calls for a 'tough-minded' rejection of ethnocentrism. On the one hand he is deeply suspicious of the concept of absolutes or transcendent values, while on the other he is forced to concede the existence of universals. Fernandez, by arguing that Herskovits's cultural relativism 'belongs to its time and should be judged by its time' (Fernandez 1990, 157), implies also that his work and contribution to the science of anthropology must be similarly judged, for it was a time when the science was establishing itself, when 'the first fruits of grounded ethnographic research were beginning to accumulate, a time challenged by European barbarism' (1990, 157).

The theme of the historical contemporaneity of Herskovits appears also in Scott's (1991) incisive essay on the problem of the African past as posed by anthropology. By linking Richard Price's much acclaimed *First Time* with Herskovits's *Rebel Destiny* (and more generally with Herskovits's work on the African diaspora, of which *Rebel Destiny* was only one), as having the same agenda, and by exposing the weakness of *First Time,* he also exposes the limitations of Herskovits's attempt to find the elusive African past. These are twofold: a reification of the past, as well as an ideological assumption that the history and culture of the African descendants in the New World require the anthropological authentication of that past. In point of fact, he points out, *First Time*, despite its compelling ethnography, presents the past through the oral testimony of Price's Saramaka informants and the written scripts of their Dutch colonizers as though they were both 'culturally different, yet conceptually uncomplicated, ways of re-presenting the past in the present' (1991, 268). *Rebel Destiny* enabled Herskovits to plot a scale of intensity of retention of the African past, on which the Saramaka are at the strong end and the American Negro at the weak. Scott is arguing more strongly than any other recent critic that the problematic as laid out by Herskovits still dominates the study of the cultures of the African diaspora. He proposes a 'theoretical relocation' of the problematic in what he calls 'tradition,' that is, 'a differentiated field of discourse whose unity, such as it is, resides not in anthropologically authenticated traces, but in its being constructed around a distinctive group of tropes or figures' (1991, 278). Thus, instead of slavery (Price) or Africa (Herskovits) circulating as 'authentic presences,' the 'tradition' trope would examine the ways in which people articulate and invest with meaning their own sense of the past, construct political communities that link past with present, and valorise the virtues of the past in the construction of personal and communal identity.

One could not agree with Scott more. When, for example, he asks 'How are the figures of Africa and Slavery employed in the fashioning of specific virtues, in the cultivation of specific dispositions, specific modes of address, specific styles — of dress, of speech, of song, of the body's movements?' (1991, 279), he is clearly pointing to a lacuna in African diaspora studies. But in a concern to avoid falling into the sin of essentialism, disclaiming both essentialism and anti-essentialism, he overlooks, it seems to me, an important angle which the comparative method can offer in understanding how cultures adapt, preserve continuities and undergo change. Thus, if, alongside the discourse of 'tradition,' which is an articulation in the present of a subjectively appropriated, therefore imagined, past, we also register a discourse of the many 'presents' scattered all over the diaspora, we may be able to understand 'the ontological status of Africa and slavery in the present of the cultures of the New World' (Scott 1991, 279) without having to make the very dubious assumption about an 'authentic' past. And both the tradition and the present apply to the continent as well, for there, since the rise of Ethiopianism, 'Africa' has been an 'imagined' past, one that has evolved its own narratives.

This chapter, then, is comparative. It compares the worldviews of two peoples: Yoruba Nigerians and Jamaicans. I argue that at the level of their respective worldviews, very important similarities may be revealed, which, in the light of its own demographic origins, may explain one of the driving forces within Jamaican culture. I arrived at the need to adopt this approach from my own discovery of the persistence of the traditional worldview of the Jamaican folk, expressed through the folk religion and system of beliefs known as Revival, within the avowedly anti-Revival and historically more recent Rastafari movement (see Chevannes 1994). What appears to be, and indeed is, a very different religion is at a deeper level of consciousness, if you will, a reformulation or reconstruction of a shared worldview.

Though conceived independently of the very important contribution of Mintz and Price (1992), it should be immediately apparent that my paradigm is an intellectual affine of the one they propose. But whereas their proposal hinges on unravelling these deeper structures at the historical points of contact, it seems to me that since, from an anthropological point of view, the value of any historical search for origins can only lie in its interpretive potential for the present, locating that quest in the domain of anthropology rather than of history might prove just as fruitful. This is not to ignore the fact that any disjuncture between history and anthropology is imagined rather than real, or that culture is nothing if not historically situated (Comaroff and Comaroff 1992).

What follows, then, is a comparative study of the present worldviews of two different cultures: Jamaican and Yoruba Nigerian (in this chapter 'Nigeria' is limited to the Yoruba ethnic group). I limit the study in the Caribbean context to Jamaica, because of my greater familiarity with the folk culture of this country than with any other in the African-Caribbean, having grown up and conducted my postgraduate research there. If the exercise is rewarding, my hope is to extend it generally through the rest of the Caribbean and possibly the rest of the hemispheric diaspora. On the Africa side, if, as Mintz and Price (1992, 45) acknowledge, there is a generalized outlook common to African cultures, then it should not matter much which ethnic group one chooses for comparison. Nonetheless, I choose the Yoruba for three reasons. First they were among the main groups which forged the new Pan-African identity in Jamaica (Schuler 1979; Robotham 1989); second the Christianity that emerged among the Yoruba was, as in the case of Jamaica, Protestant; and third, there is available a large corpus of ethnographic and other literary material available in lieu of first-hand field research.

THE JAMAICAN SPIRIT WORLD

All cultures recognize both a spiritual and material dimension to reality. Where they may differ is in the relationship between the two. Jamaicans recognize what the followers of Alexander Bedward called a temporal and a spiritual order. Seeking to reconcile the appearance at the same time, in the 1910s, of the two great leaders people regarded as prophets, namely Bedward and Marcus Garvey, Jamaicans regarded the former as Aaron, the high priest, the latter as Moses, the prophet. Where Moses had responsibility for governance, mobilization, war, diplomacy and negotiation — affairs of the temporal order — Aaron was entrusted with the task of direct representation to and encounter with God — affairs of the spiritual order.

These two orders have different modes of existence and procedures and both are focused on the human world. Put another way, the spiritual order is the more powerful, but the temporal is its end, not vice versa. In 1895 the colonial government arrested Bedward for several anti-white sermons and the society settled back into calm. In 1921 at the head of a large procession of followers, he set out on a seven-mile journey to the capital 'to do battle.' The authorities wasted no time, ambushing and crushing the 700 believers. Bedward's 'battle' however, was to be conducted on an entirely spiritual plane. The idea of spiritual battle has been a common motif throughout the historical development of the Revival folk religion to the present day, and is very much a part of Rastafari as well.

What does the spiritual consist of? First there is the existence of certain named and unnamed spirits, beginning with God. As a child I knew of him as Big Maasa. Today he is more popularly called Father or The Father, or Jah to the Rastafari. Originally conceived as a sky God, who controls the elements and human fate, through the influence of the Rastafari his abode in the sky has been downplayed and his omnipresence emphasized. But every flash of lightning or peal of thunder is affirmed by Rastafari with a roar of 'JAH! RASTAFARI!' Death by lightning is an act of The Father and usually a sign of retribution.

Since Rastafari represent a deviation from the norm, it might be useful just to say here that among this group Jah is the only spirit. But, though spiritual, he exists in the flesh in the person of Haile Selassie. Normatively speaking, though, Jamaicans believe in a multiplicity of named spirits. Besides the Father there is the Holy Ghost, or the Holy Spirit. A benevolent spirit, he possesses, as among Pentecostalists. Then there are the 'angels' and 'saints,' spirits of a Christian derivation. Revivalists add prophets such as Jeremiah and Isaiah. Other named spirits are the River Muma or Water spirit and the Indian spirit.

Satan, Rutibel and Moloch are among a group of spirits called 'fallen angels,' those ejected from heaven by God. They are earth-bound. Satan or the Devil has two sides to his character. One is malevolent, as in Christian mythology, the other is a trickster who hides things or makes one forget where one has left them, puts obstacles in the way, *etc*. A common saying on such occasions is: 'The Devil [is] strong!'

Next are the dead: the named and the unnamed. The named dead are the ancestors and known persons who have died and who appear to the living in dreams. The unnamed dead are called *dopi* (duppy). These have their own characteristics, which are generally the inverse of what is human: their feet never touch the ground, they talk with a nasal accent, roam at nights but must return to the grave by sunrise. There is an entire genre of folklore devoted to *dopi*. There is also a category of demons, called *ruolin kyaaf* (rolling calf).

All the above are spirits that can be identified. They have names. However, this is not the only way Jamaicans conceive of the spiritual order. The spiritual is above all an invisible mode of being which is essentially force or power. Every spirit has that power, by virtue of being spirit, in due measure and according to sphere of competence. But Man, that is the human being, is capable of acquiring this power. Fundamentally, this is possible because he is himself part spirit. Jamaicans frequently do not say: 'I decide to,' but 'My spirit tells me to.' However, the actualization of this potential is something else. It is the quest for and the use of this power that constitutes easily one of the most fundamental aspects of the Jamaican worldview.

> O, let the Power fall on me, my Lord,
> Let the Power fall on me!
> O, let the Power from heaven fall on me,
> Let the Power fall on me!

This is a very old Revival song which calls on God to infuse the singer with that spiritual force. Rastafari chant this identical song with appropriate adjustments:

> O, let the Power fall on I, Fari,
> Let the Power fall on I!
> O, let the Power from Jah fall on I,
> Let the Power fall on I!

The falling imagery, of course, derives from the earlier identification of God with the sky.

The acquisition of spiritual power comes about in four ways I have so far identified: through knowledge, ritual, spirit possession and charisma.

Knowledge

As the spiritual order is invisible to the human eye, so is the knowledge of it hidden from the ordinary person. From the early secret societies among the incoming Africans during the early part of slavery, to initiation into Myal, the Pan-African religion of the last decades of the eighteenth century and the first half of the nineteenth, to the fascination with DeLaurence publications such as the Sixth and Seventh Books of Moses, with Masonic lodges, Hindu mysticism, Roman Catholicism, the Book of the Macabees, and the Egyptian Book of the Dead in the twentieth, a tradition has persisted that knowledge is power, and secret knowledge is the source of feared and respected power.

By knowing how to harness spiritual power one is able to master the present life, uphold one's interests, subordinate one's enemies, thwart their machinations, and control others. Among Rastafari is a strong belief that the control over the Black man by the White man is maintained by control over knowledge. Hence the popular song by Max Romeo:

> Bring back Macabee version
> That God gave to Black man;
> Take back King James version,
> King James was a white man.

Black man, get up, stan' up 'pon yu foot
And give black Jah the glory;
Black man, stan' up an' know yuself,
And give black Jah the glory!

The King James version of the Bible suppresses the Book of the Macabees, which is included in the Vulgate used by the Roman Catholics — another reason for the fear in which Roman Catholic priests were held. Those who have this knowledge are called 'scientists.' Indeed the knowledge itself is called 'science' or the 'heights' of science. In this folk use of the word, science refers not to chemistry, physics and biology, but to knowledge of a deeper or higher level of reality, the only level that ultimately matters, the knowledge of the spirit force. Another name for a scientist is 'four eye man:' two eyes in front, two behind. He can see danger from any side.

Although acquisition of science is a technical matter that may be acquired by studying or by initiation, it is available only to those whose minds have the capacity. Some people are believed to get 'mad,' that is insane, from their inability to cope with such heights of knowledge and power. But those who do manage to remain sane are feared. Here lies the power of the *obyaman*. *Obya* is sorcery, which, due to colonial suppression, is unfortunately confused with the role of priest-healer-diviner. Consequently, some *obyamen* receive clients for healing. Whereas *obya* implies technical skill, healing and divining are charismata.

Ritual

Under ritual could be distinguished personal and collective rituals. An example of personal ritual would be fasting urged by one's spirit, or a food taboo required by one's familiar, or staring into the sun, as four-eye men are able to do. I would also include here the following example. In June 1993, a domestic helper and very devout member of the United Church (Presbyterian, Congregational and Disciples of Christ) was dismissed after fourteen years by her employer in circumstances that she concluded were unjust. Unable to reach a reconciliation, she 'read Psalm 35' in search of justice.

> Plead my cause, O Lord, with those who strive with me;
> 1. Fight against those who fight against me.
> 2. Take hold of shield and buckler, and stand up for my help.
> 3. Also draw out the spear, and stop those who pursue me. Say to my soul, "I am your salvation."
> 4. Let those be put to shame and brought to dishonour who seek after my life; Let those be turned back and brought to confusion who plot my hurt.
> 5. Let them be like chaff before the wind, and let the angel of the Lord chase them.
> 6. Let their way be dark and slippery, and let the angel of the Lord pursue them.
> 7. For without cause they have hidden their net for me in a pit, which they have dug without cause for my life.
> 8. Let destruction come upon him unexpectedly, and let his net that he has hidden catch himself; Into that very destruction let him fall.

Two or three weeks later a scandal precipitated the sudden disintegration of her employer's family. On hearing of it, she expressed satisfaction with the words: 'I did not think the Psalm would have worked so quickly!' In a separate incident, she read Psalm 37 on a vindictive tenant who in leaving had destroyed her plants. She placed three leaves of plants on the pages of the Psalm and closed the Bible. In less than two weeks her enemy was chopped up by her own friend. As proof of the power of the Psalm, 'the juice from the leave-dem suck out and cover the psalm, and the leave-dem dry, dry!' Other Psalms with a similar reputation are 7 and 109.

The Rastafari concept of 'livity' might be understood in this sense of personal ritual, insofar as 'livity' requires the observance of personal food and other taboos that enhance one's personal contact with Jah and makes one like Jah, in fact. Two critical parts of Rastafari praxis are the maintenance of the dreadlocks and sexual abstinence. The dreadlocks are not only a symbol of racial self-affirmation, but, as I have argued elsewhere (Chevannes 1995, 97-126), a reclamation of masculine power over the evil Babylon, that is white Jamaican society. The attribution of mystical power to hair, and loss of mystical power to sexual intercourse are common motifs in Jamaica. Thus, the integrity of one's hair (rationalized as the Nazarite vow of the Israelite hero, Samson) and celibacy remove one from the sphere of control of Babylon. As I will discuss later (see pages 75-6 below), the well-known salt taboo of the Rastafari may have a similar rootedness in a popular worldview.

For the most part, though, the quest for power is sought through collectively observed rituals: prayer and fasting among Revivalists, other Christians, and certain groups of Rastas, and among the Rastafari reasoning and the nyabinghi. Indeed the origins of the nyabinghi dance lay in the belief that the dancers had the mystical power to effect the death of an oppressor, hence the expression 'to dance the nyabinghi for' such a person. As for the ritual sharing of the sacred herb, ganja, the acquisition of the divine knowledge becomes the most important reason for the communion.

Spirit possession

Through spirit possession one can acquire spiritual power. In Revival, spirit possession achieves something like a calling. One never knows if and when one will be possessed, but one usually 'gets in the spirit' (*Santería* and other African-Caribbean religions speak of being 'mounted') for the first time in a ritual setting, and one is struck or laid low. Wherever the person falls, there will he or she lie, since it is forbidden to interfere with the work of the spirit. People called for the first time will remain for days, sometimes weeks, until 'released.' Thereafter, the possessing spirit becomes one's familiar or guardian. In return one may be required to perform a duty, for example an annual feast known as a 'Table,' or a food taboo, as in the case of some people who report sudden revulsion to fish after possession by the water spirit. In Jamaican Pentecostalism, which recognizes only the Supreme Deity, possession is referred to as the 'in-filling' of the Holy Spirit.

Charisma

The main charismata, or gifts, are prophecy and healing. These may be acquired under spirit possession, when the possessed travels or is taken on a journey and shown what mission is in store for him or her. Or they may be acquired in vision. Nowadays healing and prophecy are usually combined in one person, but years ago one would often see the itinerant 'warner' delivering his or her message. The early Rastafari leaders were all prophets in this sense, and two of them, Leonard Howell and Joseph Hibbert, healers as well.

The art of healing combines divination and cure. The healer is also a diviner. In Jamaican tradition, the healer first confirms the symptoms and other particulars of the client without asking questions. Healing culture is based on the belief that there are two types of illnesses, those caused by physical and those caused by spiritual forces. The two are distinguished by a temporal process which begins first with herbal remedies in the home and then by resort to public or private primary health care services. The failure of these then leads to the search for spiritual causes and cures. These cures involve certain ritual baths, prescribed prayers, and charms.

To round off this discussion of what I understand to be a central concept in the Jamaican worldview, namely spiritual power, two brief comments are necessary, the first on relations with the dead, and the second on the mediating language with the spiritual world.

Not all relations with the spiritual world are motivated by the desire to acquire power. I refer specifically to the attitude towards the dead, which, on close examination is governed by rituals of separation and distance. During the wake and *nine night* ceremonies the singers arm themselves with salt and white rum, and everyone who leaves the dead yard is supposed to make one revolution at the gate and never to look back. If the dead person was one who loved walking about the place, pins are stuck into the soles or if he was irascible, his pockets may be sewn up to prevent him collecting stones to use as missiles against the living. Grave diggers always make libations of white rum before performing their work. The dead must process feet first on leaving the church or home to deprive them of the ability to return (in the folklore they are unable to walk backwards). At midnight in the *nine night* ceremony, the house is swept, the furnishings rearranged and the clothes of the deceased packed up and left at the nearest crossroads. For one year after death widows will wear black underwear. At the end of this period of mourning, or as soon as possible thereafter, a permanent shrine in the form of a tomb is erected over the grave. Failure to perform this last act may earn the displeasure of the ancestor, who may sometimes issue warnings in dreams. Despite increasing urbanization, and with it the use of cemeteries, the traditional form of burial within the yard, in what is called the 'family plot,' still prevails. Until the rite of transition to ancestor status is complete, the dead represent raw, uncontrolled power that can inflict harm to those coming in contact with it.

This fear of contamination with the dead, I have also argued, constitutes the basis of the Rastafari rejection of death as an inevitable reality for believers and unbelievers alike. As is well known, some go so far as to avoid all foods of flesh as *dedaz*, dead things.

Communication from the spirit world takes place through dreams and visions. Dreams are manifestations during sleep, but visions occur while the person is asleep or awake. What distinguishes them is the decisiveness of their import. A dream may be a simple message, for example from an ancestor, but a vision always demands some personal decision. All conversions are the result of visions. When a person is struck by the spirit for the first time, his or her experiences are visionary. Both dreams and visions may or may not require interpretation.

Communication from the human world is effected through symbolic representation. Here I would include the use of prayer. Revival is rich in the language of symbols: sacred spaces as repositories of spirits, herbs, stones, flags, colours, water, swords, show breads (duck, crown, alligator or mongoose shaped), bottled drinks, salt, Bible, white rum, blood, gestures and other body movements, dress, dance, and so forth.

Yoruba Christianity

Like Jamaica, Nigeria was a colonial society, which conferred high status on Europeans. Also like Jamaica, a western education was, under British rule, an important means of acquiring status.

Christianity, in its Protestant variety, first came to the country in the 1840s, nearly a century after its introduction among the Jamaicans. As in Jamaica, the stress was on the Bible, God's word. The real growth of Christianity, however, came in the early decades of the twentieth century. According to Peel (1968), Western Nigeria was 74 per cent pagan in 1921, but by 1952, thirty years later, it had become 47 per cent Christian, 47 per cent Islamic and only 6 per cent pagan. Yet, Yoruba traditional religion was 'more important still today than the figure of 6 per cent would suggest' (1968, 52–3). How important he does not say, but Adewale (1988) reveals that nominal membership in Yoruba Christianity masks the dual membership in the traditional religion. He also argues that the missionary churches have had to accommodate traditional practices such as medicine, naming and mortuary rituals, and beliefs such as predestination, reincarnation and retribution. In other words, Yoruba traditional religion continues to shape the outlook of the Yoruba in very fundamental ways. As Peel put it, 'Christianity in Yoruba, both in relation to society, and in its meaning to its adherents, is Yoruba Christianity.'

The Yoruba religion has been the subject of extensive research and study. One of the caveats repeatedly mentioned by writers is the fact that there are variations throughout Yorubaland, so that in no two areas will one find identical beliefs, narratives or deities (see Hallgren 1988, Apter 1987, Olupona 1983, Simpson 1980, Akama 1987, McClelland 1982). However, it is fair to say that the Yoruba worldview has several main features. For example, through divination the harmony between man and God is maintained, and disorder and disharmony, represented by Esu, held in check. Esu is not absolute evil, however: he is a trickster and troublemaker as well, and sometimes even helps.

As conceived by the Yoruba, the human person is a composite of material and spiritual forces. The material, and perishable, parts are the body, the shadow (*ojiji*) and the mind (*iye*); while the spiritual, and immortal parts are the heart (*oka*) and breath or soul (*emi*). At death the immortal part returns to Olorun, whence it came, and becomes an ancestor. Death is not feared by the Yoruba, unless it is untimely, in which case there is a supernatural cause that can only be known through divination. Ancestors, it is believed, may be reborn in their descendants. Veneration of the ancestors is observed in two important rituals, the Egungun and Gelede festivals.

The spirit world thus conceived comprises God, the deities and the ancestors, as well as witches that may take natural forms. But what gives it its peculiar qualities are its invisibility and power. The concept of spiritual power, by all accounts, is pivotal to an understanding of Yoruba religious life. Yoruba religion, an informant tells Andrew Apter (1987, 247), referring to the Yemoja festival in which the masks dance their way from the grove into the town, 'is a form of African electronics — we are bringing electricity from the bush to light up the town.' Apter comments:

> First it underlines the conscious public attitude toward orisa worship as a flow of power, technologically accomplished rather than conceptually interpreted. Ritual paraphernalia such as brass staffs (*opa osoro*) and ritual vessels may be ornamented to please the gods, but their ritual function is practical — they transmit and 'store' ritual power (*ase*) much like modern broadcasting devices, condensers, cables and batteries. Second the analogy illuminates the 'design' of such technology. Ritual power, like electricity is 'hot,' highly charged and dangerous. Unbridled it can kill. It must be contained, limited and properly regulated and channelled to benefit human society.

Ase is spiritual power transmitted ritually. But there is another form through which power is transmitted or acquired non-ritually, through charisma. The word for this is *agbara*. As we shall see later, the distinction is important.

The idea of power flowing technologically introduces several critical ideas. First, certain ritual objects may be invested with spiritual power. Rivers, trees, groves, hills and other objects of nature sacred to the deities have *ase*. Blood has ritual power, and it is for this reason that restrictions are placed on women during their menstruation. Second, ritual, correctly performed, is one means of personally and collectively acquiring it. The words *A se* or *ebo a fin*, which end every sacrifice and prayer, mean, according to some scholars, not 'may it be so,' but 'it will be so.' Once the prescribed religious acts have been carried out, the orisas must respond.

A third idea is implicit in the analogy, namely that it is possible to acquire and control spiritual power through knowledge. Babalawos, the Yoruba priests of Ifa, acquire such knowledge through a life of training beginning from seven or eight years old, passing through four stages of knowledge and culminating in a rite of initiation and transmission of power lasting seven days. Babalawo knowledge, as also the knowledge of the orisa cults, is secret only to the initiated. Babalawo literally means 'father of secrets.' Even so, it is distributed according to seniority, the more senior the deeper the knowledge. Thus the power that comes with knowledge derives its potency from its limitation and depth.

The focus on spiritual power brings to the fore a central preoccupation in Yoruba religion with all forms of disorder, moral, cosmic and physical. The Yoruba see the world as preserved in balance between the forces of order and disorder. Creativity, progress and social and physical well-being derive from the containment through appeasement of chaos and disorder. Rituals of divination and healing are therefore the most pervasive, and the Babalawo the most important religious functionary. He both divines and prescribes the right ritual sacrifices and medicines, through a highly sophisticated system of divination that rests on a corpus of 16 sets of verses known as *Odu*.

Such was the worldview that Christianity and Islam changed in a most dramatic way in the three decades from 1920. What concerns me here is not the factors which have brought about this change, but the shape of the changes. It is on this that any comparison with Jamaica rests.

Much has been made of the process of the rationality of conversion to Christianity in Africa (Horton 1971, 1975; Peel 1968, 1977, 1990). When people adopt a new and alien belief, they do not thereby jettison their old worldview lock, stock and barrel, but are compelled to make a new rearrangement of it. Only by reinterpreting past experiences, by bringing new insights to bear on them, in fact, does the new religion become a new imperative. It would have been a great surprise, therefore, were important aspects of Yoruba traditional worldview not found in the personal conversions and careers of the men and women, the prophets, through whose tireless effort and devotion Christianity spread through Yorubaland. For example, the hunter Egunjobi, five years after his baptism in 1907, was hunting when an angel appeared and commanded him to preach of God's anger and of 'the coming war and epidemic' (Peel 1968, 59). Egunjobi did nothing until a year later, when compelled by repeated dreams. Still a Baptist, he preached the power of prayer, but, says Peel, 'he did not ban healing herbs; he mixed them with water, and added a psalm to be said, emphasizing that it was the power of Jesus which healed.'

For this and other prophets, the new Christian religion made old problems intelligible, as the old religion failed to do. The personal God, Jesus, the word of God, the Bible, the power of prayer — all new elements — and the gift of healing, were incorporated within the traditional language of visionary experiences and dreams. Even as Yorubaland became Christian, the traditional Yoruba worldview was finding fresh ways to express itself. Peel explains this as due to an accommodating approach by the native Christian evangelists, who looked for Yoruba equivalents of Christian teachings and practices. Thus the Bible replaces Ifa divination, while Christian symbols such as Christ's sacrifice or the power of the Psalms are given a Yoruba interpretation.

Peel studied two Aladura churches, the Christ Apostolic Church (CAC) and the Cherubim and Seraphim. In the interest of brevity, I focus on the CAC. It was founded by Sadare and Sophie Odunlami, both members of a praying band within the Anglican Church. They fell out with the Bishop of Lagos after declaring infant baptism wrong, a position they had reached through visions, following the death of some infants. The Bishop 'praised the high morality of the Society but objected to its insistence on the exclusive use of faith healing, its opposition to the baptism of infants, and its reliance on dreams and visions for guidance' (Peel, 1968, 63). Leaving the Church Missionary Society, they contacted an American sect called Faith Tabernacle. What initially drew them was 'the emphatic and confidently Biblical assertion of the effectiveness of prayer' (Peel 1968, 64). This, says Peel, was the main element passed on to CAC from Faith Tabernacle, though there were other beliefs, some of which were rejected, like the forswearing of property in preparation for the millennium. Others, deriving from or more in keeping with Yoruba traditions, like baptism of the Holy Ghost and reliance on visions, the CAC founders insisted on, and as a result, broke with Faith Tabernacle. Seeking European sponsorship as a necessary way of gaining legitimacy under Nigerian conditions, they linked up with a British Pentecostal group, the Apostolic Church, from which they split in 1940 over the question of divine healing. The English missionaries did not forbid the use of all medicine, and indeed themselves took quinine as a prophylactic against malaria. The founders objected and broke with them, taking the name they are now known by, Christ Apostolic Church. Yet, they nevertheless institutionalized the instrumental use of *omi iye* (water of life).

Examining the process whereby these Nigerian Christians attached themselves to, and detached themselves from missionary Christianity, we may detect a cultural imperative in the search for effective means of dealing with sickness and disease. This they found in prayer.

The name Aladura derives from the Yoruba word for prayer, *adura*, and came to be applied to these Yoruba Christians because of their emphatic rejection of all other means of healing. Adewale (1988) refers to them by their alternate name, 'Prayer and Faith Healing Churches.' Most Christians treat Christian symbols in a 'technological' manner, 'in that they assume that the process of getting what [they] want is partly like following a recipe or operating a machine, and partly like asking someone to do something for you' (Peel 1968,121). If I interpret Peel correctly, the attitude of Yoruba Christians to prayer is more in line with the traditional religion than with European Christian orthodoxy, in their emphasis on prayer as protection against evil and evildoers.

Prayer in the Yoruba religion was also aimed at seeking knowledge of God's will, and was closely linked to dreams and visions, media through which the spirit world communicates with the living. What is new among the Aladuras is their conscious seeking of visionary experiences through prayer and fasting. Here too, reliance on dreams and visions is more in keeping with the traditional religion than with Christianity. The Yoruba display greater faith in dreams and greater readiness to interpret them. In other words, dreams and visions are quite normal, because the spiritual world is a normal part of everyday reality. Notwithstanding the relatively little research done on dreams in Africa (Jedrej and Shaw 1992), and his own caution concerning the influence which the investigator's own interests may have on whether dreaming is ubiquitous or not in the given situation, Charsley (1992, 156) nevertheless admits that 'if Africa is viewed as a whole and contrasted with Euro-America, the attachment of significance to dreams in Africa is considerable.' They are experienced as significant phenomena at all levels of Yoruba society and through all walks of life. Politicians, students, professionals attach as much significance to dreams as do prophets and visionaries.

In Yoruba theory, if the cause of disease is a natural agent, the cure is to use proper techniques, such as modern medicine. If, however, it is of evil or divine origin, the Yoruba turn to traditional medicine and divination. But there is also an order of appeal. Simpson (1980, 136), whose research was conducted in 1964, reported that 84 per cent of 184 respondents in Ibadan said that their last resort in a serious illness would be the dispensary or the hospital. However, this must be balanced against the finding that 52 per cent of those who used the hospital or dispensary also consulted babalawos or used magical protection. He therefore agreed that Nigerians resorted to the babalawos when their home remedies failed, and further demonstrated that they also availed themselves of western healing.

For their part, the Aladuras' response is not uniform. Though both trends, CAC and Seraphim, hold to healing by faith, Seraphim is not averse to medicines, and indeed uses *omi iye*, the water of life. CAC, on the contrary, bans all drugs and medicine as weakening faith in Christ. Aladuras hold the same theory of disease aetiology as among pre-Christian Yoruba, but differ radically in what they conceive of as the cure. Witches are believed to exist as surely as physically caused illnesses, and, says Peel (1968, 96), 'it is natural that the source of spiritual power unleashed by the Aladuras should be used for countering the former as the latter, particularly since ...the [Aladura] revival was seen as a battle against the Devil and his works — which included evil-thinking, idol-worship and witchcraft equally.'

Thus, one of the main concerns of Yoruba religion is healing. It was 'the main occasion of the emergence of the Aladura churches' (Peel 1968, 127), which turned to prayer and *omi iye* because these were more powerful than traditional medicine. Healing therefore rests on spiritual power.

Both Seraphim and Christ Apostolic feel themselves to be the recipients of *agbara emi*, that is, spiritual power. Their most frequent epithet for God in Aladura hymns and prayers is *Alagbara*, the Dispenser of Power. The great prophets were *alagbara emi*, men of spiritual power.

This way of expressing what religion is about is certainly in line with traditional Yoruba religious views, according to which a whole range of people had 'power' of one kind or another: obas, babalawos, witches, men with powerful juju (Peel 1968, 135). So important a concept is 'power' in Yoruba thought that the English word itself has become a catchword even among non-English speaking Yoruba.

What is the nature of this power? From a reading of Peel, one may conclude that there are three aspects. Power is life: *iye*. This is the quality most associated with God, Olorun Alaiye, the Dispenser of Life. Second, power is also charisma, *agbara*. *Agbara* is the spiritual gift that the healers and prophets had, not only with respect to their miracles and prophecies, but also with respect to their personal authority. As such, it is distinct from *ase*, which is 'legitimated *agbara*' (Peel 1968, 137) that one would receive when ordained as a priest. *Agbara* is from God, *ase* is from man. According to Olupona (1983, 113), however, Olodumare (or Olorun, God), the orisas and the king are all thought to possess *ase*. Indeed, he reports that the Celestial Church of Christ observe a distinction between spiritual power conferred by anointing and that of the founding prophets. Thus, there may not be a contradiction as such, but a way of expressing two different means of transmission of spiritual power, whose ultimate source is God. Spiritual power that is transmitted direct from God to any individual He chooses is *agbara*, charisma. Spiritual power transmitted ritually is *ase*.

Third, there is a sense in which spiritual power is conceived as a substance, something that is transmissible from father to son, or from drinking *omi iye*, or from saying a prayer or pronouncing certain holy words, or through the gift of tongues.

Spiritual power may be acquired in a number of ways: first by isolation and seclusion, in sacred places such as groves and mountain tops; second through transmission, as we have already seen, whether from ordination by a prophet like Babalola, or through inheritance from one's forebear; and third, through knowledge.

In this last, the Bible (and for that matter the Koran) is a most powerful source, whose words are invested with special power. In this respect, knowledge of the Bible is to power 'what a handbook of electrical engineering is to electricity' (Peel 1968, 141). And not only the Bible but other documents, such as Blavatsky's *The Secret Doctrine*, or *The Sixth and Seventh Books of Moses*, or S.L.MacGregor's *The Kabbalah Revealed*. 'Rosicrucianism which 'unlocks the hidden powers of the mind' has a considerable following among Yorubas' (Peel 1968, 142).

To summarize, at the centre of Yoruba worldview are concepts about the nature of the spirit world, with a particular focus on power. This power is the most important attribute of that world. It gives the spirit world its peculiar advantage over the world of living human beings. Its acquisition and disposal by humans form the most important rationale for religious observance and ritual. Based on traditional concepts, it has so far shaped the way Nigerians have adopted Christianity. It is this preoccupation with spiritual power that apparently gives Yoruba religious life, both traditional and Christian, its this-world orientation. Whether this is a function of the social or the economic stage of development of Yoruba society, or of both, need not concern us at the moment. What is important is the identification of the features of this aspect of their worldview.

TRANS-ATLANTIC SIMILARITIES

It may seem obvious, but, in light of the line of argument being pursued, it needs to be reaffirmed that the Nigerians and the Jamaicans whose worldviews I have been exploring have different cultures. One only needs to consider the important role of the lineage in family and social life, as is common to most African societies. In the Yoruba's patriarchal society the lineage extends its influence beyond its role in kinship and marriage into even the prayer bands. In Jamaica, on the other hand, its role is limited to the expression of solidarity in mortuary rituals and affirmation of symbolic corporate identity through the institution of family land. The languages are different, the myths are different, the religions are different.

That said, it is clear that there are remarkable similarities and recurrent themes. The most profound is the conceiving of spiritual reality as power and organizing to tap into it as a means of controlling and influencing daily life. Consistently, both cultures share the following understanding about the nature of this power. First, it is impersonalized force: *agbara* (Yoruba), *power* (Jamaica). The assumption is that it somehow constitutes the nature of spiritual, invisible reality, such that merely being a part of this reality endows one with power over the visible social and material world. The masks when they perform have this power, and so do the recent dead until the rites of passage have been performed. Second, it may be personalized. The Holy Spirit is the principal spiritual force here, but there are 'angels' also. Revivalists have a pantheon that includes Old Testament prophets, the water spirit and others. But Jamaican Pentecostalism, in which Revival has transformed itself, adheres only to the Holy Spirit, in much the same way the Yoruba Christians do.

This power can be acquired. One way is through a special calling or gift. In both cultures the role of prophet and healer generally begins with a demonstrated claim of direct experience of the spiritual world. Healing rituals in Jamaica and Nigeria vary, but whether they take the form of an internship or a consultation at the healer's headquarters or the Pentecostal and Evangelical type crusade, the pattern of centring on the special powers of a special individual through whose touch, or word or presence the power over illness and all forms of affliction is transmitted is the same.

Another way of acquiring power is through knowledge. In both cultures there is widespread belief in the existence of bodies of knowledge, which are a source of power to those initiated few privy to them. The babalawo's knowledge is the result of his long years of training. One of my informants left the company of early Rastafari leader, Joseph Hibbert, because Hibbert failed to share his spiritual knowledge. Akama (1987, 124) tells us that one of the reasons for the great success of the Evangelist Adam Igbudu, whose mass movement started as a prayer band within the Anglican Church, and who was practising faith-healing right up to the 1970s, was the widely held belief of the Araya people that the missionary Bible was a substitute for the true one. It was thought that the true Bible which had been discovered by an illiterate woman in her field was hurriedly shipped away to England by the white missionary who realized its 'unusual power and significance.'

Closely connected to the acquisition of power through knowledge is the acquisition of power technologically (to borrow a term from Peel), as when people manipulate certain passages of the Bible, or perform certain rituals, to achieve desired ends. The difference is that such knowledge is common property, and not that of an initiated elite.

Acquiring power through social positions of authority, for example kingship or chieftainship, or, as Mbiti (1969, 197–8) argues, through age is, as far as I know, missing from Jamaican practices. According to Mbiti, the words of a senior to a junior person and the words of a parent to a child may have mystical power of blessing or curse, but among the Jamaican folk, respect according to age ranking, both within as well as outside the family, still flourishes, as those of younger age must by virtue of being younger accord respect to older ones.

Another similarity in how both cultures view the spiritual world lies in its directedness towards the present world, or, to use the more conventional term, its this-worldly orientation. Whether expressed as a deity or deities, or as impersonalized power, human relations with the spiritual are aimed primarily at achieving ends in this world, rather than in the next. What the meaning of a this-worldly emphasis in religion might be I would like to discuss later, but for now we should note two things. The development of an 'other-world' outlook that posits as the main ethos of religious life the ensuring of salvation in the next is not incompatible with an outlook that also views the satisfaction of earthly needs and advancement of well-being as guaranteed by religious belief and practice. One of the signs of predestination held by the Calvinists was the accumulation of material wealth as a result of hard work and thrift, though its enjoyment was not much a part of the Puritan ethic. In the Jamaican worldview, and I would opine in the Yoruba as well, the pleasure derived from honestly gained wealth is very much a part of the happiness of the saints on the earth.

Given that these two societies examined are not homogeneous, either in terms of religion, ethnicity or class, it might be useful to point out that many of the assumptions are common to a wider range of people than suggested by our focus on particular religious or ethnic groups. This certainly is the case among the Jamaicans and seems to be the case among the Yoruba as well. For Jamaica, as I have already said, the worldview is shared by people who neither are nor were themselves members of Revival churches, orthodox Christians even. Erskine (1978) makes a similar point. Crises have a way of peeling off formal beliefs and practices to reveal underlying links to the cosmology of the folk. It certainly is current enough for politicians to exploit (see Senior 1973). Wedenoja (1978,190ff) finds the main seekers after DeLaurence-type 'science' to be the new middle class. A possible reason, he suggests, is that 'science' may be a more modern and therefore acceptable form of quest for spiritual power than sorcery, or, one might add, than Revival, given the low status of the latter.

In Nigeria the point may be even more strongly sustained. The concept of power was central in the charismatic movement among Nigerian students (Ojo 1988), while Hackett (1989,119) reports that 'Prayers for protection and deliverance became the central religious activity as well as a yearning for more spiritual power' in Calabar during the civil war. Currently there is widespread interest in spiritual science groups like the Rosicrucians as a way of increasing personal power.

But if ideas about the spirit world are uniformly held among the Yoruba, they are also common to other parts of West Africa. We find similar emphases and assumptions of the nature of power, how to access it and what to use it for in Ghana (Baeta 1962, Mullings 1979, Wyllie 1980); Ivory Coast (Walker 1965); Liberia (Stakeman 1986); the Koongo (MacGaffey 1983). Indeed, so common is this throughout the continent that Mbiti (1969,197) could say that 'there is no African society which does not hold belief in mystical power of one type or another.'

My point here is not to argue that this belief is peculiarly African — indeed, all beliefs in the supernatural presume its superior power — but to demonstrate the similarities at the level of worldviews between a sending culture in Africa and the diaspora, which similarities, it may be inferred, are the results of a shared heritage. If it is difficult to identify with certainty most of the cultural practices among peoples of the African diaspora, it is equally difficult to believe that the millions who came to the New World, not to be integrated into but to be segregated from the new European societies for most of their four hundred years here, would have reconstructed their own world based on everything else but the ideas, values and practices with which they came. This is hardly in doubt. What has been in doubt ever since Herskovits is what those ideas, values and practices are.

An example of the difficulty posed by the search for survivals and retentions, and at the same time the possibilities of the approach adopted in this chapter, is useful. The salt taboo among the Rastafari, Roland Littlewood (1995) argues, may not be the retention of an African practice, as some might argue, but of a perverse affinity to a dominant tradition. Inherent in the relations between the ruler and the ruled is an identifiable structure, which, when opposed, results in a given pattern of opposition. Given the common experience of the dominant tradition of British rule, given also common tools of redemption in the form of Christianity and the Bible, Puritan and Rastafari oppositions exhibit remarkable similarities to each other. A salt taboo is one of them; others include certain verbal shifts and figures. Thus the Rastafari salt taboo may be an example of continuity not with Africa but with a Puritanical tradition.

But what is the evidence of an African link? As Schuler (1980) has shown, BaKoongo captives freed on the high seas by the British and brought to Jamaica in the decade after the 1838 Emancipation retained a strong belief that ingestion of salt would deprive them of the mystic power through which they could one day return home, which, we know from MacGaffey (1983) and Bockie (1993), is the land of the living. To argue convincingly that this is the source of the Rastafari practice would require being able to trace not just a Koongo influence among them, but specifically the salt taboo. We know now that the origins of the peculiar Rastafari drum tradition are in part traceable to the Kumina ancestral cult (see Moore 1953; Bilby and Lieb 1986; Chevannes 1994), an ancestral cult of the BaKoongo descendants in eastern Jamaica. The salt taboo could plausibly be similarly connected. But to be absolutely sure one would have to be able to establish this link through Leonard Howell, the Rastafari founder whose membership included Kumina people, to the general membership of the Rastafari. Till then, as unproven as Littlewood's theory is, it cannot be dismissed, although the retention theory is the more plausible.

Generally speaking, the linkages sought between the New World and Africa have been of the nature of itemized practices like the salt taboo, notwithstanding important exceptions like Thompson (1984), Alleyne (1988) and Warner-Lewis (1992 and 2003). However, a second problem with this approach is that of situating the particular item within the overall social, economic or cultural life of the diaspora community being studied. 'Morning sport' is a form of cooperative labour derived from similar West African practices like the *dokpwe*. So what? How important is 'morning sport' in the rapidly changing economy of peasant agriculture? And when the practice of 'morning sport' dies out, where will be the 'African heritage?' Again, we know that the silk cotton tree was believed by Jamaican peasants to be the domicile of certain spirits, and therefore before they could fell one to build a dug-out canoe a sacrifice had to be made at the root of the tree. These beliefs are quite clearly similar, if not identical, to those held by some West African peoples. The BaKoongo, for example, believe that the cotton tree is a coven for witches. Good. But then in Jamaica this belief has fallen into desuetude with the modern outboard engine which virtually all fishermen now use. What then? Has another link with Africa been severed? And what of the fact that many of these beliefs and practices are themselves rapidly changing among the continental Africans themselves?

This is where I think the worldview approach accomplishes far more. It allows for greater explanatory value in the processes of both change and continuity. A persistent theme in the literature on the new religious movements in Africa is the doggedness and persistence of old religious needs and concern. The impetus to adopt Christianity is driven mainly by what has been referred to as a this-worldly orientation, namely an approach that focuses the quest for spiritual power on the needs of current life. At the same time, conversion to Christianity is forced by its greater explanatory power over the traditional. The former type of conversion derives from what, as I have already pointed out, Peel calls a technological or instrumentalist conception of religion, the latter type from an intellectualist conception. The debt which this debate on conversion owes to Peel (1968, 1977, 1990) and Robin Horton (1971, 1975) is recognized by everyone who has commented on the subject. Peel, arguing from Weberian premises, situates the difference between the two types of conversion from traditional to world religion in the degree of rationalization undertaken by the new convert to harmonize radically his or her personal morality in line with his or her new beliefs, doing so either radically or only partially. Most Yoruba, he shows, settle for partial rationalization and in so doing retain a this-worldly character in their religion. A small minority, however, undergo the type of radical conversion that bases moral life on an absolute faith in the Supreme Being, not on the power of ritual. With the advance of industrialization, particularly literacy, this in his view is the trend of the future.

Horton, on the other hand, advances his 'Intellectualist Theory' that locates the cause of conversion in a cosmological shift from the microcosm of community to the macrocosm of a wider world in which the cult of the Supreme deity replaces the more localized deities in order to give greater coherence to the more widened social relations. This shift is an inherent logic of widening social relations, whether through long-distance trade or other forms of communication, and does not depend on exogenous causes. Christianity and Islam are only catalysts. He agrees therefore with Peel's identification of conversion to Christianity with industrialization, but disagrees that such a development will necessarily entail the loss of a this-worldly focus. Distinguishing two components in the religious experience, namely 'explanation-prediction-control' and communion, he believes that African religion combined both in a this-worldly way, as did Western Christianity in its earlier history. What Western Christianity has relinquished is 'all pretence of providing a theory of how the world really worked, or a recipe for controlling the course of its affairs'

(1971, 96). This African religion must also do, but if it is to survive it must focus on this-worldly communion.

If a this-worldly orientation is a characteristic feature of African religions, and if, as I hope I have convincingly shown, the conceptualization of the spiritual as power lies behind it, it becomes easier to see why the Christian religion in Jamaica has taken the forms that it has. It becomes easier to understand the high religious mobility between churches, the dual membership phenomenon of the recent past whereby people became members of the mainline churches, in order to access channels of upward mobility and status, but retained their orientation and allegiance to the traditional, in order to access channels of spiritual power and satisfaction — both phenomena common to West Africa as well (see Hackett 1989, 348; Adewale 1988, 37). The worldview approach to African-Jamaican religion (and by extension African-Caribbean and probably African-American, as well) enables us to understand better than we have hitherto been able to why the Jamaicans converted to Christianity, late in the eighteenth century, and why they retained the religious forms they did.

But we should not view this matter of continuity and change in any but dynamic terms. For the shape of African Christianity in Jamaica over the past 200 years has not been the result of that initial missionary impetus alone. Throughout these years the Africans there have constructed and reconstructed forms of Christianity that arise out of a Pan-African imagination, that is an imagination common to all who came, not just Yoruba or BaKoongo or Ashanti. And in the reconstruction, in yet another typically African way, they borrow and create. An 'Indian spirit' joins the pantheon of spirits, Chinese *dopi* are invested with greater power than ordinary (Black) ones, adjustments are made so that Pukumina, a religion that pays ritual obeisance to amoral and malevolent spirits, can coexist with Zion Revival, a religion that does not; and now, as I have recently found in contemporary urban Kingston, both share ritual space with Kumina and Bongo, two ancestral cults. Fernandez (1982, xix) prefaces his great work with the following remark:

THIS BOOK is about efforts at "world reconstruction" that have been going on in small and often isolated villages in the Equatorial Forest of West Africa. The word "reconstruction" brings to mind great wars and great depressions and attempts by mankind to repair and overcome the grievous damage to peoples brought about by these events...

The 'world reconstruction' undertaken by the Africans in Jamaica, in the wake of the grievous damage done them by the great 300-years-old war called European slavery, was accomplished in the isolated villages of a free people on the foundation of worldviews taken with them across the Atlantic. I do believe it continues to provide the dynamism in what is indeed a modern culture.

Chapter Three

Ambiguity and the Search for Knowledge

When asked what he does for a living, Ted Chamberlin (1999) replies that he tells stories. Professor Chamberlin is an expert on Caribbean storytelling, so he is quite aware that *story* sometimes means *lie* in our part of the world. But that is not what he means. In an excellent address on 'the university' he describes what we all do here as storytelling. It is fitting, therefore, that I begin with a story my siblings and I grew up on as children deep in the then remote hills of northern St Catherine, with ghosts and rolling calves outside and storytelling inside.

> Once upon a time there was a woman who had two girls. One of them was her own daughter and the other her stepdaughter. She used to ill-treat the stepdaughter. She would give her all the hard work to do, cleaning the house, fetching the water, while her own daughter would remain idle. When she cooked beef soup, the daughter got all the yams and dasheen, while the stepdaughter got the meat already boiled out and trashy. The child suffered all this in silence.
> One day she decided to turn the child out of the house, telling her to go and look life, and not to come back. 'Poor mi little one,' the child sang as she went obediently on the way. She walked and walked, until she came upon an ugly, old woman sitting by the wayside.

'Maanin, granny!' she greeted the old woman.

'Maanin, mi chile!' the old woman replied. 'Where are you going?'

'My stepmother send me out to go make life.'

'Alright, mi child, but come 'cratch granny back fi her.'

'Yes, granny!' the child replied, and proceeded to scratch. But the old woman's back was not only tough, but rough.

'Not dere so, up so more! Over to the side! Yes, down de so!' The child scratched and scratched, until her fingers started to bleed.

'What's the matter, child?' the old woman asked.

'Nothing, granny,' she replied.

'Are you sure?'

'Yes, Granny!'

'Thank you, my child. Here, take these three eggs. When you reach the first crossroad, break the first one. When you reach the second crossroad, break the second one, and when you reach the third crossroad, break the last one.'

'Thank you, granny. I'm gone, granny.'

'Walk good, mi child!'

The stepdaughter walked and walked. When she came to the first crossroad she began wondering which way to turn, and had almost forgotten what the old lady had said. She broke the first egg. Suddenly a horse and chariot and servants appeared and took her off. At the second crossroad, when she broke the second egg, she received a lot of gold and riches. At the third crossroad, a handsome prince appeared, took her home to meet his father and mother and married her.

Concerned that her family should benefit from her great fortune, she returned to her stepmother and told them her story. But the stepmother was incorrigible. She turned her own daughter out thinking that she too would return rich and famous.

The daughter did not want to go at first, and she kept complaining all along the way. The road was too lonely, the bush too thick, the flies a pest. Then she spied the old lady. Her first remark was, 'What a ugly ol' woman!'

The old lady, pretending not to have heard, said to her, 'Maanin, mi child!'

'Maanin,' she replied grudgingly.
'Where are you going, my child?' asked the old woman.
'None of your business,' she replied rudely.
'Never mind, mi child, come 'cratch granny back.'

Remembering the reward she would get, she complied. But she could not avoid grumbling. She complained that the old lady's back was too rough, that the old lady did not know which part scratching her. By the time her hand began to bleed, she had had it all.

'Look how you cruffy ol' back come cut up mi hand!'

'Never mind, my child. Here take these three eggs. When you reach the first crossroads, break the first one....' She hardly finished. The girl grabbed the eggs from her and went her way.

'Walk good!' the old lady called out.

And so she walked and walked. She was about to complain about the long distance, when she came upon the first crossroads. She could hardly wait. Her fortune was at hand, she thought. But instead of a chariot and servants, a lion came after her. At the second crossroads, she suddenly found her clothes transformed into rags. But on breaking the third egg, a pot of tar fell and covered her all over. She returned home covered in shame.

As told to us children, this story was a deliberate device to reinforce in us such important values as respect for age, good manners (note that the heroine greeted the old lady first, whereas the anti-heroine did not), obedience and respectful silence towards the disabilities of others. Like many other Anansi stories, they were extensions in the night of teachings and attitudes taught and formed during the day. Anansi was for us not just a little devil we encountered after the sun went down: he actually lived in the ceilings and nooks of the house, and we would see him there in the days.

However, as children we missed two important aspects of that Anansi story, or rather, I think they burrowed themselves into our subconscious — the fact that the travellers were sent on a journey to find their fortune, and the fact that it was at the crossroad that the fate of each of the two girls was sealed. Both of them undertook the very same journey, but for one of them, the crossroad represented good fortune, and for the other, misfortune. One realized the start of her happiness, the other the beginning of her tribulation. Buried there in the subconscious, the crossroad resurfaces every so often as a *leitmotif*, a sort of backdrop to the radical turning points in everyday life. I suppose through stories like this we must have acquired the implicit knowledge that nothing happens unless we are prepared to travel, and nothing will be discovered unless *at the crossroad*. Just as nobody had to tell us how important it was to respect and not speak ill of the elderly, so also nobody had to tell us that the crossroad represented both good and bad. So that when people spoke of travelling and coming upon the crossroad in dreams and visions there was nothing strange about it. It made sense. We knew it all our lives.

In Jamaica's folk religion, those called by the Spirit, whether to be healers or diviners, always set out on a journey, during which they encounter 'a man,' or 'a woman,' invariably at a crossroad, where they are questioned as to the purpose of their travels, and given gifts to accompany them.

And in the days before medical care became easily available, one method of dealing with a protracted illness was to give the patient a bath and then take the bath water and pour it in the nearest crossroad.

Nothing can be more everyday than death, yet it marks the final and decisive turning point in the life of an individual and his/her family and community. In the *nine night* ritual completing the separation of the deceased from the living, at midnight the spirit is invited and enticed with libations to join the procession to the nearest crossroad, where after encircling the square three times the processants smash a glass of water and enjoin the spirit to go which way it will, but not to return. They then return to the house, where the rooms are swept, the furniture rearranged, and the clothes disposed of.

Anansi is our crossroad deity par excellence. Of course, as children we did not acquire any knowledge of him as a deity. Nobody worshipped Anansi. He inspired no fear — quite the opposite: he made us laugh because he was so clever and those who suffered by his cleverness so stupid, simple or nowhere near as smart. Yet it is by the power of his intellect that decisive turning points in the character and identity of those who people the world came about. Tiger was a handsome and civilized suitor until Anansi turned him into a creature hiding his shame in the darkness of the forests. Cockroach and fowl were even friends until Anansi made them enemies.

Interestingly, all stories are Anansi stories, even when, like the one above, Anansi does not figure in them.

The power of ambiguity and paradox in Anansi is not Jamaican alone, but is a common heritage of the Afro-Caribbean, a legacy of the West Africans who were enslaved here. In place of the Akan Anansi, there is the Yoruba trickster deity, Eshu, and the Fon trickster deity, Legba. Legba, the lame beggar, is the keeper of the gates. All are guardians of the crossroads, that meeting place of the cardinal points, which is simultaneously both ingress and egress, good and bad, loss and gain, joy and sorrow, sacred and profane.

Nor is Anansi the only crossroad deity in Jamaica. In my first fieldwork experience as a young social anthropologist, a young Revival Zion leader was possessed by a deity that hobbled as he danced around extending his hand in a begging gesture. Yet nowhere in the literature on Zion, or on Pukumina for that matter, is there any mention of Legba, the lame guardian of the crossroad, as he appears in vodun. And then, of course, there is 'the man,' or the 'woman,' or the 'old lady,' who appears in the visionary experiences and Anansi stories.

At the 2000 Caribbean Studies Association meeting in St Lucia, a Cuban scholar prefaced his paper with a very suggestive thesis that Elián González was Elegua, the Cuban version of Legba. He was referring not so much to the deification of the boy by the Miami-based Cubans as to the fact that the fate of Cuba hung in the balance over his fate. The Cuban administration understood this, and therefore spared nothing in order to get him back. The power of this suggestion is evident when one considers what would have happened had the outcome been different, had the child and his father chosen to remain in the United States, or the American courts ruled in favour of their Miami-based relatives. No sooner had this Cuban crossroads been negotiated than three members of the United States Congress visited

Cuba and spoke favourably of normalization of relationships, and others have apparently joined in.

The propulsion of these trickster deities into cultural life — Legba/Elegua in Haitian and Cuban folk religions, Eshu in Trinidadian and Grenadian orisa, Anansi in Jamaican folklore, speaks to the centrality of the crossroad in Afro-Caribbean worldview, and of the place of ambiguity in the structure of everyday life.

It is a feature of many cultures to have a trickster-god — Hermes among the ancient Greeks, Janus among the ancient Romans, the coyote among Native Americans, all presiding over the same basic feature of life: ambiguity. This is another way of saying that ambiguity is a part of human reality, but a part that, lying outside the realm of reason, cannot but assume divine, superhuman characteristics.

What is remarkable about the Caribbean is not only that the trickster heroes and deities have survived but that important aspects of Caribbean reality itself belong to the crossroad. The four cardinal points meet here. Many of those who travelled them have broken their egg and returned with their wealth and their stories. Others, finding no satisfaction, pass through to other crossroads. But for most these islands-crossroads have become home. And herein lies the complexity of the Caribbean. Who are these people? Where did they come from? Are they a people? If they are a people, what defines them as a people? How do they define themselves? These are questions of identity, answers to which are by no means simple and straightforward, even if they appear so. Eighteenth century historians and visitors 'passing through' or seeking their fortune, like Bryan Edwards (1966 [1973]) and Edward Long (1970 [1774]), have given their versions; nineteenth century missionaries and visitors, like Lady Nugent (1966 [1839]), Reverend Hope Masterton Waddell (1970, [1863]) and Reverend J.M. Philippo (1969 [1843]) have given theirs; twentieth and twenty-first century scholars and writers, like Melville Herskovits (1958), M.G. Smith (1965), Sydney Mintz and Richard Price (1992), Vidia Naipaul (1962), Derek Walcott (1992) and Kamau Brathwaite (1971, 1984), have taken over and dominated the discussion. The claims are as many as those who have come —

northerners, like Morris Cargill, who edited *Ian Fleming Introduces Jamaica* (New York: Hawthorn Books) — an interesting title, for Fleming only wrote here; *southerners*, like Olaudah Equiano (1995 [1789]) in the eighteenth century and Marcus Garvey in the twentieth, like the Rastafari in Jamaica and Black Stalin in Trinidad and Tobago; *easterners*, like Ajai and Laxmi Mansingh (1999). Only *those from the west*, the native peoples of the Americas, make no claim, although their ghosts still haunt the crossroad in the jerk and the bammy, the casreep and maroon heritage.

Of contemporary political scientists none has devoted more time in seeking answers to the question of who we are than Rex Nettleford, and yet none is more difficult to read on the subject. But it is to him that I owe this concern with ambiguity. I have read or consulted his celebrated first book, *Mirror, Mirror,* many times, and my reaction always has been the same — a very difficult, tortuous discourse on a subject that by my thinking ought to have straightforward answers. As a result, at the end of any one of the four essays that make up the book one is asking, so what is Nettleford's position? What did he say? And knowing his creative genius as a choreographer and dancer, one is tempted (and I know other members of the academy who do) to say that as he dances so does he write — you cannot pin down a dance, it is constantly in motion. Yet, as the late Derek Gordon and I agreed, no other scholar has done more to keep alive the centrality of race in Caribbean identity. Then one day some four years ago in one of those Archimedean moments of serendipity it occurred to me that one was dealing here with a man who was a master of ambiguity as a method or a praxis for understanding relationships and identities that were themselves ambiguous, and that this was the source of our difficulty with him.

I confirm this by a brief deconstruction of the most influential and enduring of his essays, 'The Melody of Europe, the Rhythm of Africa,' to suggest that because ambiguity is a lived reality for the African-Caribbean peoples the social sciences have much to learn, for notwithstanding their theoretical insights into Caribbean reality, they are unable on their present epistemological foundation to incorporate or make sense of this reality.

EUROPE'S MELODY, AFRICA'S RHYTHM

The subtitle of this essay is as important as the title, *But Every John Crow Tink Him Pickney White*. The very first sentence of the essay reads:

> The BLURRED focus of the Jamaican's perception of himself frequently invites metaphors for description. 'Every John Crow tink him pickney white' is still among the most expressive and has been for generations the most brutally accurate. (Nettleford 1998 [1970], 173).

In a footnote explaining the proverb he writes:

> "[E]veryone thinks what belongs to him is of the best (literally, every John Crow thinks his child is white)." ...To call one a John Crow is to equate him with a scavenger, a low-bred, worthless fellow...." (p. 173).

Note that the essay begins with an oxymoron, 'blurred focus.' Jamaican identity is by his definition not susceptible to the discrete light of political science discourse and so requires metaphor to be described. So, 'Every John Crow...' is a metaphor that is a 'brutally accurate' description of 'the Jamaican's perception of himself.' As if blurred focus and metaphor are not hard enough challenges, the proverb is itself ambiguous. Does the proverb mean white, as in status, or white as in colour? But, one could retort, there is no difference. Well, if there is no difference, the Jamaican THINKS what belongs to him as a part of his identity is white, whether it is really white or not. Which is to say that if high status ascription were defined by something else, every Jamaican would think what belongs to him to be that *something else*. This is similar to Nettleford's later idea of *smaddisation* which in his new 1998 Introduction he footnoted as getting from Tony Laing (p.xvii), his good friend, cultural activist and radio talk-show host. But the point is that *that something* happens to be white and we cannot escape the ambiguity of white as status, and white as colour; the ambiguity of white as sign of ambition and white as sign of delusion. And there the matter rests, forever ambiguous.

Turning to the title, 'The Melody of Europe, the Rhythm of Africa,' he notes that the phrase seeks to catch, in less spontaneous and 'all too inadequate' language, 'the dynamic of the quavering existence that some people loosely label "Jamaican."' Blurred and quavering — his own description of a rapidly moving, indistinct phenomenon. The quaver, one-half of a semi-crotchet, or a quarter-note, follows through on the general music metaphor. As a notation it is fleeting. But as a verb the word also means to shake, quiver, or flicker. So, which does it mean? What kind of political science is this?

But that is not all there is to say about the subject matter. Nettleford introduces an enigmatic twist to the already ambiguous subtitle. Normally, the relation of a subtitle to a title is one of amplification or explanation. Titles are generally intended to catch the eye or the ear, while the subtitles explain the content. Thus, the catchy title *Mirror, Mirror* (with the rest of the rhyme left unsaid but its biting irony understood) is amplified and explained by the subtitle, *Identity, Race, and Protest in Jamaica*. But in the essay in question, the subtitle/metaphor is conjoined to the title by the word 'But' — But Every John Crow Tink Him Pickney White. Why 'But?' Why not 'Or?' As a speech event, 'But' introduces oppositionality, qualification. This subtitle is not an explanation of the music metaphor, but an independent insert intended to qualify all there is to say about how much of Africa, how much of Europe there is in the construction of Jamaican identity — ambiguity within ambiguity.

To summarize, then, according to Nettleford, Jamaican identity is by definition ambiguous, and to describe it he has to resort to a brutally accurate proverb and metaphor. In other words, he has to step outside the range of conventional social science language when dealing with Jamaican (and probably West Indian) identity.

But how does a political scientist go on to describe an ambiguous existence, if the language of conventional political science is inadequate, if he has to resort to metaphor? Can one arrive at truth through metaphor? Is understanding derived through metaphorical relationship between subject and predicate the same as knowledge derived through identity between the two? And how does the social scientist wade through?

A careful reading of 'The Melody of Europe, the Rhythm of Africa' uncovers a number of devices Nettleford employs to lead the reader through the complex range of issues. It is these devices more than the fact that the subject matter is ambiguous that make the reading difficult. Victor Turner, and before him, Van Gennep have described the ambiguity of liminal existence, but, in my view, in language that is committed — one, two, three. These anthropologists use categories of thought that bring a sense of order to what is outside of order, thus to increase our understanding. With Nettleford, however, the devices themselves are somewhat open-ended, generally lacking in certitude and fixity.

The first device is detachment or distancing. As the writer he presents a line of argument but without committing himself to a position on it. A good example may be found in the early part of the essay, where, in elucidating the title he presents four different interpretations that 'some people,' or 'music purists,' give to the relationship between melody and rhythm, but without saying which is the correct or preferred. Another way of achieving distance is the use of the phrase, 'so goes the argument,' or some such formulation to indicate that the particular line of argument is not necessarily his own.

Similar in its open-endedness is the use of the subjunctive, that iffy, perhaps mood, which allows for possibilities rather than indicative closure. For example, in pursuing the point that multiracialism is more of an aspiration than a fact, he writes: 'The black majority may find little cause to feel that multi-racialism has anything to do with them when "multi" conjures up a complex in which they hold an inferior position on grounds of class which in turn dovetails with race origin.' At best the *may find* is suggestive of the author's own point of view, at worst it leaves open the possibility that the black majority *does* find, or does *not* find.

And the third device is the 'segue,' that moment or movement in a dance when a pattern/theme/flow is seamlessly transformed into another. As a literary device, what this does is allow the author to glide into related discussions, without having to justify the change through logical nexuses. In *Dance Jamaica* he is somewhat explicit about the lessons of creative dance for politics and governance in the Caribbean.

The effect of these devices is to cover all the contradictions but avoid closure, and to make his own position open — to both attack and defence. In what is perhaps the central part of the essay he writes that of all comers to the plantation, the African slave has been:

> the prime agent of creativity through which all the experiments in the new living have been carried out. He therefore becomes the richest expression of all the contradictions, the failures, successes, the fears and hopes of the new society. He is black man, white man, brown man and all the 'in-betweens' rolled into one. He is Europe's melody and Africa's rhythm, at once the dissonance and the harmony. He thinks 'him pickney white' fully knowing that everyone else knows he is black and that he would probably prefer to have him 'brown.' It is through the negro, then, that the new society is said to express itself most. Negro does not mean exclusively African and could never mean exclusively white — it is the other dimension emerging from these dominant elements. (p.185)

Here the Negro is defined as a cultural hybrid. But on the very same page, Nettleford writes:

> Yet despite all these cultural claims made on behalf of the negro he still finds himself fighting for recognition and status more than a century after legal emancipation. His own racial identity still coincides, naturally, with his society's fight for independence....

Here, in this second quote, Negro is not white, brown or in-between, but black. Taking both quotes together, we read that the Negro is both black and non-black, African, but not African. On one and the same page, Negro shifts in meaning. Nettleford is both for and against multiracialism, against the dominance of Europe, but against the dominance of Africa. The ambiguity is striking. Interestingly, he apparently does not believe that this condition is necessarily and existentially permanent. The way he would see it is for an identity that is neither Europe nor Africa, but for 'the two together interacting into a powerful other dimension and reinforced by newer elements operating in the service of our present and generating at least some of the goods of our future.' And it is this something else, the 'powerful other dimension' that he believes the 'artist-citizens' have been striving for — Mais, Hearne, Bennett, Lamming, McKay, Brathwaite. Implicitly, it is to art and not to social science that one has to turn.

The Social Sciences, as also western science in general, are founded on what Oudemans and Lardinois (1987) call 'a separative cosmology,' as distinct from an 'interconnected cosmology' that still nourishes art, morality and literary creation. All cultures share the need for differentiation and separation. Without differentiation humankind would be lost in chaos, hence the categories of thought which demarcate clear lines of separation in all the spheres of human life — between man and nature, man and the gods, between man and man (for example, marriage, blood ties), between life and death, law and order, and, according to the authors, between darkness and insight, for 'man can only hope to maintain balance between the categories which determine his identity if he has the ability to gain insight. Without this quality there would be no religion, no marriage, no burial, no justice' (Oudemans and Lardinois 1987,31). Differentiation is thus a common feature of human life.

But what distinguishes separative from interconnected cultures is how differentiation is made. The trend in European thought is to differentiate entities and categories and to unify them subsequently. Differentiation and unification may be complementary, but they embody opposing tendencies as well: whenever entities are arranged in different categories, their similarities tend to be effaced; whenever they are put together in one category, their differences are prone to disappear.

An important trend in European cosmology seeks to solve this paradox in a specific way: by separating entities from all obscurities until they are totally transparent, and by separating them from all implicit metaphorical comparisons with other things, until all entities are completely distinct from each other. The separation of the unclear from the clear, and of the indistinct from the distinct, takes the shape of an abstractive reduction, disregarding the diversity of the individual. Confusing aspects of entities are eliminated until a clear and distinct hard core has been distilled. Such a description does not speak of a 'threatening thunderstorm' but of electric discharges which have been stripped of all connotations of fear or cosmic violence. Water has numerous associations: bathing, flooding, drinking, drowning. In a clear and distinct description it is stripped of these metaphorical garments until it is reduced to its molecular or atomic skeleton.

When abstractive reduction succeeds, it may turn out that the reduced entities are identical with respect to their hard core. Unification then becomes feasible. The power of such unification is tremendous. Newton was able to unite falling apples and falling stars in one law of nature (Oudemans and Lardinois 1987, 31–32).

The philosophical underpinning of this rigorously reductive rationality is, of course, Descartes. Cartesian cosmology rationalizes insight and 'leads to knowledge without vagueness, confusion, metaphors, ambiguity or paradox. This implies that the reduced cosmos itself is without disturbance or internal hostility. Nature, God and man being carefully distinguished, potential conflicts between them are precluded' (Oudemans and Lardinois 1987, 39–40).

In interconnected cosmologies, however, the distinctions between entities and categories are not absolute, and differences can be transposed from one category to another. Incest, for example, violates the cultural demarcation of the boundaries between family and marriage, but it may signal also the 'intrusion of untamed nature into culture' (p. 48), which could have consequences for the fertility of women, or the fertility of the land, and involve the gods as well.

Because separation is categorical, whereas reality is not, human thought is always confronted with the marginal, the in-between. Cartesian cosmology excludes marginality and contradiction, whereas interconnected cosmology accounts for the marginal in the cosmology itself. And not just the marginal, but the contradictory, as well, that which transgresses boundaries. To Cartesian, separative thinking, it is incomprehensible and irrational that the same entity that pollutes can also purify. But to the interconnected mind, blood carries both opposite and contradictory meanings — it is ambiguous.

If, as Oudemans and Lardinois argue, 'to be permanently confronted with the power of ambiguity' is to remain uncivilized, it is equally true that human life is impossible without some acceptance of ambiguity. It is not that modern European cosmology is devoid of interconnected thinking, but that in the modern European Cartesian mind vestiges of it are relegated to art, religion, politics, and philosophy.

Caribbean thought is thought, but will never be Caribbean unless it embraces the power of ambiguity. This is my reading of the power of Anansi, Eshu and Legba, these trickster-gods that permeate social life, making it possible to live in what is, as it were, a permanent crossroad, where space is west and east at the same time, and the sun rises from the west (the West Indies), unlike other parts of the world, where order is forever contested and stretched, where, as Simone Schwarz-Bart (1992) says, the end is only a beginning. Ti Jean, her Guadeloupean hero, is the son of chaos, being born of his own sister into the marginal space between the memory of the Africa of his father, Wademba, the Immortal One, and the Europe of the colonizing power.

Ti Jean is called by destiny to slay the great colonizer beast that has swallowed the sun, the giver of life and light, but in so doing he too is swallowed up. It is there in the belly of the beast that he is transported back to the land of the ancestors, seeking his father who had assured him on his dying bed, prior to his own return:

> It was long, long ago when I left my village, Obanishe, on the bend of the Niger, and all those who knew me sleep in the dust. But if one day you ever go there, you or your son or your grandson, down to the thousandth generation, just say you had an ancestor called Wademba and you will be welcomed like brothers. For I belong to a blood that is very heavy and slow, a race that has a very long memory and forgets nothing, not even the flight of a bird through the sky. Don't forget – Obanishe, on the bend of the Niger (Schwarz-Bart 1992, 43)

There in the land of his ancestors Ti Jean learns the bitter truth that the people of Wademba's own village had 'shot Wademba with their arrows.' 'The Sonanke say slavery is a leprosy of the blood, and if any of them is taken by the enemy, even if only for an hour, he cannot return to the tribe. For they say his is already defiled' (Schwarz-Bart 1992, 105). There, in the land of his own ancestors, Ti Jean finds that he, too, cannot return, that death awaits him. He dies, is killed, stoned to death, and finds himself in the Kingdom of the Dead, searching for his father, Wademba. Centuries and eternities later, our hero emerges from the Kingdom of the Dead, wearing the smell of both death and life, and finds himself in France. There he encounters the old Sorcerer from Guadeloupe, Eusebius, with whose help he slays Death and sails again to Guadeloupe, disguised as a crow. Eusebius remains in France, from where he will continue the search for Wademba, his old friend and mentor. In farewell he said to Ti Jean:

> '[T]his old duffer of a Eusebius has decided to play the lunatic, but it's been proved that the world can be more lunatic than the human heart. So, if ever I should meet Wademba at the end of my foolishness, have you got a message for him, a good word or two?'
>
> Ti Jean smiled at the incredible fantasy concealed in that poor old brain, beneath the appearances of knowledge and reason.
>
> 'The only word I know,' he murmured at last, 'is that the soil of Guadeloupe was generous once, before the sun disappeared. If you cut a branch off a tree and just stuck it in the ground, and if

the virtue of the branch was still intact, it always sent out its own roots in the end. Tell him that.'

'Old warrior,' said Old Eusebius, 'I'll tell him about the branch.'

'Tell him,' went on Ti Jean with a pang, 'tell him that perhaps we are the branch cut from the tree, a branch swept away by the wind and forgotten. But perhaps in the end it will send out roots, then a trunk, and new branches with leaves and fruit. Fruit that will be like no others, tell him' (Schwarz-Bart 1992, 184-5).

The hero returns, slays the beast and brings back the sun. Then he realizes that what was to be the end 'would be only a beginning: the beginning of something that awaited him there among the groups of tumbledown huts, those makeshift shelters beneath which people quietly told each other their stories, and dreamed, and already eagerly invented life anew by the light of torches stuck in the earth' (Schwarz-Bart 1992, 212).

In this powerful epic, Schwarz-Bart searches for meaning, for truth. If every end is a beginning, there is no end and no beginning, only the eternal reaffirmation of life. A cast-away, windswept and forgotten branch can wither and dry up. But it can also live. These people have a story to tell, because the virtue of the branch remained intact, a virtue inherited from a tree that shares no responsibility for the new life. Thus, we are swept by the power of art, its license, its compelling imagination, to concede that though African, the African peoples of the Caribbean are not African; that they are, as the title of the novel so matter-of-factly states, *Between Two Worlds*. And in this in-between, liminal state, the forging of new identities becomes an open-ended adventure of imagination.

PART II
The Spider God

Chapter Four

Rastafari and the Paradox of Disorder

Jamaica is a great paradox, as well known for its cultural creativity as it is for its deadly violence. A Caribbean island country of 2.5 million people, with a rate of between 35 and 40 homicides per 100,000 population per annum it has a reputation outmatched by only two other countries, South Africa with a population of 45 million and a history of apartheid, and Colombia with a population of 44 million and a history of cocaine production and trafficking. And this rate excludes the 150 or so extra-judicial killings by the police. For such a small country, there must be only a relatively few people who have never personally known a homicide victim. How, one is frequently asked, can such a small country murder so many of its citizens? Don't you all live in fear? What is of course not much known to the outsider is the fact that the violence is for the most part concentrated in 'the ghetto.' I am not sure precisely when this term crept into local discourse but I am fairly certain that the black ghetto of the American city was the model, used to emphasize the conjuncture of black skin colour and the appalling poverty and subhuman conditions under which some Jamaicans lived. 'The ghetto' is mainly that relatively small area of downtown Kingston, the capital city, a narrow ribbon stretching 15 kilometres along the waterfront to the west. In recent decades Spanish Town, the old capital and now part of the Kingston Metropolitan Area, has its ghettos, as does Montego Bay also, the city on the westernmost end of the island.

Yet, the ghetto was where modern Jamaican music was born, nurtured and developed, and from where it has pulsed into the heartbeat of millions of people all over the world. From ska to rocksteady to reggae and now to dancehall, Jamaican music has achieved immense popularity, capturing a share of world popular culture far out of proportion to the size of the country. Bob Marley is only the best known of a constellation of Jamaican artistes that continues to stir the imagination of young people the world over, and through his fame Trench Town, where he once lived, has become the symbol for all ghettos. This flowering of musical creativity and of the genres of dance and fashion that have accompanied it has been a constant in the Jamaican landscape for over 40 years, and has been very closely associated with the disorder and chaos that the ghetto has come to represent. The transition from ska to rocksteady was associated with the rude-boys of the 1960s, while now the transition from reggae to dancehall in the 1980s has carried with it an explosion of sexual vulgarity in both lyrics and performance, and gun violence. Right up to the very recent past applause at dancehall concerts used to be expressed by gun salutes, or with simulating gestures and shouts. Now as a matter of routine everyone entering a dancehall concert is searched for firearms.

Remarkably, this paradox of creative and destructive energy not only emerging from and coexisting together in the same space, but in fact also mutually feeding on and reinforcing each other may not seem so strange at all when considered against the background of Rastafari, a symbol of and source of inspiration for that creativity, but at the same time itself a powerful embodiment of disorder. Georges Balandier (1988) reminds us that disorder is an inevitable part of the order of things, or that they are both two sides of the same coin, or *indissociables*, a truism that modern society has somehow forgotten but of which traditional society was keenly aware. In the myths of origin, not only was the world thought of as created out of disorder, but its development 'est conçu "comme une perpétuelle remise en équilibre, et le désordre comme un ferment de civilization." 'C'est pourquoi Dieu n'a pas anéanti le Renard' (Balandier 1988, 22), symbol of disorder among some West African peoples.

A more relevant personification of disorder for the purposes of this paper is Anansi, the spider-hero of the Ashanti we met in the previous chapter. As I suggested there, West African trickster-gods together crossed the middle passage of the European slave trade and have since gone separate ways — Legba to Haiti and Cuba, Hare to the United States, Eshu to Trinidad. Anansi took up residence in Jamaica, where he not only creates laughter by his outrageous individualism, and respect for his use of wit to triumph over the more powerful, but reproduces himself in certain local personalities who use guile to deceive others for their own personal advancement. As long as he remains a hero in the stories that celebrate his triumph over tiger, or his escape after stealing alligator's eggs, he is the source of merriment, but when he incarnates himself in the *samfai* (conman) and the *jinal* (trickster) he presents a challenge to the social order, though not the kind of challenge that seeks to destroy it. In 1999, in the wake of the widespread concern over the deterioration in traditional values and the rise of coarse and antisocial behaviours, a call was made at the Annual meeting of the Jamaica Teachers Association to 'ban Anansi.' The JTA member did not say how. As Pelton (1980) shows in his study of Legba, Eshu and Anansi, these tricksters serve a social function. They are part of the creation of the social order by their introduction within it of disorder, which tests and extends the limits of what is sanctioned.

Within the colonial and the non-revolutionary postcolonial order, Rastafari has served as the focal point of disorder among the urban masses, expanding the limits of traditional conventions and mores, and in some respects succeeding in subverting them. In doing so it supplants (or maybe is the modern personification of) Anansi, by accomplishing the transforming trick through the power of the song. It therefore is destructive of one order while at the same time creative of another, a position of ambiguity that gives the movement the liminal character from which it derives its compelling power.

The Background

The island of Jamaica was captured by the British from the Spaniards in 1655 and at one time became for them what Haiti was to the French, their most profitable slave colony. Sugar was king, and under its sway was a large slave population drawn from West and West Central Africa. Britain's rule, however, was never entirely secure, and the colony was dogged by a rebellious slave population with more revolts and plots than any other slave colony, except Brazil. A long drawn out series of Maroon wars led by Kojo in the west and his sister Nanny in the east resulted in 1739 and 1740 pacts which gave freedom and autonomy to three groups of Africans on lands relinquished by the Crown.

Nanny, Kojo and their brother Accompong, after whom the main settlement in the west was named, were Ashanti. But by 1760, based on the development of an apparently new religion called Myal, a Pan-African revolt swept the entire country. Although the rebellion was suppressed, Myal was to prove a source of inspiration in all subsequent revolts. Its success must, among other things, be attributed to its capacity to absorb ideas: in the first instance, the Protestant Christian message that was carried to the slaves first on a small scale by the Moravians in the 1750s and on a large scale by the Baptists and Methodists in the years immediately following the American Revolution of 1776. In a succession of adaptive transformations, Myal inspired the 1832-3 Rebellion led by Sam Sharpe under the guise of the Native Baptist Movement, an uprising that hastened the declaration of Emancipation in 1834; the Morant Bay Rebellion led by Paul Bogle in 1865, which resulted in the dissolution of the Assembly and imposition of direct rule by the Crown; and, under the guise of the Revival religion, the sedition of Alexander Bedward in 1895 and his abortive march on Kingston in 1920 'to do battle with his enemies.' By 1920 Bedward was the second most powerful black Jamaican, after Marcus Garvey. Bedwardites looked on Garvey as Moses to their leader's Aaron: one the prophet, the other the priest (a trope that has been passed on to Rastafari, who by identifying the third in the trinity have continued the formula of redemptive action: prophet, priest and king). According to Bedward's followers, they were both destined by God to lead black people into the promised land.

The idea of return to Africa had never completely died, and was kept alive ironically by the absorption of the Christian message with its narrative of captivity and exile and the promise of return. The late post-Emancipation influx of Central Africans as indentured labourers also contributed to the idea, for they seemed to have revived the tradition of abstaining from salt as a way of acquiring the spiritual power to return (see discussions of the origins of the salt taboo in chapter1 and chapter 2). In any event, Garvey's Pan-African activities lent themselves to this interpretation given by Bedward and his followers. Indeed, Garvey's middle name was 'Mosiah,' a remarkably suggestive combination of 'Moses' and 'Messiah'. Garvey's United Negro Improvement Association (UNIA) was very large. It had branches all over the United States, where Garvey had set up his headquarters, and from where he presided over hundreds of branches all over the Pan-African world: the Caribbean, Central and South America, West, South and East Africa. His back-to-Africa movement, intended to make a bridgehead on the continent as the first stage of building a united Africa capable of influencing world affairs, captured the imagination of the people, and fired their spirits when they caught sight of the ships in his Black Star Line plying the Atlantic.

It was the fulfilment of his prophecy about the rise of a Black King and Queen of Africa that was to provide the spark that ignited the imagination of some of his followers, leading them to the creation of a new vision, Rastafari. 'Look to Africa for the crowning of the King and Queen of Africa to know your redemption is at hand.' These words attributed to Garvey may have actually been taken from one of his plays, *The King and Queen of Africa*. We know that it was staged at his headquarters in Kingston, Edelweiss Park, where following his deportation from the United States in 1927 he implemented programmes of cultural and educational activities; and that it culminated in a coronation. When, therefore, in November

1930 Ras Tafari Makonnen was elevated to the imperial throne of Ethiopia in a widely publicized ceremony that attracted royal and state dignitaries from the centres of power in the West, many saw in it the moment Garvey had foretold. Ras Tafari, as was customary among kings and emperors, appropriated names and titles. Tafari assumed the imperial name of Haile Selassie, which means 'Power of the Trinity,' and the title King of Kings, Lord of Lords, Conquering Lion of the Tribe of Judah, Elect of God, Light of the World. These were almost verbatim references used by the Old Testament prophet Isaiah, referring to the Messiah. Haile Selassie's family had for centuries traced its genetic line back to Menelik, the son of Candace, Queen of Sheba, and King Solomon, conceived on her state visit to Jerusalem. As the son of David, Solomon belonged to the tribe of Judah, from where Jewish thought held the Messiah would come.

And from what was the Messiah expected to deliver God's people? The bondage was both a physical and a spiritual one. Slavery in the new lands of the west was forced exile away from tribe and nation. Long before Garvey, the homeland used to be referred to as 'Guinea.' The name 'Ethiopia' seemed to have entered the slaves' imagination as a result of their contact with European Christianity and was, as in ancient Greece, used as a generic name for the *burnt face* people. 'Africa,' to quote Mudimbe (1988) was an invention, and although Garvey's movement made very ample use of it, there was no doubt that it was an interchangeable reference for *Ethiopia, the Land of Our Fathers, the Land where the Gods love to be* — the opening line of the UNIA's national anthem. This was the promised land of return.

But as a slave the African or Ethiopian had been refashioned into a status of inferiority and contempt precisely for having a *burnt face*. Capitalism, Eric Williams (1964) has argued, was built around slavery, but it was not enough to rule by force of arms: the ideas of racial inferiority were as important and integral a part of the rules of the slave order, and in this way they entered the discourse on the making of the modern Western world (Gilroy 1993). *Black* and *white* were developed into binary opposites and the fountainheads of a series of opposing ideas that can be traced in the discourse of philosophers and essayists, historians and missionaries, planters and bookkeepers: savage and civilized, Africa and Europe, ugly and pretty, bad and good, dark and fair, coarse and fine, ignorance and knowledge, child and adult, laziness and industry, flesh and spirit, nature and culture, impulse and rationality, immorality and morality, impurity and purity, heathen and Christian, hell and heaven. These ideas were not the accidental results of naked force. ' "Our rule exists in the last resort," says Bodilly, "on a carefully nurtured sense of inferiority in the governed. As soon as we lessen that we lessen the security of our laws" ' (*Daily Gleaner* November 2, 1932, 12). Commander R.C. Bodilly had served as Resident Magistrate in Jamaica.[4]

The ideas of white legitimacy, power and righteousness became normative. Myal's incorporation of Jesus, John the Baptist, and all the Christian prophets and archangels did nothing to indigenize them in the way, say, Ethiopian Christianity indigenized them in their own Ethiopian iconography. To this day, the icons of Jesus adorning the altars of Revival churches and inside-covers of that powerful instrument of the word, the Bible, remain very much the same as he was presented by late eighteenth and nineteenth century missionaries — white and very Italian. Revival's greatest-ever prophet, Alexander Bedward, told ethnologist Martha Beckwith that when on the appointed day in 1920 he would have flown to heaven his skin would be transformed white like hers.[5] The equating of black skin colour and African phenotype with ugliness and sin is a deeply unconscious reflex widespread throughout the Caribbean. A frequently recited prayer in contemporary Revival churches asks God to wash us 'clean, whiter than snow.' Herbert DeLisser would describe Revivalism of the early twentieth century as 'the mud,' contrasting it with 'the gold' of civilized (and civilizing) European religion. By the end of the century black women were caught up in a skin-bleaching craze.

Real life is never completely the way the mind conceives it. Not surprisingly, the master-slave/white-black opposition was unable to prevent the *métissage* of the bed. If mixing the races served to reinforce the prevailing ideas by introducing a system of graded valorization of skin colour, it also served to undermine the ruling power to the extent that the colonial order refused the incorporation of the children of mixed race into its ranks. The story of the struggles against slavery, and in the aftermath of Emancipation, for social, economic and cultural advancement, is not without examples of both betrayal and trust, of both distancing and solidarity, on the part of the mixed group — the ambivalent effect of the Spanish machete. Not surprisingly also there were always present those unimpressed by the ruling ideas. Paul Bogle, in rallying the people of St Thomas to 'war' in 1865, devised the slogan, 'colour for colour,' while exactly 30 years later, the same Bedward, who expected his skin to become white, was making the seditious call for the 'black wall' to surround and crush the 'white wall.' The persistence of a conviction in the wholesomeness of blackness has been intractable throughout Jamaica's history, and was the basis on which Garvey was to elaborate his mission. It continues to the present in the power and appeal of the Rastafari.

Nonetheless, the colonial order was maintained by the force of arms, or threat of force, in times of uprising, and by the idea of white legitimacy and black unworthiness, in times of peace. As Lloyd Braithwaite (1953) argued, far from being a plural society Trinidad was integrated by a commonly held value system in which everyone, black, white, Indian, and mixed agreed on one thing, namely that the ideal was white. If this was true of Trinidad with so brief a history of plantation slavery, it was doubly true of Jamaica with 300 years of British attempt to control the mind. The apparent success of that control may be gleaned from the 1921 or 1943 censuses, which in listing the religious affiliation of the population showed the leading denomination to be the Church of England, once the religious arm of the colonial state. It was followed closely by the Baptists, whose popularity derived from their close association with the final struggles against slavery, then by the several other European religions. All together European religions, Protestant and Catholic (Anglican and Roman), accounted for over 90 per cent of the population at mid-century, the remainder going to miscellaneous groups, including Revival.

The Church provided the colonial order with sobriety, authority and stability, ritualized in a number of ways. There was first of all the Sunday ritual. On this day of the week you wore formal attire to church — hat and stockings, handbag and fan, jacket and tie. Even Sunday dinner was special: rice and peas, served with chicken or beef. But the reach of the Church extended well beyond Sunday, into the primary and secondary school system, into which religious practices and knowledge were well integrated. School began and ended with prayer, and the study of the Bible was and still is a subject matter alongside English, Mathematics and History. And although the Church of England had been disestablished in Jamaica late in the nineteenth century, state ceremonies were all duly sanctioned by the Church, as its celebrants in the name of all His/Her Majesty's loyal subjects invoked the favour of Almighty God.

The insane and the criminal

Then — it could have been early 1931 — intrusively the quiet, sedate order of a late Sunday afternoon promenade around the Parade in the heart of Kingston is broken by the single voice of a clearly mad man. His words are strange and unintelligible. Ras Tafari is God. Ras Tafari is the returned messiah prophesied by Marcus Mosiah Garvey. God is black. The living God is an African, an Ethiopian. The moment of fulfilment of the longed-for promise of the children of Israel is here. The voice travels. Soon it is heard. Soon it becomes a chorus. The voices are recognizably Jamaican, Leonard Howell still there, strongest and loudest of all, but the strains of their song are discordant. King Ras Tafari is our God. God is a black man. We have our own King. The chorus is now an entire congregation. And the colonial government begins to take notice.

Edna Manley, reflecting in an entry of her diary on the Rasta man she had come across one morning, thought that one of the most revolutionary portents was the affirmation that God was black.

Howell, Hinds, Dunkley, Hibbert, Napier, Powell and all the early founders of this strange doctrine were subverting the colonial order by repudiating the basis of its legitimacy. In a single article of faith they inverted the hierarchy in which everyone knew and accepted their place. If Almighty God is black, where does that leave the white Jesus, or the very image of God the Father presiding over creation? And where does it position those who are white and derive their status and legitimacy from being white? And if God is the black man to whom the Duke of Gloucester went to pay homage at his coronation, where did that leave him, when he became King, and those who would sit on the British throne? Throughout the history of the Rastafari movement hundreds, probably thousands have endured imprisonment for beliefs of one sort or another. But in the early years of the movement, the declaration of allegiance to anyone but His Majesty the King of England, and encouraging people to withhold taxes from His Majesty's Government were crimes of sedition.

But the Rastafari went further still. Since God is black and King, then those who are black are a royal people. And they ritualized this in the uniforms, wooden swords and regalia they wore on ceremonial occasions, quite in keeping with the Garvey tradition. But in their daily presentation of the self, Howell introduced the wearing of the beard. This was another radical and ominous violation of the social order. In Jamaica of the 1930s men, white or black, did not wear beards (See Chevannes 1995, 97–126); cultivated moustaches, yes, but beards, never. A beard, especially if left untrimmed, as it was among these new cultists, was a threatening symbol of being beyond the pale of the social order, and therefore of trying to introduce the crackling static of a different code, of crossing of signals of communication whereby all statuses and places, with their attendant praxis, were understood. More than a mere belief, it was the first and most serious outward sign of the breakdown of order. According to a newspaper account of the day, the thought among the Howellites was that those wearing beards would be miraculously empowered to cross the sea and return home to Africa. Whether so or not, the reality was the threat posed by the simple cultivation of a beard by black men, and its association with the unfinished business of slavery. The day the so-called repatriation was to have been effected was none other than the one hundredth anniversary of the Declaration of Emancipation.

For a generation or so the Rastafari became known as the Beard Men. The makers of public opinion, sensitive to the slightest waft that could disturb the status quo, equated Bearded men, or 'the Beards' with mental insanity, a description that was to remain for a long time, and in due course receive academic sanction.[6] Madness is the first declaration in the marginalization of disorder. This had been Alexander Bedward's fate.[7] Frank Jan van Dijk's very careful documentation of the available data makes it quite clear that the colonial government was very much on top of the development of this group of black men and women whose vocal denunciation of the British throne, equating it with the apocalyptic references to the whore of Babylon, was one of the reasons for the not infrequent street battles with the police. But when it became clear by the growing weight of numbers that there was a threat here, criminality was added to insanity. If they were not insane they were criminals.

I believe the addition of 'criminal' was made early in the 1950s. It involved the criminalization of a plant. As simple as that. *Cannabis sativa*, known in Jamaica by the Hindi name *ganja* because it had been introduced by Indian indentured labourers in the nineteenth century, was one of the substances banned under the Dangerous Drugs Act in 1924. Incorporated into the pharmacopoeia of the rural and urban working people, ganja was widely used for colds, flu, fevers, asthma and other illnesses. Suddenly and without medical evidence it became a serious crime to cultivate, sell, possess and use ganja.

George Lamming (1992 [1960], 38-9) makes the point that:

> the novelist was the first to relate the West Indian experience from the inside. ... He looked in and down at what had traditionally been ignored. For the first time the West Indian peasant became other than a cheap source of labour. It is the West Indian novel that

has restored the West Indian peasant to his true and original status of personality.

The novelist in the case of the Rastafari was none other than Roger Mais, whose *Brother Man*, published in 1955, cast the preacher of this new sense of self into a Christ figure. (See the next chapter, 'Rastafari and the Critical Tradition' for more on this novel.) But as Kamau Brathwaite (1986,172-3) revealed, brown middle-class Mais was on the way to his Damascus to enlist in the reserves in support of a colonial order threatened with disorder when he was struck by that blinding vision of the new and black redemption. Brother Man, the character, becomes the double victim of betrayal. First he is made into a common criminal, treacherously found in possession of a quantity of the banned plant, ganja. Then he meets his crucifixion at the hands of a vengeful mob, many of whom he had healed with his own prayers and touch, in reprisal for a foul murder allegedly by a member of this new and dangerous cult. Mais collapsed into a single image the profile of the enemy within — the ganja-smoking murderer.

This was the beginning of the era of the Dreadlocks, which I discuss below, a period that also saw the final push to Independence, first in the short-lived Federation of the West Indies and then as an island-state — a transition fraught with the danger of abortion. And one nearly took place. Or so thought the still-colonial state. A preacher by the name of Reverend Claudius Henry returned home from the United States, met and married Edna Fisher, the leader of a local UNIA branch, and with her membership established a Rastafari church. Henry gained great publicity when in taking up Howell's drive for repatriation he announced October 25, 1959, as the 'Day of Decision' when Africa's scattered children would leave for home, and to this end he distributed blue cards in lieu of passports. His notoriety soared the following year when police discovered arms and a letter inviting Fidel Castro to take over Jamaica prior to their departure for Africa. The society went into shock.

Greater shock was yet to come when, appeased by Henry's arrest and arraignment for treason, the public was now confronted with the discovery of an armed guerrilla group operating out of the church.

The leader was Ronald, Claudius's son, who with some black American colleagues had been training the group in the uninhabited scrublands of Red Hills, overlooking the city of Kingston, where they had uncovered and killed the police informer. Two British soldiers were killed in the military operation, which ended with the capture of Ronald and his two American colleagues, betrayed by the frightened peasant in Sligoville in whose yard they had fallen asleep exhausted (See Chevannes, 1976; Meeks 2000).

In the two weeks between the skirmish and the capture public hysteria reached fever pitch. The only parallel was the Morant Bay Rebellion of the century before. The hysteria at that time had allowed Governor Eyre to butcher 436 peasants and burn over 1,000 of their houses. In the rage, the brown middle-class George William Gordon, who had sided with Paul Bogle and the St Thomas peasantry in their petitions for justice, had been hanged without any evidence presented against him. The Assembly had dissolved itself and virtually begged for the imposition of direct government from Whitehall. One of the first Acts passed by the new Legislature as a means of buttressing the colonial state was the Treason Felony Act. The only time in its history the Treason Felony Act was ever called into force was in the case of Regina *versus* the Reverend Claudius Henry. But for the public hysteria, which was abetted by the circulation of all kinds of wild rumours, such as the Rasta's plans to poison the reservoir that supplied Kingston with water, and which was finding release in behaviour reminiscent of *Brother Man*, it would have been clear to any reasonable mind that a couple of revolvers and some dozens of conch shells stuffed with dynamite could not in the wildest of imaginations have posed a serious threat of any sort to the colonial government, and that there must have been more to the letter purporting to invite Castro to take over the country. That letter, in fact, bore the mark of Rastafari cosmology, in which Fidel Castro represented the native peoples of the Americas who were dispossessed by the Europeans. The Rastafari think of repatriation not only as the return of Africa's scattered children to Africa, but also in terms of the restitution of the Americas to their rightful owners, and consequently the return of the

Europeans to Europe. Blinded by fear of the disorder, of the unknown represented by the Rastafari, the society was in no frame of mind to see reason. But so violent was the storm that the brethren sought the refuge of the only sanctuary they could find, the University. The University Report of 1960, the result of a rapid appraisal, was the fruit of that overture.[8]

By then, however, the menace had already achieved symbolic status. I refer to two practices aimed at overturning the prevailing order, which were regarded as signs of the criminal mind. The first was the sacralization of ganja. How this came about is a story of what Jean Besson has called the 'culture building' of the Jamaican peasant, though it took place not in the rural countryside but in the urban yards of the 1950s. The culture-building components were the ganja plant and smoking implements fused with African traditions of smoking, reasoning and, possibly, implements as well.[9] The law against ganja dates from 1912, when for no apparent reason other than the whimsical abuse of power the Jamaican Legislative Council included ganja among the substances to be banned by the Opium Convention that Great Britain had sent around to be ratified. There might have been rumours of an association with murder. Definitely that was the association made fifty years later in the real murder case fictionalized in *Brother Man*. Then in 1924 a Dangerous Drugs Act was drafted and passed into law. It was amended five times, each time with stiffer penalties, until finally ameliorated in 1972 (See chapter 10 for more on the history of legislation concerning ganja).

By ritualizing ganja as a sacrament that they compared to the wine of Christian communion, the Rastafari elevated disorder to a new level, forcing back at great expense the boundaries of the social and moral order. They challenged the state to show just cause why a plant whose growth was as natural as any other should be criminalized; and, satisfied from folk wisdom, social practice, and Biblical knowledge that there was none, they concluded that the real aim of the law was, as it always had been since the time of slavery, the suppression of black people. But for the obligations to the international conventions governing the control of psychotropic substances, it would indeed be very difficult for a postcolonial democratic state not to repeal the law. Ganja smoking has become so widespread, with the infusion of the Rastafari worldview into the popular music, that were the police to arrest every offender they confront, the entire system of justice in Jamaica would collapse. The flaunting of the Dangerous Drugs Act with ganja smoking has become routinized at reggae concerts and football matches and on the street corners of inner city communities.

Following the recommendations of a National Commission to decriminalize the private and religious use of ganja, (see chapter 10) the Jamaican Government is contemplating an amendment to the law. Anansi stories explaining the nature of the world and the relations and places of the beings in it, prior to declaring the end say, 'Is Anansi mek it!' If and when it is no longer a criminal offence to use ganja in private or as ritual sacrament, it could truly be said 'Is Rasta mek it!'

The second practice was, and remains a far more complex issue: hair. I have elsewhere (Chevannes 1995) traced the reasons why. Whereas the focus of the struggle to use ganja freely was and continues to be the organs of the state — its laws, the courts, the police and the prison system — the hair culture that has become universally known as *dreadlocks* is targeted at no one in particular but at everyone in general. Looked at against the background of a prevailing system of public morality it has to be seen as a brilliant representation of the contempt for the social mores and of the disorder and confusion it was the mission of the Rastafari to scatter in the midst of society. Breaking no law, the dreadlocks broke 'unofficial law.' Society felt suddenly unsafe. What sort of law could there be against a hair culture that violated the freedom of no one? But the dreadlocks did violate the freedom to regulate social statuses. It broke through an invisible but real barrier, crossing the boundaries that set the limits within which the black self was to be conceived and represented to both self and society.

As I have said, this was a period of transition. The white guardian was preparing to hand over his guardianship to native hands, satisfied that these were well schooled in the traditions of the finest democracy devised by mankind. But, as Katrin Norris (1962) was to find on her brief journalistic visit on the eve of Independence in 1962, there was a crisis of identity, of a black country searching everywhere except within — Canada, Australia, even the United States — to find the model for its future. And along comes this positively black, insanely, criminally menacing group, eyes inflamed from the excessive smoking of ganja, disorder read unequivocally and in wild profusion in their gnarled, knotted locks. No law broken of God or man, but the society felt threatened. When, therefore, the first chance arose to ensure that 'temporary arrangement for our safety,' in the Claudius Henry affair, it let loose the full extent of the 'official Law,' and went beyond it in the forced shaving of the dreadlocks — like Samson's, the dreaded seat of power.

THE DISORDER OF LANGUAGE

As a mode of communication the dreadlocks were a ritualized way of reproaching a society insecure in a black identity. It would have been a matter of time before the more direct mode of communication, language, took on a similar form. This was what the *dread talk* was all about, a subversion of the linguistic codes governing social relationships within a hierarchical order. The disorder represented by Jamaican creole had already been corralled and confined as bad English, unfit for public speech or for communicating with people of higher class. It was the language beaten into submission by teachers and admonished into confinement by upwardly mobile or already-arrived parents. What the Dreadlocks began doing in their urban camps of the late 1940s and early 1950s was to reject the complicity with the status quo implied in the submissiveness of the dialect to an inferior place. But they went further and began the subversion of the English language itself.

Benjamin Whorf proposed that language structures the way we think, and therefore the way we perceive reality. English, for example, obliges us to think in terms of subject + verb + object. 'Thus we are compelled in many cases to read into nature fictitious acting-entities simply because our sentence patterns require our verbs, when not imperative, to have substantives before them. ... *A change in language can transform our appreciation of the cosmos'* (Carroll 1956, 203; my emphasis). Exploiting the trick implied in a homonymic appreciation of sound and in other word plays, the Dreadlocks began to expose the deception of the English language. For example, reversing the meaning of *up* and *down* revealed the true meaning of *downpression*; reversing the meaning of *under* and *over* revealed what it truly meant to *overstand*. In a creative stroke of genius they dispensed with the objectification of the self implied in the positioning of the personal pronoun *me*, replacing it with the subject of agency and *overstanding — I*. An entirely new cosmos revealed itself: the *I* of sight, of Selassie *I*, looking down from the *I*-er *I*tes of *over*standing (the trick relies also on the proclivity in Jamaican creole to misplace the aspirant *h*: *high* becomes *'igh, heights* becomes *'eights*). The brilliance of the change was publicly acknowledged when the Prime Minister in a retort aimed at quieting the Opposition's call for a general election in 1971 declared, 'Is only one man can call election, and dat man is I man!'

Revealed also in that new cosmology was the true meaning of slavery: the captivity of *Babylon*. *Babylon* represented an entire system of conspiracy: the white establishment of wealth and privilege, served by the state; the agents of the state, especially the police; the Church, especially the Catholic presence of Rome, the whore and *down*pressor whose apocalyptic downfall was already assured by prophecy; the *head*ication (education) system that filled up the head of black people's children with falsehoods and inanities like 'the cow jump over the moon,' and 'Dan is the man in the van.'

> By the rivers of Babylon, where we sat down
> And there we wept when we remember Zion.
> For the wicked carried us away in captivity
> Required of us a song
> But how can we sing Rastafari song in a strange land?

Singing a song in a strange land meant singing in a strange language.[10] It meant perceiving the world in a strange and alien way. The basic intent of *dread talk*, therefore, was to destroy the polish and legitimacy of Standard English, and, by inventing a new truth out of its subversion, to reclaim an African way of perceiving and ordering the world.

Undoubtedly the most offensive word-weapon in Rastafari assault on the social order was its legitimization of the *badword*, the vulgar expletive. Equipped with an arsenal of words and expressions drawn from both Standard English and the creole, an angry Jamaican can be offensive to the quick. The most venomous words are the creole words *bombo*, of Central African origin, meaning the vagina, and *raas*, a word for anus, both combined with *klaat*, the creole for *cloth*. In colonial days, such words and expressions were called forty shilling words, in reference to the fines they fetched. To the Dreadlocks no word could of itself be offensive. If it was, it was because the hearer was trapped in a colonization of the mind. So-called badwords could not be bad if actually they referred to normal things. Morality lay in the actions and intentions of mind, not in the word. In placing a ban on words Babylon was only revealing its ignorance.

The reggae king of the badword was none other than the famous Wailer, Peter Tosh, who recorded an entire song with the two most offensive expletives, *Oh bombo klaat, Oh raas klaat!* Tosh's explanation was most revealing. Once when troubled by an evil spirit the only way he could think of to get rid of it was to shout out a string of bad words. The effect was salutary. What Tosh in fact did was to revive a piece of Jamaican folklore that badwords effectively spoken can drive away duppies (ghosts). In the explanation he implied that the duppy troubling him was none other than the *shitstim*, his own neologism for the Babylonian *system*. The law remains in effect and has been invoked in recent times against dancehall artistes who spice their public performances with badwords. Their use is an offence against public order.

Trickster and Trick

One of the ways any society, traditional or modern, deals with disorder is through repression — the witch, the adulterer, the criminal. Short of totalitarianism, success at repression requires public acceptance of the threat posed by the disorder, and belief in the correctness of the measures to deal with it. But what happens when disorder becomes, or threatens to become, itself a new order? The result is a very interesting dynamic. Such has been the case of Jamaica, where for the past 30 years within the urban ghettos Rastafari has provided the prevailing ideology of disorder against the postcolonial Babylonian state, without crossing the boundary into outright rebellion. I found during my fieldwork in the mid-1970s that belief in the divinity of Haile Selassie was as natural to children in some of the urban ghettos as belief in the divinity of Jesus Christ was to children of my generation in the rural countryside. A new generation of children has been finding attractive many if not all aspects of the beliefs, iconography and ritual practices of the Rastafari, while as a living organism within the body politic it remained as marginalized. And not just the children. Important defections from the brown middle class have been taking place and are most evidenced in, but not confined to, the Twelve Tribes of Israel.[11] The awful and awesome *dreadlocks*, for example, began to be visible outside the black ghettos, eventually becoming by the 1990s such a fashion that with the expense of a few hours in a hair salon one could transform oneself into a Dread. How was such transformation of disorder into order effected?

The answer lies in the performance of the trick by the trickster. I borrow Diane Austin-Broos's insight into the way Anansi transformed American Pentecostalism into an essentially Jamaican religion. Pentecostalism came to Jamaica in the early decades of the twentieth century, steeped in the rational, other-world ethics of Puritan traditions, and there it encountered Anansi, the spider-god of disorder within a single universe of order and disorder. In a this-world-oriented cosmology, the lines drawn between flesh and spirit in the moral order of enlightenment rationality out of which Pentecostalism derived its meaning, do not exist. Instead the moral order is realized in a union of flesh and spirit expressed as the marriage between the believer and Jesus, between the brides (the saints) and the divine bridegroom. The instrumental trick effecting this subversion is, as it always was in the Anansi folktales, by the song. The magic lies in the song. And so, Austin-Broos demonstrates, Jamaican Pentecostal worship is driven by a *eudemonic* ('a fleeting "happiness" experienced in both rite and performance' [1997, 249]) of song and dance, whose rhythm and movement unite bride and bridegroom: in this world, not in another.

Rastafari represents a new trickster, but the trick remains the same — the song. It is through the song that the boundaries of the postcolonial order, challenged by the politics of disorder, have been extended. The binary opposition of order and disorder is often expressed as an opposition between society and nature, civilization and savagery, village and forest. As a new trickster-god, Rastafari emerges from the pale, where he appropriated the profile of the natural — unprocessed foods, natural substances, a return to nature. However, no better symbol of this appropriation can be found than the dreadlocks. It is through the uncultured, natural dreadlocks that he deliberately assimilates the profile of the king of the forest — the *lion*. This iconic representation gains additional currency from the nurtured presence of lions in the palace of His Majesty Haile Selassie, a symbol of his claim as the *Conquering Lion of the Tribe of Judah*. In a book that deserves to be read far more than its self-published status has allowed, Dennis Forsythe (1983), a sociologist and now practicing attorney-at-law and a Rastafari, was the first to *sight* the role of Rastafari as the *lion* challenging the *spider*. Where Anansi accomplishes his feats by spinning his webs of deceit, prevarication and circumlocution, Rastafari the Lion is able to confront, to be direct, to inspire by awe. Forsythe would therefore say that Rastafari has no need of a trick. And he would be right, in that Rastafari is uncompromisingly honest. But when without a single change to its 'official Law' a society awakes to find within its own sons and daughters, so well socialized into its mores, the carriers of the very disorder it arranges protection from, a trick, a brilliant magician's trick has been accomplished. And all through the magic of the song.

Two streams converged at a point in the history of Jamaican music to produce a great confluent. Rastafari was one; the other was the rise of Jamaican popular music. Drawing heavily but briefly on Steve Barrow's excellent description in the four-volume release *Tougher than Tough: A History of Jamaican Music,* one can trace the beginnings of Jamaican popular music to the 1950s, a period which, as Barrow puts it, saw the fusion of the powerful creative impulse of the urban ghetto youths bursting to express themselves, technological advancement first in the form of the sound system, and then in the production of vinyl, and talented producers and arrangers.

Prior to this, Jamaican popular music was *mento*, touched by the strong beat of the Revival religion. In mento the accent is given not on the first beat, as in European music written in 4/4 time, but on the fourth beat, the one that has the slightest emphasis. The typical mento band comprised the banjo, the fife, the guitar, the shaka, and the rumba box (a large thumb piano with four notes providing the bass). Street bards used to compose in this style, sell their tracts and sing on the street corners.

With the sound system, a wider audience began to be reached, but with it also came exposure to American rhythm & blues. Except for the folk songs and songs by the street bards, Jamaican compositions were, up to the late 1950s, copies of American R&B, but it was not until 1960 that the idea of emphasizing the afterbeat, mento-style, instead of the downbeat, using the guitar, first took root. Thus was born a new sound: *ska*. Ska spread literally like a wild fire carried by the wind — its tempo was quick, and it burned up all in its path. The beat had all the life and promise of a nation just born in 1962, and that was what Derrick Morgan saw in his song *Forward March*. The euphoria of Independence was, however, short-lived, as little happened to ease the crushing poverty, and the divide between the social classes widened. For the elite, ska was too loud, and its beat too monotonous.

But the climate was changing. Ska began losing its appeal among the urban, unemployed ghetto youths, some of them not long come from the countryside. Mid-1960s was their season of discontent; they took on the name *Rude Boys:* surly, deliberate, ominous, the 1968 Rodney Riots[12] just around the corner. And the music changed with them: surly, deliberate, ominous — *rock steady*. But as the music industry matured, competition became stiff, especially among producers, constantly on the lookout for something new, for an edge. It was in this context that they found a faster and tighter rhythm, but not quite as fast as ska. Clancy Eccles, who, like many other singers was also trying a hand at producing, claims to have invented the name *reggae*, from *streggae*, a street girl.

Thus was born a sound which has broken the barrier of nationalism and race. Only the compelling international reputation of Bob Marley by the end of the 1970s could have forced the recognition by the establishment of the creative contribution to world culture by the poor and dispossessed. Bob Marley received the highest possible order of recognition from the state, the Order of Merit, but sadly the religion that inspired his lyrical passion and power was denied recognition by the same Parliament that in the very same debate gave recognition to the Mormons. The Mormons until very recently preached that Black people had to satisfy themselves with a different and less glorious heaven from Whites.

To the alienated Jamaica, particularly the youth, the regard for Rastafari was quite different. Unemployment had doubled through the decade of the 1960s, and hope was in scarce supply, except among a group of people who had upheld the traditions of Marcus Garvey. Garvey had by then been given the nation's highest honour of National Hero, his remains exhumed from an obscure London cemetery and interred with much celebration in the Park of Heroes. Surely, there was hope here. Then in April 1966, their God and King came — on a state visit, as Babylon was forced to bow to his power. They reported that it had been raining while the state dignitaries and ceremoniously dressed military regiments stood awaiting his arrival, when the rain suddenly stopped, the cloud broke open and out of the heavens descended their God and King, the Alpha and Omega. The mighty Dreadlocks went wild with enthusiasm and, surrounding the plane, began offering up incense of smoke of the holy weed. And nothing happened, no fire. Another miracle, many proclaimed. God is with us.

By the end of the seventies, nothing could persuade an ever-growing generation of disenchanted youths that Haile Selassie was not God. The churches tried to get him during his four-day visit to disclaim his divinity, and arguments have continued to this day, and will continue for some time. The Rastafari became for the youths the only hope.

The way this was reflected in the music was, at first, in the names of the many groups and artistes: the Abyssinians, whose song, *Satta-a-masagana*, became an all-time classic:

There is a land, far, far away
Where there is no night, there's only day
Look into the Book of Life and you will see
That there's a land far, far away.

The King of Kings and the Lord of Lords
Sit upon his throne and he rules us all
Look into the Book of Life and you will see
That there's a land far, far away;

Burning Spear, a son of Marcus Garvey's home town, St Ann's Bay — 'The Burning Spear' being Jomo Kenyatta's *nom de guerre;* The Sons of Negus — Negus being the Ethiopian word for King; The Ethiopians. The focus was on Africa. Many in this way made their connection with the land of the ancestors, adopting names that established their personal identification. By 1972, the year Michael Manley came to power, most artistes and musicians were already Rastafari and dreadlocked.

When Bob Marley, Peter Tosh and Bunny Wailer first came together and recorded hit songs like *Simmer Down* and *Long Time*, they were a young, gifted and dynamic group, but far from the warriors they were later to become. Then the locks began to sprout.

A consciousness had taken hold of them. In Trench Town, Marley came under the influence of one of the leading Elders of Rastafari, Mortimo Planno. In the decade of the 1960s into the decade of the 1970s, Planno was by far the most influential Rastafari Elder. He had been one of the three Rastafari on the nine-man delegation sent on the Mission to Africa by the government of Norman Manley, following on the recommendation made by the University scholars who had carried out the study requested by the Rastafari.[13] The Mission was much publicized, as were its two written Reports, one by the six non-Rastafari members and the other by the Rastafari. But even more than his role in the 1961 Mission, Planno was the one called upon by His Imperial Majesty to request the Brethren to clear the way to allow him to deplane at the start of his historic visit to Jamaica in April 1966.

As Marley's consciousness grew, so did his locks, and so did his music. *Trench Town Rock, Get Up Stand Up, Concrete Jungle, Burnin' and Lootin', Small Axe, Them Belly Full, Crazy Baldheads, War. Get Up Stand Up* was composed by the razor sharp Peter Tosh. Through songs like this, Trench Town became the symbol of the marginalized Jamaica, with an aesthetic and an ethos of its own. Later, in his *No Woman, No Cry*, the Govament Yaad in Trench Town would add to the mystique about this little ghetto, inducing thousands to trek, just to see and experience what could have been so magical about its First Street and Second Street, its poverty, squalor even. Perhaps it was the experience of the night, sitting in the yard, keeping the fire burning, cooking and eating the meagre fare of cornmeal porridge, drawing the chalice, reasoning about man, God, nature and politricks. This was Trench Town, the signifier of every ghetto in Kingston, east and west.

And the locks grew — luxuriant, phallic, life. This was the voice of the Rastaman spirit, proclaiming 'Babylon, yu throne gone down, gone down,' who could connect with the universal soul of the mother weeping for her son shot down in the street like a dog, who, like the spirit of the God within can console universal woman — woman anywhere, woman everywhere, 'for every little thing's gonna be alright.' Thus was the trick made. The locks became an outward symbol of an inward commitment, as reggae artistes found satisfaction and fulfilment in the vision of the still relatively new religious movement.

> And I
> Rastafar-I
> in Babylon's boom
> town, crazed by the moon
> and the peace of this chalice, I
> prophet and singer, scourge
> of the gutter, guardian
> Trench Town, Dungle and Young's
> Town, rise and walk through the now silent
> streets of affliction, hawk's eyes
> hard with fear, with
> affection, and hear my people
> shout: ...
>
> So beat dem drums
> dem, spread
>
> dem wings dem,
> watch dem fly
>
> dem, soar dem
> high dem,
>
> clear in the glory of the Lord.

This is poet Kamau Brathwaite in an excerpt from one of his poems in his *Rights of Passage* celebrating the power of this 'prophet and singer' to elevate and transport the spirit of the afflicted out of their affliction, through song of voice and music of drum.

Conclusion

Only a reductionist reading of Jamaica's contemporary social problems would attribute the urban rage and violence to the Rastafari. The problem is quite complex. There is the suicidal role played by the political parties in the initial training and arming of urban gangs in their mad quest for power. There is the widened and still widening gap between the rich and the poor. And now the devil himself disguised as a harmless-looking white powder called cocaine. These cannot be ignored. Violence of the type being suffered by Jamaica is not unique. It is part of the disorder of modernity and, as Balandier would have it, 'Le désordre ne se cantonne pas.'[14] What I hope I have succeeded in explaining is the paradox of the powers: the power to destroy and the power to create charged from the same source. This, in the final analysis, is what development and change is all about. Which is to say that Jamaica is still a work in progress; that looking down the road of its future from the present vantage point the shape of the kind of society it develops into will much depend on how it incorporates the disorder represented by the Rastafari. It will not be enough to deify the messenger but kill the message.

Chapter Five

Rastafari and the Critical Tradition

A few years ago George Lamming, the father of the modern Caribbean novel and leading critic, gave a lecture at the invitation of the History Department of the University of the West Indies and the Barbados National Cultural Foundation. The lecture, titled 'Western Education and the Caribbean Intellectual,' has since been published with an accompanying piece, under the title *Coming, Coming Home: Conversations II*, and the subtitle: *Western Education and the Caribbean Intellectual Coming, Coming, Coming Home*. It is, for me, one of the most penetrating analyses of the role and main task of the Caribbean intellectual, an essay that to my mind is undeservedly still relatively unknown, a condition that represents a part of the very problem as he outlines it. He couples the Caribbean intellectual with a return migration of endeavour, implying a movement away from alienation to integration. I discussed this book briefly in Part I, Chapter 1, 'Africa and the Caribbean.' In this chapter, I present Lamming's main line of argument as a frame for the achievement of the Rastafari as intellectuals. The Rastafari as intellectual is absolutely central to the critical quest, the critical question.

Lamming's reminder of Gramsci's advice to compile our 'inventory' out of the 'infinity of traces' left us by the confluence of historical processes begs the question: what are some of the traces deposited but not yet inventoried by our history? They begin with events and processes deposited by a minority of men, Europeans, that form part of their inventory, their consciousness of themselves, but to us an infinity of traces. They begin, says Lamming, with the crimes they committed on a landscape they controlled but never considered themselves a part of. They begin as well with their own sense of a moral obligation to justify their immorality. Our traces begin with the Admiral Columbus, who in the same breath in which he waxed lyrical about the beauty of the landscape and the people he found in it, made his intent clear: 'They would make fine servants.... With fifty men we could subjugate them all and make them do whatever we want,' words which, observes Lamming, compressed the entire fifteenth century into a single moment. The crime was genocide, and the moral justification, the myth of the Noble Savage, a 'dreadful concept ... most necessary to the White man's experiment in civilization, and quite dispensable at the slightest sign of resistance to White conversion.'

> The Admiral of the Ocean Sea, a man who sailed with the absolute conviction that God had destined him to be His divine instrument for spreading the faith; this sailor had hardly set eyes on those noble savages before the thought occurred, and most naturally, "... we could subjugate them all and make them do whatever we want." Subjugation and servitude became the logical instruments of social intercourse between Europe and all others. From the day of Columbus's arrival, the ideology of racism became the foundation of all Caribbean history which, for the next three centuries, would be decided by force (page 6).

Behind every crime has been an idea, 'an unselfish belief in the idea — something,' Lamming is quoting Marlow, 'you can set up, and bow down before, and offer a sacrifice to....' Following close on the Admiral's genocide was Juan de Sepulveda's idea that '[i]t does not appear to me contrary to justice that they be taught just and humane ways...under the authority of civilised and virtuous princes and nations....' Two hundred years later it was Lord Acton in defence of empire: 'Subjection to a people of higher capacity for government is of itself no misfortune; and it is to most countries the condition of their political advancement.' And so powerful has been the idea that even Joseph Conrad, the novelist, who was hardly able to stomach the 1890s Belgian atrocities in the Congo, could nonetheless betray where his loyalty lay, when it came to Boer independence versus English imperium. Wrote Conrad: 'they have no idea of liberty, which can only be found under the English flag all over the world....'

And as the era of imperial responsibility passes with the end of colonialism, it is Henry Kissinger who now succinctly reformulates the moral justification for the same world order but packaged anew, when in his 1974 essay on 'Domestic Structure and Foreign Policy' he divides the world between the West with its Newtonian view of the world, and the pre-Newtonian cultures. To the Newtonian West, writes Kissinger, reality is external to the observer, to the pre-Newtonian it is 'almost completely internal.' Thus, right down to the very age in which we live, the idea of the civilized West and the uncivilized rest remains, albeit in new formulation, as the central moral justification for the White man's insatiable drive for economic conquest of the globe.

This, concludes Lamming, is our legacy, this text of race and class stratification, and, with its 'formidable historical and philosophical monument of knowledge and power,' the context in which 'the Caribbean intellectual was formed and in whom was deposited "an infinity of traces, without leaving an inventory" of its own' (2000 [1995],12).

The task is therefore clear. It belongs to the intellectual, who must begin to create that inventory out of that infinity of traces bequeathed by history. But who is this intellectual, asks Lamming, and proceeds to identify four senses in which the term is used. In the first sense, the intellectual is a philosopher, one concerned with the history, origin and influence of ideas, the way knowledge is acquired, the relationship of appearance and reality. Here you find Whitehead and Russell, Marx and Toynbee, C.L.R. James and W.E.B. Dubois. The difference between the Jameses and the Duboises, on one hand, and the Toynbees and Whiteheads, on the other, is not their range of interests but their motivation. James's *Black Jacobins* and Dubois's *Soul of Black Folk* began at the very beginning of that critical elaboration, namely by initiating 'the inventory of a folk whose humanity had not been validated' (Lamming 2000 [1995],12).

A second if less rigorous use of the term 'intellectual' refers to people like artists, teachers, technocrats, academics: people 'engaged in work which requires a consistent intellectual activity' (p. 13). Often highly competent specialists, they are not necessarily intellectuals of the first kind, in that they eschew the exploration of the connectedness of ideas and disciplines. In an implied criticism that becomes explicit later on, Lamming notes: 'It is not difficult to find in our ranks a historian or social scientist who has very little knowledge of the imaginative literature or the general cultural history of the region whose past he is reconstructing' (p. 14).

In the third and more generalized sense, 'intellectual' describes a wide cross section of people 'whose tastes and interests favour, and even focus on, the products of a certain intellectual activity' (p. 14). These are the music, literature, theatre and art lovers. They do not make their living from intellectual production, but as its consumers they overlap with some of those who belong to the second type, together with them constituting what Lamming calls 'the domain or area of mediation' (p. 14).

Mediation is the forging of 'vital links between sources of knowledge and the wider consumption of facts' (p. 15). This is a difficult role because part of the imperial legacy is to regard knowledge as property and to restrict it to the intellectuals: intellectuals discoursing with intellectuals. But where this bit of the infinity of traces is overcome, mediation becomes 'a force of resistance against Western hegemony,' for through it the majority of the people become part of the process of continuing self-definition. Without that incorporation, without that mediating bridge, an inventory in and of itself is of little significance. It remains to us a trace deposited by someone else's history, not a part of the heritage of the Caribbean people.

It is this mediation Walter Rodney understood so well and devoted and gave his life trying to accomplish. For he understood that the ordinary fisherman and farmer were also intellectuals, who constitute what Lamming calls 'the most dynamic force of transformation.' They are, and indeed ought to be respected as, intellectuals in the widest possible sense of the word, for no form of labour is possible 'without some exercise of the mind.' Until intellectuals in the traditional and narrower sense of the word begin the inventory, until they transcend the 'smell of bandages emanating from those accumulated footnotes, [that] certain odour of morphine linger[ing] over the average thesis' (p. 16), and integrate their endeavour with that of the also-intellectuals, the farmers and fishermen, until they come home, there will be no knowing 'thyself,' no consciousness of what or who we really are, no critical elaboration.

Lamming ends:

> I do not think that there has been anything in human history quite like the meeting of Africa, Asia, and Europe in this American archipelago we call the Caribbean. But it is so recent since we assumed responsibility for our own destiny, that the antagonistic weight of the past is felt as an inhibiting menace. And that is the most urgent task and the greatest intellectual challenge: how to control the burden of this history and incorporate it into our collective sense of the future (p. 25).

As I have said, the essay deserves to be much more widely known. I would even go so far as to say that there is no other *raison d'être* at this juncture of our history for the Caribbean intellectual. The intellectual legacy of the Caribbean, particularly at its academic and professional levels, excluding its impressive literary tradition — that's why Lamming implies in the title that the journey home has already begun, has no sense of itself other than through the reflections, the categories of thought, of the West. Unlike our literary colleagues, the farmers and fishermen provide no source of inspiration for our conceptualizing or theory building, and we, who should be the interpreters of the traces left us by a past that cannot be relived, are ourselves caught in a spider's web of interpretation of the spider itself.

But there is one group that deserves to be treated as intellectual in a sense separate from the four described by Lamming, and that is the folk philosopher. This is no teacher or academic, nor consumer of intellectual production in the general sense used by Lamming. However, but for the fact that his or hers is an oral in contrast to the scribal tradition, he or she could well be placed alongside the Jameses and Duboises. This is the sage, the village lawyer, the counsellor, the healer, the religious leader. I suggest, however, that insofar as orality constitutes a different genre from the written tradition, in much the same way that the griot differs from the academic historian, the folk philosopher is an intellectual in a fifth sense. For one thing, the folk philosopher's philosophy is generally speaking the result of, or an exposition in, a discourse. It is delivered in argument, and may be the result not even so much of personal insight as of collective wisdom, which to some extent is Lamming's point. Moreover, one could object that if Socrates was a philosopher rather than a folk philosopher, there is no reason to patronize the folk with a fifth category. And I would not much debate the issue, though the fact that a written and unchanged text attributed to the teachings of Socrates has become part of the corpus of Western philosophy has made a profound difference. The point I want to emphasize is that there is an intellectual tradition among farmers and fishermen, separate and apart from the general understanding that because work involves intellectual ideas, the worker is thus both a consumer as well as originator of ideas. This is where I situate the legacy of the Rastafari, for the most part men consumed with ideas — not any ideas, but ideas central to the consciousness of self, and hence central to critical elaboration.

As I have implied, the Rastafari were not the first folk intellectuals in Jamaica. Those Africans who spun around the subjugation of the enslavers with the wit and web of the Spider God, those *bricoleurs* who recreated a culture of word power and signification out of a lexicon drawn from the oppressor himself, who dreamed of a free society and fought to bring it about, who listened and took the message from the messenger to create new ways of finding spiritual empowerment, who debated on the meaning of Africa and redemption — all these were intellectuals. So the Rastafari were not the first, and they are not the only folk philosophers. But, having said all this, it is no doubt a remarkable achievement in the intellectual history of the Caribbean that a group of unlettered farmers and fishermen could out of the yards and street corners of the Dungle and slums of Kingston have developed a coherent body of thought about the world, of such compelling power as to be forging mediating links with teachers and lawyers and professionals, with the consumers of ideas, in a remarkable reverse of the expected flow of influence. The most attractive quality of Rastafari is not so much its agenda of change and social transformation as its new elaboration of an architecture of the self.

Although one of the first members of the intellegentsia to take critical note was the artist Edna Manley, who as mentioned in the foregoing essay noted how revolutionary the Rasta idea of a Black God was, it was the journalist and novelist Roger Mais who first undertook an inventory when he made a Rastaman, Brother Man, the hero of his celebrated novel of that name. Set in the early 1950s, before the sacralization of ganja and the dreadlocks had become generalized throughout the movement, when the beard was the Rastafari's self-defining feature, *Brother Man* is a story of the triumph of decency and trust and faith in the human spirit over deceit, treachery, anarchy and death in the everyday life of urban tenement yard dwellers.

The first time we meet Brother Man he is on his cobbler's bench working, with a Bible lying open on a stool beside him. At his feet assisting him sits Minette, once the young girl of 17 from the country who, in an apparently not uncommon gesture of desperation, had begged him for shelter and protection two years before, and now the woman secretly in love with him. He belonged, the author tells us, 'to that cult known as the Ras Tafarites, and some people said he was mad. Others again thought he was a holy man and a healer, and many came to him, secretly, because they feared gossip, to heal their sick, and for advice and encouragement when things were going wrong' (Mais 1966, 22–3).

Brother Man is different, not because the author tells us so, but because his words and actions are different. Barely had he finished defining, in answer to Minette's question, what love is — 'Love is everything. It is what created the world. It is what made you an' me, child, brought us into the world' — than he was again teaching her a lesson about life. A bird flew into the window glass and fell stunned, almost dead. Brother Man took it up and held it cupped in his hand for a long time, his head bowed over it, in trance almost. It dies. Minette is querulous that he should have set it down on the bench beside him, and he explains: 'It is one of God's creatures, and it was alive a little while back, and now it is dead, an' it didn't do no harm' (p. 26). Here is a man who is not ordinary, who searches for meaning in the very simple sudden innocent death of a small creature: it was alive just now, and now it's dead, 'an' it didn't do no harm.' Brother Man eventually finds in the incident, not the existentialist despair of meaninglessness, but 'a signal purpose in the ways of God going about the world he had created, and somehow it stirred him' (p. 31).

Brother Man is a teacher who draws on living experience to teach profound lessons. It is crab season, and a boy is on his way home with a crab whose claws he managed to make grab each other. 'A han-cuff him,' he explains, 'by mekin' him grab-hol' him own claw, dat way Ah can carry him easy as anyt'ing, him caan do me nutt'n 'tall.' Brother Man buys the crab for sixpence, releases the claws and sets the creature free. 'What you do that for,' the boy asks incredulously. 'Crab feel pain, feel 'fraid, same like you an' me. ... Eat dem is one t'ing, han'-cuff dem an' ill-treat dem is anodder, son. ... Po' li' crab don't do you nutt'n, why you should han'-cuff him like a t'ief?'

Intrigued by the simple wisdom of this strange and different man, the boy — Mais does not even give him a name; he could be anybody — picks on his outstanding characteristic to ask of Brother Man why he wears a beard. And so he hears of, even if he does not fully comprehend, the power of the Nazarite, Samson, who because the spirit of the Lord was with him was able to slay a thousand men.

> 'Is dat why you grow you' beard? 'Cos you want to be like Samson?'
> 'De spirit of the Lawd went over into Ethiopia when Israel was parted among the nations. De twelve tribes were scattered an' lost. But the spirit of the Lawd passed over into Ethiopia, after the Queen of Sheba came to Solomon and learned all his wisdom, an' passed over back to her own land. So it was black men out of Africa who became God's chosen people, for they had learnt de Way.'

This is obviously an early variation of the myth of origin, which by the time Prophet Gad emerged in the late 1960s-early 1970s, was representing the twelve tribes as being in truth the Black men and women in the diaspora, awaiting their day of redemption. But with Brother Man it was the spirit, and not the identification of race, that defined Blacks as beneficiaries of a special relationship with God. That State Visit of the Queen of Sheba to the sacred King of Judah had resulted in the transfer of spirit. Blacks now had it, and the wisdom of Solomon too.

> There was a man who had been living with his sweetheart for some seven years, three years of which he had spent in jail. He had never had any children by the woman, but while he was in jail, that is to say during the second year of his sentence, she had had a child.
> He had forgiven her unfaithfulness, and they were living together again as man and wife, but he was not prepared to go to the length of supporting another man's child, what with the cost of things what it was in those days.
> When the man was finished speaking Brother Man asked the woman if she had anything to add.
> She hung her head and said, no.
> Then Brother Man told the husband to fetch three paving stones, and to see that they were flat on both sides, top and bottom.
> He made him place the stones one on top of the other.

"Can you remove the middle stone without disturbing either of the others?"

And the man said, certainly sure not, that couldn't be done.

Brother Man looked at him and asked him again if he was perfectly sure of that, and the man said he was perfectly sure.

Then Brother Man said that he himself had judged this issue and decided it already, and he should do according as he had judged.

"For," said he, "these three stones are as yourself and the woman and the child. You on top, the child in the middle, the woman at bottom."

And the people who were standing by applauded his judgment as it might have been the judgment of Solomon, and they laughed richly, and clapped the man who thought he had been wronged on the back, and made loud talk, and laughed, and the man himself started laughing, and soon he forgot that he ever had a grievance at all (pp. 122-23).

The plot of the novel revolves around the clash of good, represented by Brother Man the wise judge, the healer whose fame in curing a dying child once forced him to flee the adulating crowd into the Wareika Hills in order to regain his composure of simplicity and peace, against the force of evil, represented by Papacita the lecher, gambler and counterfeit dealer who must satisfy his lust for Minette. He schemes to have Brother Man arrested and destroyed for counterfeiting, but himself becomes the victim of his own excesses as his abused girlfriend kills him in a spirit of revenge. Mais weaves into the plot a factual event, the widely publicized double murder of a young man and his sweetheart along the Palisadoes Road by Wapi King, a bearded man. The result was a sudden backlash against all bearded men, for decades despised as antisocial and criminal. His reputation for good now darkened by the clouds of suspicion as a counterfeiting criminal, Brother Man, the bearded doer of good, finds himself a victim of hysteria and is stoned almost to death, fouled and defiled, but is rescued by love, the love of Minette, now his woman, and Jesmina, a devoted follower.

My point in recounting this tale is by no means to critique the novel as novel, but to show how and why an intellectual, in the person of a literary artist, undertook the still incomplete task of critical elaboration, by valorizing a marginal existence in which he found a great and compelling future.

But Roger Mais goes further to suggest that in Rastafari is the only future, and he does it by making Brother Man, the healer, miracle worker and sage, a Christ-figure. Brother Man's faithful friends washed and bound his wounds and laid him in bed, keeping watch at his side, in action reminiscent of Jesus's crucifixion. 'On the evening of the third day, at sundown, coming out of a deep sleep, he opened his eyes...' It was his resurrection, and the future was now assured. 'They'll all come crawlin' to you yet,' Minette, now his woman, assured him, 'an' beg you to forgive them.' ... 'He saw all things that lay before him in a vision of certitude, and he was alone no longer' (pp. 190-91).

Mais's choice of a Rastafari as hero was not accidental. *Brother Man*, to paraphrase Norman Manley in the Introduction to the *Three Novels*, was the result of a young man plunging deep into the lives of the people to perform a great service by 'interpret[ing] that other world to which the majority belong for the rest of us to see and understand' (p. vi). But even before Mais had completed Brother Man a new and more powerful vision had begun to take hold of the Rastafari: the Dreadlocks emerged.

It would be superfluous to trace the origins, development and meaning of the trend that swept through the Rastafari movement from the 1950s into the early 1970s. The story is sufficiently known. A composer in a creative undertaking searches for the right melodic flow and feeling to accompany the words of a song and bring out its meaning. He or she searches, and every try could work, possibly, but is just not it. And then, in an inspired moment, it presents itself, as if from nowhere because it always was, with a logic that seems so easy, so natural and eternal. And as if to validate its timing it becomes an instant success, a song in the hearts and on the lips of every lover of music. So was it with the Dreadlocks. So natural, logical, eternal, that every artist is suddenly finding that he is already a Dreadlocks.

The Dreadlocks gave Rastafari its name, its signature. The revolution in the meaning of negroid hair, the revolution in the concept of the self, and the sacralization of a forbidden herb constitute a monumental achievement in critical elaboration. Out of the infinity of traces deposited by the White man's rape of Africa in Africa and the Caribbean, the Dreadlocks Rastafari compiled an inventory of meaning aimed at the critical question confronting all philosophy: *gnothi seauton* — know thyself.

Rastafari philosophy does not come out of nowhere. It comes out of the detritus of our history. It is forged in contention with a hegemonic order that legitimized and continues to legitimize its crimes with the help of morality and religion. The religion has been easy enough to spot and unmask, but the morality is ten times more difficult because of its customization and general acceptance. At the foundation of that morality is the demonization of Africa and all things black, which is to say the demonization of the Black self. Franz Fanon (1967) analysed for us the perversion that results from this alienation, and would have had something to say about the bleaching of the black skin, which now reaches epidemic proportions. But is not this the same self that is driven to resist the demon, and to impose its own creation and worldview on the hegemonic order? How else are we to make sense of the survival of Vodun and Santeria, Orisha and Revival? And what do we say of the gift to world culture in the form of the steel pan and reggae, music from the ghettos of Port of Spain and Kingston?

A certain ambiguity about the self has been an inherited trace of our history. The self has been about personal power, the spiritual empowerment through which man becomes god, the mover, the seer, the healer, the conqueror. Armed with their own religion the Africans of the diaspora nurtured a sense of self that gave them feelings of confidence and invincibility. Religion enabled them to undertake the arduous task of taking on the system, and every revolt, every act of defiance was rooted in the appropriation of an empowered self. Grandi

Nanny caught the bullets with her buttocks; and as Boukman was to do later in the Bois Caïman in Haiti, Taki first sought spiritual power prior to the 1760 uprising; Sam Sharpe was already a spiritual leader when he swore death rather than return to the plantation; and so was Bedward when he declared the power of miraculous flight and an end to the world.

But one did not change the self the same way a witch changes skin in order to confront the social order. The self is, as well, a construct of negotiated engagement with the other, in this case the hegemonic other, who has established a(n) (im)moral order of safe self-actualization. If and when it works you do not need a police force; if and when it does not you need an army. That (im)moral order, as Lamming reminds us, has been based on racism, which in its many forms, confronts those destined to be black by virtue of birth with a wall of social powerlessness and personal inadequacy.

Revival religion did not quite know how to deal with this aspect of the construction of the self. Bedward inveighed against the social order, not because of its fundamental immorality, but because it denied him the equal status it monopolized for itself. He denounced the entire establishment, from governor to parson, because, among other things, it refused him the right to marry people. Marriage was at that time, in the 1890s, an indication of social status. It remains so. Then as now, poor people never married until they had realized a rise in material substance. Marriage is not the doorway to sexual cohabitation and family, but the climax of social stability and approval. A license to marry would have been a sign of legitimacy for a church steeped in African ways of empowerment. The hegemon knew he could not co-opt in this way and still retain the hierarchy of status based on the ascriptive condition of race and colour.

Rastafari, however, took a radical turn. It approached the question from within. It immediately rejected the blueprint, rejected the ambiguity of the self. It confirmed the appropriation of spiritual power but negated the alienation from social power, thus retaining the integrity of the self — a self that escapes the vulnerability from the (im)moral order by denying it the legitimacy to be defined by it. Rasta has nothing to gain from the society. It respects none of its values, indeed it denounces them, exposing their fraudulence and inhumanity. It thus finds itself in the margin, beyond the pale, mad, a scandal to everything and everyone that is respectable, but whole, wholesome, at peace.

The dreadlocks phenomenon, symbol of marginal status, is also sacrament, the outward sign of an inward grace — the grace of the *I*. One does not become a Rastafari by wearing locks, but one wears locks by becoming Rastafari. The *I* is, in the first place, the African *I*, the *I* whose history, quite correctly, begins not with the crimes of Europe but with life in the idyllic forests and savannas of the motherland continent where humankind began, the garden of Eden, where man is at peace with God, beast and fellow man. To know thyself is to appropriate this denied, denigrated, deposit of history. Thus every Rastaman is first an African, 'no matter where yu come from.' Here is the locus of the social values of self-construction — the Bongo of honorific stature, as in Bongo Natty, or Bongo Time, the Princes of Egypt and Patriarchs of Israel, the Elders of African social order, the Rasses and Empresses of great Ethiopia, where the gods love to dwell. And every Rasta family is founded on the appropriation of a social order ruled by a benevolent King and Queen, whose subjects are the willing, self-directed Princes and Princesses.

The *I* is as well total subject, subject without object, mover without being moved, God without being God. For to realize the self as subject is to be responsible for oneself, to be unmoved except by oneself. Man free. Man free because God free, because the spirit of God, Jah, dwells within the spirit of man, is man.

And as it is with an ontology that is beyond the reach of the White man and his philosophy, so is it with an epistemology. In Western philosophy of education knowledge begins with treating the unknown as object, and knowing as the process of appropriating it. It is essentially all about acquisition and power, ownership and possession. One knows when one possesses the other. But what if the other is also subject and cannot be objectified? How is knowledge possible? Rastafari answer that knowledge is not an acquisitive process in which the unknowing enriches itself by possession of the unknown, but a revelation of divine oneness, the *I-nity* that makes the *I* of every you, that makes of every object a subject. True knowledge is based on what already is within seeking to manifest and reveal itself. One therefore does not become a Rasta, one already is Rastafari from the very beginning but one manifests the truth in the fullness of time when the self attains consciousness of itself.

How then does one attain consciousness? In the West one goes to school and acquires the consciousness of someone else. But consciousness cannot be acquired, bought, paid for. It comes through the process of reasoning, with the assistance of the holy herb of wisdom, given to man by God, first discovered on the grave of the sacred King, Solomon.

In 2001 an Elder of the Nyabinghi Order from the Pitfour Tabernacle near Montego Bay explained to the National Commission on Ganja the place and significance of this daily ritual among the brethren. I share some of what he said:

> The Rastaman in his philosophy is conscious about God. He is the temple of God — the Rastaman, not this building. It is within us He dwells, His energy. So we become an instrument of Him, thereby we show Him the divine work of us. So we would burn this fragrant incense within this temple unto Him, the Head, the Divine, the Highest Thought of Man, to stimulate this inner being above all this [that] you call political and them thing. We go about it in spiritual discourses, [so] that we will sit here for the whole day, and despite all of the noise and all of that, we are not moving from here. We will be here all night, we will be here, right here, and we reason and have tea. This is what you call the most integral part of the Rastaman, to really sit and reason and come into one common interest and whatsoever, whether it is political, economical, business, or about the state of the Jamaican Government. ... So it is that herb now, and that chalice now, is the balance that keep us there, the whole holy herb, because when we read the Book we see where they say Moses saw God from the burning bush. The Rastaman himself believe that Moses saw God from burning the bush. He

must have taken a spliff, because there was no God in no bush. We read the Bible biblically, prophetically, literally, and so on. So when we look at it, we see [that] it is a cup, a chalice, and when him [Moses] sit up inna himself from a panoramic vision, he sees.

.... Within that now we find divinity in man, and you become a monosystem that God is one. We know God is one, but God is also found in man, and it is out of that consciousness and presence of God in man that the Rastaman function and go and live day by day, now that He [God] is dealing with him and direct him. And he could sit down with his own herb and his consciousness within him, and you find that the brethren walk five, ten miles, to share that with his brethren — just to burn a spliff or chalice.

This deposition is a brilliant exposition of Rastafari philosophy of knowledge. Knowledge derives from a process that involves the ritual reasoning under the facilitating sharing of the holy herb. Reasoning is discourse, but discourse elevated above the 'political,' the mundane. The sharing of the herb transports *I an' I* to a plane where *I an' I* find and become one with the God within. It is there that true knowledge is revealed, whether about politics, economics or the state, or how to interpret the meaning of the Holy Bible. Thus, Moses could not have seen God from the burning bush, as this passage of the Bible is traditionally interpreted, but from burning the bush, the weed, the holy herb of wisdom. The need to attain such heights of knowledge will cause 'a brethren' to journey far distances to commune with his brethren in holy reasoning.

These farmers and fishermen have inventoried the infinity of traces left by our colonial history. In the White man's own inventory of that history, the Admiral Columbus and those who followed — Drake, Hawkins, Morgan, Cortes — are the heroes who have changed the world forever. In Rastafari critical elaboration, however, they are exposed as the criminals of genocide and greed. But so fundamental is this elaboration that the Rastafari challenge the very thought processes that justify and defend wrong. Henry Kissinger's Newtonian versus pre-Newtonian reformulation of what Lamming calls 'the old dichotomy of civilised and uncivilised, Christian Prince and Noble

Savage' is described by Lamming as 'a more palatable and deadly device of neatly carving up the world' (Lamming 2000 [1995],11). More palatable because it is no longer politically correct to call people uncivilized or savage, or primitive, for that matter, but more deadly because of its capacity for destruction, even destruction of the possibility of life itself. The intellectual challenge mounted by the Rastafari rejects the objectification of reality and instead connects all creation into one. There is where its critical elaboration begins.

CHAPTER SIX

Fatherhood in the African-Caribbean Landscape

A Jamaican newspaper in 2000 reported that

> More than a third of Jamaican children whose paternity is questioned in court were not fathered by the man named by their mothers, according to scientists at paternity testing labs.
> Of every 1,000 samples tested by the lab at the University Hospital of the West Indies (UHWI), 340 or 34 per cent show the man to whom fatherhood is attributed is indeed not the child's father.
> The bulk of paternity tests done by both the UHWI lab and the National Blood Bank are ordered by the family court in cases where mothers take the 'fathers' to court for lack of maintenance of children. Of the over 1,200 cases that arise in the family court monthly, about 80 per cent are for child maintenance. Of these, approximately 30 per cent will generate orders for paternity tests....
> Local labs also handle a significant number of requests from foreign embassies and high commissions seeking to confirm paternity in cases where fathers living in other countries file for immigrant status for their 'children.' Scientists say the fate of misattributed paternity in these cases is also about one in three.
> 'Normally, the embassy would order a test when they have doubts about an application, like when the father's name is not on the birth certificate or the mother calls the child by a "pet name" which is different from the name they have,' says Sonia King, head

of the UHWI lab. 'It doesn't take much for them to have a doubt. And they're quite often proved right.' (The Sunday Observer, February 8, 2000, p. 1).

The *jacket* phenomenon is well known throughout the Anglophone Caribbean, and goes by the name *ready-made* in some islands. (A *jacket* or a *ready-made* is a child whose biological father is other than the one named by its mother). Based on the scientific evidence, the newspaper article claims that one in three contested births are *jackets*, and suggests that the same ratio could be applicable throughout the general population. This is astonishing — not the fact that women have outside relationships, but the extent of it, given the widespread belief that outside affairs are really the domain of men. But perhaps even more astonishing is the fact that the report elicited no public response. There are ten radio stations operating in Jamaica, with twice as many talk shows in stiff competition with one another. Normally, an exposé of this magnitude would provide enough grist for the talk mill to last several days. There was not even a whisper. Two weeks later, however, the Women's Crisis Centre threatened to close when the workers there were threatened for providing shelter to a victim of rape. The public outrage allowed the issue to be sustained on the talk shows and print media for over a week. It is perhaps unfair to compare the two issues, for where the second speaks to crime and violence and summons forth anger and outrage, the first elicits laughter: one portrays woman as victim, the other portrays woman as clever trickster. No doubt there are those who would find in the response to the *ready-made* phenomenon added proof that women are never taken as seriously as men, but to my mind the issue raises questions about female sexuality, as distinct from male sexuality, answers to which may throw light on important aspects of fatherhood in the African-Caribbean context. Following this discussion, I go on to treat the meaning of fatherhood in its varied contexts, and conclude with some considerations on the *trickster* motif in the construction of African-Caribbean folk culture, but with particular reference to sexuality.

THE *JACKET* OR *READY-MADE*

It seems a tautology to say that the fact that *jacket* or *ready-made* is entrenched in African-Caribbean folk cultures means that extra-union affairs by women have also been entrenched. But it needs to be said, if for no other reason than the popular perception that the outside affair is a male, not a female, attribute. The calypso, *Shame and Scandal in the Family*, derives its punch from this underlying assumption.[15] And it makes sense. For if the male-female population ratios are pretty stable at 50:50, certainly not greater than 49:51, and if most or all, or even a substantial proportion of men have multiple partners and relationships, then it stands to reason that a substantial proportion of women also have multiple partners and relationships. Unless, of course, a tiny handful of women are the partners of a large proportion of males. There is no evidence even to support speculating thus.

Chambers and Chevannes (1995) found that women do enter into outside partnerships, and for two reasons: sexual satisfaction and economic support. If an economically stable union lacks sexual fulfilment, they may look to an outside relationship for satisfaction. On the other hand, a sexually enriching union may be unable to allow them the measure of economic freedom they need, which they may find in an outside relationship.

In a family or household structure, and in a society, in which the locus of power, both moral and physical, is balanced on the side of the male, female outside relationships are possible because they are conducted with discretion. Men, also, do exercise some discretion in their extra-union affairs, but they derive positive valuation from its becoming public knowledge, or certainly little if any negative sanction, whereas women derive shame. Both types of outside relationships are possible because males and females control and derive their own power from different domains: males the public, women the private. The dichotomy is not as clean and simple as all that, for men do exercise power in the private domain — responsibility for economic support, titular headship, and so forth — while women, in African-

Caribbean cultures, are able to extend their power over into the public domain, as well. But as normative behaviour, it helps to explain why men are less involved in the day-to-day running of the household, or why public leadership is disproportionately in favour of men.

Men and women understand these spheres of power. That is the basis for doubting and contesting paternity, especially in situations where the relationship is tenuous. Roberts and Sinclair (1978) argued that a case could be made for a fourth type of union, the casual, which precedes the visiting, because the latter often develops out of the former, and children are often the products. A relationship could be defined as casual if there is no commitment, no affectivity even, between the partners. In such a situation a man would want to make certain that the pregnancy is really his. If he is satisfied that it is, he accepts and that is that. If he is not, he will deny. But, as the Jamaican folk will say, *ef yu neva go deh, yu name couldn call* (had you not slept with her she could not call your name). Denial or no, only two verifiable options are open. One is the paternity test, which medical science now makes possible, but at great cost. The other is time, as in a few years genetic resemblance or peculiarities will close or widen the gap of uncertainty. By then, however, paternal bonding with the child could suppress the desire for a response.

A woman, on the other hand, cannot doubt her own pregnancy. The only room for doubt is for whom. And whoever is the sire, she remains the mother. The *jacket* or *ready-made* phenomenon gives her the power to name the father. If, then, a woman has the power to determine who the father of her child is, then in a very real sense she controls, at least in part, the first principle of what constitutes fatherhood among the African-Caribbean peoples, namely the bloodline.

According to Raymond Smith (1970), in the Caribbean every child has a father, whether or not he is present, or is known to the child. In this sense, fatherhood begins with paternity. It rests on the ontological principle of blood, through which a child is incorporated into a lineage. The blood principle governs the way people conceive of the kinship group. Half-siblings do not exist. What exist are siblings by father's side, or mother's side. It is through this blood principle that eligibility to family land is determined. (See chapter 10 for a detailed discussion of family land.) As an institution found throughout the Anglophone Caribbean, family land may be passed on through the matrilineal or patrilineal connection. It makes no provision for fictive relationships. Thus, stepchildren and children who belong to a family through folk adoption, by which they may even retain their own names and knowledge of their own blood kin, are excluded from inheriting family land.

With ideas like this a man has to be quite certain that his children are indeed of his bloodline, otherwise he is under no compulsion to play the role of father. In Dominica, it is customary for the infant offspring of a casual or visiting relationship to receive a visit from the man's mother, aunt, or other kin, in order to look for resemblance of one kind or another and, finding it, to claim the child as a member of their kinship group. This, whether or not rumours fly. In Jamaica establishing paternity is not as ritualized, but is as compelling, and both men and women speak of men confirming or rejecting paternity through intuitive knowledge. I am told that the practice exists elsewhere in the region.

It is certain, however, that many men ignore rumours or even the confirmation of *jacket* and accept paternity for the child. We know why. Children are part of the construction of manhood. In the study of Jamaican fathers by Brown, Anderson and Chevannes (1993), a consistent seven or eight out of every ten men claimed they would have had negative feelings about themselves had they not been able to have children. The powerful and even primordial feelings which men held about fatherhood came tumbling out in response to the question 'How would you feel to be without children?' This intensity was evident from the language in which they framed their replies:

> 'I would feel like a bird without a wing'
> 'I would feel like a tree in the forest without leaves'
> 'I would feel no good as a man'
> 'Like a eunuch'

'I would feel haunted'
'Like I am wasting my time'
'Jealous of others who have'
'I would run away from my wife'
Other adjectives included: useless, empty, lonely, embarrassed, irresponsible, unbalanced, strange (Brown et al. 1993, 138–9).

Provided a man's social standing is not threatened, owning up to a *jacket* means confirming one's status as a man.

In this section, I have examined the phenomenon of the *jacket*, or the *ready-made*, to make a case that fatherhood in the African-Caribbean cultural context is not a matter of a functional role only, which is how scholars and social advocates conceptualize it, but a question of identity, as well. Many see in the denials or contesting of attribution of paternity a moral flaw embedded in the male psyche, the action of men who want to enjoy sweetness without responsibility for consequences. I contend that the matter is far more dynamic and complex than that. And it is to this I will return later.

FATHERHOOD, UNIONS AND THE FAMILY

If throughout the Anglophone Caribbean fatherhood is a status, it is also a role which men are expected to play. There are two generally recognized aspects to that role, namely providing for one's children and being the guardian of their moral development, particularly the boys. How these roles are fulfilled is determined not only by the prevailing notions of patriarchy, but also by the structure of the family at a given stage in the domestic life cycle.

From an abstract point of view, men are believed to be the heads of their families. This represents an ideal, not so much in the sense of a desirable state of affairs towards which everybody should strive, as in the sense of an ideology, an idea held to be naturally and self-evidently true, even if disconfirmed by reality. In the African-Caribbean world, the Bible is cited as the ultimate authority on which men's moral leadership over women rests. Nonetheless, the realities are otherwise. The male dominance which patriarchal authority implies is tempered, erased even, not only by other cultural norms that confer on women the position of dominance over domestic matters, but also by the situation of the family in its development cycle.

Early childbearing has up to the present time been a feature of the African-Caribbean reproductive pattern. The growing concern of late with teenage pregnancy and childbirth is a function of the now universally accepted expectations about preparation for adult life through long years of education. Most pregnancies at this stage of reproductive life are unplanned, and the source of great personal trauma, but one which accomplishes the transition of a girl to full womanhood. According to data from Jamaica (Chevannes 1995), the overwhelming majority of babyfathers of teenage mothers were on average between six and seven years their senior. Whether the partners were intimate lovers or only social friends, the pregnancy and birth were accepted as bestowing status on both girl and boy. The girls reported that their relations with their own mothers were generally better than they had been prior to the pregnancy. Eight or nine out of every ten girls reported that the young men not only accepted the paternity once they knew of the pregnancy, but provided the moral and material support they needed at the time. Many of them had been totally rejected by or alienated from their immediate families, and in addition had had to bear the humiliation that an in-school pregnancy carried. The father's support for the baby continued after birth.

For girls who are able to return to secondary school to continue their education, or to go elsewhere to learn a skill or begin a career, the babies are taken over by their families of socialization. If the young man's relations with his babymother and her family remain good, he will have visiting rights, and the child will know its paternal kin. If the relations are acrimonious, he may be deprived of all rights to the child. The worst possible humiliation a young man could suffer would be to be denied the right to pass on his name to a child he knows and accepts as his own, especially if it is his first.

Young men and women entering the initial stages of a developmental cycle of reproductive and affective life are particularly vulnerable. The young woman's vulnerability derives from being trapped into too early dependency on a spouse who has himself not yet attained social and economic security. Chevannes (1995) found that those babymothers who did not enter the programme of counselling and re-entry into the secondary school system were living in common-law unions with their first babyfathers, had had subsequent pregnancies, and were receiving lower wages than those who had been counselled and placed. Roberts and Sinclair (1978) reported that many women actually preferred visiting unions, because it gave them a greater degree of freedom from the control of a co-resident spouse, yet still allowing the babyfathers to spend on average fourteen or fifteen hours of contact per week with their children, two-thirds the norm for all fathers. In a visiting relationship, it is the man who visits. He supports the child but cannot dictate anything else. He certainly cannot abuse the mother in her own yard.

But the young man is also vulnerable. The younger he is, the greater the likelihood of being unemployed, underemployed or unskilled. Lacking ability to take care of his child, he *ipso facto* lacks authority over both child and babymother. If being able to exercise the role of father means so much to a man's identity and self-esteem as Brown *et al.* (1993) have shown, what does it do to a man who is unable to mind his children? For one thing, he will seek to absent himself, rather than face an unsympathetic babymother.[16] The incidence of single female-headed households has been linked to poverty from as far back as the research of Edith Clarke (1957). And unless he can contribute to the child's upkeep, he will be denied access to him or her by his babymother. The child becomes a big loser, as well, for without the opportunity for contact the father-child bonds will be weak.

Yet with changing demographic patterns new ways of expressing the status of father are being found. The rapid decline in the average rate of childbirth to women means a decline in the average rate of childbirth to men, as well. If children mean so much to men and men are having fewer of them, it is reasonable to assume that they would expend more interest in the few they have. In Jamaica, at least, there is evidence of men engaging in such nurturing roles as playing and counselling, although, culturally speaking, they receive no credit for it, as the provider role remains their principal charge. But more research is needed to determine whether and to what extent these more noticeable behaviours, such as attending child health clinics, are due to demographic shifts, or to social and economic factors.

The incidence of visiting unions gives way quickly to co-residential units, both of the married and common-law varieties. Common-law unions reach their highest incidence among African-Caribbean women in their mid to late twenties, probably a little later for men. By then, the first child or first two children are in the yard stage of development, during which time they learn the gender-segregated roles they see and are taught. The girls pattern their behaviour off their mothers, and are the object of a protective axis between home and school, while the boys pattern theirs off their fathers, older males and their peer group. Boys learn quickly that they are free to absent themselves from the home, provided that they carry out their assigned chores. The gender ideal, held by women and men alike, discourages a boy from being tied too much to the yard, for fear he should grow into a *makoman*, or a *maamaman*, a feminized and domesticated man. Naturally, women do not expect their own spouses to be *mako*. Apart from the stigma, such men undermine their power by interfering in the female domain. Thus, the more they grow, the more boys experience freedom from maternal control. A great part of their socialization is accomplished outside the home, in public spaces and among their peers. At this point it is a father's responsibility to exert control over his son, in order to ensure that he grows up into a socially responsible person and that he does not deviate from the values taught in the home.

Fathers are thus expected to be authority figures, a status that is not consonant with involvement in the daily running of the household, or with affectivity. He thus appears to be distant. But in that seeming distance, marginality or absence, often lies the effectiveness of his authority role, whether as an arbiter on behalf of the children against the decisions of the mother, or as disciplinarian, the threat of whose sanctions is often enough to enforce rectitude. It is the boy child that most feels his disciplinary hand. His tactile contact with his daughters would have begun to diminish from the beginning of their yard stage of development and disappears altogether the nearer they get to puberty.

As a man settles into some gainful employment, and passes the stage when he can no longer compete physically with his young adult peers, he begins to acquire a degree of social respectability. Although he may not be married, younger children and adults generally begin to address him in terms which couch intimations of expected behaviours more in keeping with someone socially responsible and deserving of titles of respect. Critical in that standing is his control of his yard, which first and foremost demands being able to provide, but which also requires being unchallenged by his spouse or his children. By the time adolescence creeps up on a boy, a good father is one who not only provides, but one whose son is socially well adjusted.

Marriages do not remain at common law forever. They generally move into lawfully recognized unions. Of the three types of unions, marriage is the only type that exhibits a steady rate of increase through the life cycle. It is therefore seen as a permanent state, towards which couples aspire, rather than one they begin with. Among the differences with common law is the enhanced respectability that the family all round acquires. The married status is befitting the couples' movement upward in age. But the factor most critical to making the transition is the man's economic prospects, which do not necessarily translate into having a house, but require a fairly stable income or the ability to source money when needed.

All unions, but especially the co-residential marital and common-law ones, afford a man opportunities to develop affective relations with his children. A significant aspect of fatherhood is the special and particular bonding with some or all of his children, derived from their face-to-face contacts and presence,[17] their match of personalities, particular events in their lives and how they deal with them, and any number of unstructured factors. The point is, men are human, and just as they find idiosyncratic ways to express their affection for their spouses and partners, so also will they find ways to express their paternal instincts towards their children. It is in this regard that the outside child surfaces as problematic.

ANANSI AND THE *outside* CHILD

In Brown et al. (1993,172), the highest level of dissatisfaction over their role as fathers was expressed by fathers with outside children. They visited and played with their outside children less frequently than they would have liked, and those who were themselves outside children regretted most the fact that they never grew with their fathers.

Since a child remains with its mother on separation from father, the outside child is outside its father's existing union. There are two ways in which a child achieves this status. The first is through a previous relationship. Several factors determine a man's own disposition towards such children. One is the nature of the break. If it was acrimonious, the chances of him cooperating willingly to support and bond with the child are low. If, however, the break allows for amicable relations, he is more likely to play a constructive paternal role. But his present spouse often becomes a factor discouraging contact with a previous rival, and in the interest of preserving stability, he will comply and refrain from visiting or maintaining his outside child. From a different angle, but with the same fear, the male spouse of the man's babymother will also want to discourage contact.

The other way to beget an outside child is through a casual or steady relationship outside the existing union. Raymond Smith (1988) discusses the practice of middle-class married men keeping outside women, and the interplay of hierarchy based on colour and social status, which keep the kept women and their children apart from their half-siblings. But the practice is not confined to relations between middle- and upper-class men and lower-class females. It is generalized through all social strata, and among the peasant and working classes it has its own meaning. The common stereotype of every man having more than one woman applies especially to the working classes, though the evidence shows that at most the proportion that actually do is no more than one-half (Chevannes 1985). Middle-class men, by keeping a completely separate household in another social class altogether, and because of their patriarchal dominance at home, are able to avert the unwelcome social problems that would arise from full public exposure of their affairs. A working-class man, on the contrary, moving within the same social stratum, though not necessarily within the same community, must devise ways and means to prevent his affairs coming to the attention of his spouse. One is talking here not of the casual relations, which can be dismissed with the resignation that men in general, or this man in particular, is wild. Rather, the kind of relationship that brings domestic disputes is the steady, outside woman variety, whether or not it produces a child.

Multiple partnership is a recognized feature of the conjugal and mating patterns of the African-Caribbean peoples, but one which is more prevalent at the lower than at the higher end of the mating cycle, and therefore more related to the visiting and common-law unions. As forms, these unions coexist with marriage, which is not only legal, but given hegemonic status. As I have said, marriage bestows respectability on a man and his family. But the 'price,' so to speak, is monogamy, an order of morality that is also sanctioned by the Church as one ordained by God. All other types of sexual union are considered 'living in sin' by all the churches, whether established or new. The established ones routinely deny their common-law members communion, while the newer ones constantly preach against 'fornication,' or sex outside of marriage. But the fact that multiple relationships flourish in populations that are largely Christian indicates a lack of cultural congruence with hegemonic values.

Outside relationships, however formed, involve varying degrees of deception.[18] The *jacket* is the female counterpart to the outside child who is the product of a man's outside relationship. A woman gives her spouse a *jacket,* he gives her an outside child. Both contravene the moral order, but whereas the *jacket* is the subject of amusement, the outside child is not. What elicits the humour is not the fact of the child but the deceptive sexuality of the mother.

There is at work here in the kind of sexuality that produces both *outside* child and *ready-made* the same trickster ethos discussed above in 'Rastafari and the Paradox of Disorder' where reference was made to Diane Austin-Broos's study of Jamaican Pentecostalism. Anansi opposes the Western European ethical rationalism of 'the idea of marriage, work, and a sober life as integral to Christian being' (Austin-Broos 1997, 50) with an ethos of play and pleasure that acquires ontological status. This produces in Jamaican Pentecostalism an intrinsic tension between the two moral orders, which is never resolved in the triumph of one over the other, but is lived in the ever-present cultural need of women to establish their fecundity, coexisting with the spiritual call to be saints, the tension between backsliding and rebirth. Austin-Broos gives to the Anansi aesthetics a centrality of place in Jamaican culture, infecting it with a taste for irony, ambiguity and play.

Her analysis owes much to Robert Pelton, whose interpretation of the cosmological meaning of the trickster-god embraces the two other West African figures of Eshu and Legba. The tricksters reproduce in human life the contradictory forces of the cosmos, constantly extending limits into the realms of possibility, creating at the same time as they destroy. Eshu, for example,

> embodies sexuality as unleashed desire — not lust merely, nor even avarice, envy, or greed, but that passion for what lies outside one's grasp which the Greeks saw in some sense as the sovereign mover of human life. Eshu is agile: he is moving always to challenge, break open, and enlarge every possible structure and relationship (Pelton 1980, 161).

Anansi, for his part, 'is master of wisdom because he yokes together the mysterious ambivalences of ordinary life — speech and pain, emptiness and fullness, wisdom and waste' (Pelton 1980, 41). He evokes laughter, 'but his funniness has nothing earnest or one-dimensional about it. He is no sweaty metaphysical pioneer hacking the actual out of the jungle of the possible, nor is he a good-natured cosmic mechanic, revving up the motor of social order by injecting a richer mixture of chaos into its fuel. He does these things, but his style is radically oxymoronic' (Pelton 1980, 48).

From its West African-derived ethic and aesthetic, the cosmology of the African-Caribbean peoples, as we discussed in Chapter 3 and again in Chapter 4, embraces a worldview that maintains in everyday life a creative tension between order and disorder. The *ready-made* and *outside* phenomena are, typically, expressions of a people who push the moral order beyond its limits to reveal the infinitely larger possibilities of human life. Against the immorality of deception is pitted the power to widen human intercourse and relationships, and to create new life, even as it destroys. This is what life is all about, affirming while at the same time challenging the values of social order.

The *outside* child is thus a foil for the *inside* world of structured relationships on which the social order rests. It is for this reason that the *jacket* elicits no negative social response: the child is already entrenched within the nurturing embrace of the family. Fatherhood of *outside* children, on the other hand, presents and represents a challenge. It challenges men to invent ways of fulfilling their sense of duty towards their own blood. But at the same time, it is an inevitable and intrinsic expression of an impulse within African-Caribbean culture towards contradiction and ambiguity.

PART III
THE MORAL ORDER

CHAPTER SEVEN

The Evasion of Moral Responsibility: A View from Within

Our Standard 6 English teacher at my elementary school was the headmaster himself, Mr W.A. Smith. He was an effective and highly rated teacher. All the basic rules of the English language — the first rule of concord, for example, were drilled into us. We knew *how* English was supposed to be spoken, even if we did not speak it. He often taught by gathering us in a semi-circle around his table. One day as the group assembled around him, he looked down and saw that the leg of one of the two Beryls in the class had been bleeding. 'What's wrong with your foot?' he asked. The Jamaican word 'foot' means thigh, leg and foot — a legacy of West African ancestors. Beryl looked up nervously and replied, "It cut, sir." Teacher Smith, our English teacher, looked contemptuously at Beryl, cut his eye in true Jamaican fashion, and said, 'I suppose it must have cut itself!'

Poor Beryl! The rest of us were quite happy that the spotlight was not on us, for I am now quite confident that we all would have given the same reply. It would have been decidedly quite awkward to say, 'It is cut, sir,' using the passive voice, a circumstance that was quite obvious to Teacher Smith, who by his sharp retort made it clear that what he was looking for in the answer was *agency*. In later years following my transformation into a bilingual speaker, I learned from hearing first-language speakers of English that Beryl's answer should have been something like: 'I scraped it on the fence, sir,' or 'I fell and cut it, sir!' or simply, 'I cut it, sir!'.

But the problem is not simply one of translation. There is a deeper significance here. For, who in her right mind would cut her foot, or scrape her leg just so? We do not inflict pain and injury on ourselves for the sake of doing so, therefore it is not right to say, 'I cut it!' *I* did not cut it. But if I did not cut it, who did? Not who did, but what? The creole speaker can and does in fact address this, and instead of saying, 'It cut!' has the option of saying, 'Bakl [bottle] cut me!' which addresses the question of agency, but immediately raises another question in the mind of the anglophone speaker, namely how could an inanimate object have the animus to inflict a cut.

Example No. 2. A glass or plate falls from the hand of a domestic helper and breaks:

'What happened, Mavis?'
'The plate brok, mam!'
'How did it break?'
'It drop out of my hand, mam!'

Who, except the most wilful and malicious, would deliberately drop a piece of crockery, and endanger her job? Therefore, Mavis's answer assumes that her mistress understands that it was not a deliberate act on her part. Were she an anglophone speaker Mavis would probably in one speech act say, "The plate *accidentally* fell from my hand, mam!" I emphasize the word *accidentally* to suggest that this qualifier is admissible in anglophone speech, but not in the creole, unless by switching to explain to an agitated mistress of the house, 'Is a accident, mam!' I cannot think of an equivalent in Jamaican, or a speech act in Jamaican that would make use of the word *accidentally*. Philosophically, accidents are chance occurrences, which need no further explanation, because they are assumed to be part of the 'order of things.' They are random. They just simply happen. If I am right about Jamaican, however, there are no 'accidents,' in the sense of random occurrences. 'Things' are not ordered that way.

Example No. 3. A regularly scheduled country bus leaves for town without Maas Joe. As he returns home, Maas Joe explains to a surprised wife: 'The bus lef' me!' There is no direct English equivalent, unless there is an implied deliberate intent on the part of the driver of the bus (not the bus itself) such that: 'I was standing by the bus stop and the driver sped pass without stopping. He left me!' But that is not what Maas Joe means. 'The bus lef' me!' implies that the bus passed by the stop before Maas Joe reached it, but Maas Joe does not say, 'I was late for the bus!' Instead he sidesteps the issue of his own responsibility by making himself a victim. I am certain that is how the anglophone speaker would interpret it.

These three examples of speech events in Jamaican creole, 'It cut!', 'Di plate brok!', and 'Di bus lef mi!' are fairly common in the language. They raise issues of agency and responsibility, and are a source of misunderstanding and conflicts. There are three ways of approaching them. One is to regard them as Jamaican creole ways of expression, which one could appropriately translate. Clearly, I do not believe that that is what they are, even while admitting the peculiarities of the creole. The second is to treat them as raising an issue of morality, which is how they have been treated by planters and missionaries, who throughout the history of contact, have seen black people as evasive and irresponsible. The fact that this is the way an entire people speak means that an entire people are categorized as evasive and irresponsible — a national or racial character flaw.

There is a third way, and that is to treat them as *sui generis*, expressions of their own kind, in a somewhat similar way to the demographer George Roberts's treatment of the illegitimacy issue. In the early years of West Indian scholarship, Roberts rejected the notion of moral turpitude on the part of the majority of black people, and advanced the position that an illegitimacy rate of over 70 per cent in some instances in the Anglophone Caribbean pointed to a mating pattern *sui generis*. Through the work of Raymond Smith on the domestic cycle (see 'Law and the African-Caribbean Family,' Part IV), scholars have since acknowledged the *sui generis* character of the conjugal behaviour of the African-Caribbean people, and accepted Roberts's naming of the extra-residential mating that begins the cycle as the 'visiting union.' Thus, instead of seeing the expressions as indicators of moral irresponsibility, we could explore them for some other functional significance, which is what I propose.

Each of the examples I cite has a philosophical base somewhat different from the others. The base of the first — 'It cut!' — I would describe as fate. In Western secular thinking, we would be inclined to call this an accident, and I have no problem in doing so, except that we would need to distinguish this kind of accident from the base of the second example, "The plate brok!" Presumably, one has less control over setting one's foot down on a piece of bottle one did not see or is prevented from seeing, than letting a plate slip from one's hands while washing up dishes over a sink. In Western secular thinking, both are chance occurrences, but I think they are distinct. I use 'secular' to identify a post-enlightenment rejection of a religious tradition that saw fate as *Dei voluntas*. And both of these are somewhat different from the third. 'Di bus lef' me!' is not fate, not the will of God, at least not on the surface. It becomes fate only when later events either on the road or at home reveal that the failure to get on that bus was crucial. For example, missing the bus would be a blessing in disguise if the bus met with a terrible accident, or a curse, since in staying home Maas Joe slipped, fell, broke his neck and died.

There are differences. But there is an important common thread that runs through these three speech events. Each implies a lack of *intent*. Whatever we can say about each, as a way of expressing a happening, it implies that the speaker had no intention of effecting the outcome. Intention is the subjective orientation of an actor *qua* actor, and if the outcome is not what was intended, then s/he cannot be morally responsible. Western jurisprudence acknowledges this in the concept *mens rea*, but does not absolve the actor as blameless if the sequence of his/her actions leads to injury. S/he would be lacking in intent but blameworthy by negligence, the philosophical base being that s/he is a conscious initiator of his/her actions.

Thus, there is no difference where both Jamaican and English are concerned. As many of us found out when we were children, one can be guilty by being 'kyeelis' (careless), especially if plates are frequently broken or buses frequently missed. In Jamaican thinking, however, the issue goes beyond this. I want to suggest two interrelated types of explanation.

The first type of explanation rests on the simple premise that we are not the masters of our own destiny. Karl Marx said as much when he wrote that ends are intended, but results are not. The medieval scholar put it thus: *Homo proponit, Deus disponit*. The Jamaican versions are *Man plan, but Gad mash dong plan*, or *Man write an Gad wipe out*. For Marx, the difference between ends and results lies in the intervention of class interests, and for the medieval scholar and Jamaican worker, in the intervention of spiritual forces. And therein lies what is peculiar to the Jamaican. His/her personal world is shaped by forces that interact with his/her own will to produce results that are therefore not entirely his/her responsibility.

The following is a common enough experience for many of us who have not severed our links with the poor and dispossessed. A young man you have not seen for months, maybe years, meets you and even by his body language and the way in which he expresses the customary pleasantries you know what he is coming with next: a favour, either money or a job or a contact for a job. But whatever is the favour his rationale will invariably be: 'Yu waan si, notn naa gwaan fi mi.' Transliterated it means, 'You see, nothing is going on for me,' but this does not convey the meaning, and in fact is misleading if taken to mean 'I have not been lucky.'

What does it mean? It could mean one of two things. The first is, 'Nothing has come my way,' as in the spider waiting patiently to trap an errant fly. There is an attempt to evoke our sympathy, which if he succeeds in doing traps us into doing him a favour. At this point it becomes pointless to ask 'What if you didn't see me?' or 'What if I hadn't passed this way?' To ask such a question is to seek refuge in a way of thinking that allows the possibility of chance. But our friend's thought is at a different level: 'Is the Faada sen' yu, Jah know!'

A second possible meaning is, 'I have tried, been here, there and everywhere, and still cannot find a break,' and is tantamount to saying 'Mi bad lukid!' (I am unlucky) or 'Mi salt!' especially if the experience included many a near miss, which is what our 'chance' meeting would become if we refuse to help. There is a strong Afro-Caribbean tradition of viewing salt as dispiriting, and the word has become commonplace among Jamaicans. Whether the first or the second sense of the phrase is intended, the point is the same: one is a victim of external, usually spiritual, forces which cannot be combated without external help. One therefore guards one's daily life by prayer and ritual, by charms and amulets, to appease, amass, or otherwise control, those forces. Going to seers and healers to get a reading is itself an interesting practice, since behind it is the notion that one can in fact alter one's fate, though 'what is fiyu kyaan bi anfiyu' (what is yours cannot not be yours). Undergoing the ritual bath is of the same order. As a water ritual it cleanses one of malignant power and insures one.

Most forces are external to the individual, but there is one that is internal, and that is one's spirit. The spirit is conceptualised as independent of the actor, influencing him/her by advice on the course of action to take, or persons to be wary of.

The individual is often the victim of the external forces, for the want of which the end result would have been the end intended. As Dean of Faculty, with authority to grant or deny students courses over the approved norm, hearing their explanations as to why they failed or did poorly can be quite instructive. My part-time students do not deny that it is they who attempted to juggle the full load with the demands of the workplace, that they were well aware that they could have been called on at any time to put in some overtime on the job, that the traffic coming up to the campus was always heavy after 4 p.m., that it was they who arrived at the examination hall late, and therefore it was they who failed or did less well. They know this, but they do not accept the consequences of it. Or, to put it more accurately, they accept the consequences imposed from outside, but do not internalize responsibility: they are not morally responsible. I cannot recall a single case of appeal for consideration for extra credits that factored in the contingent. So despite having failed or done poorly, they *know* they can handle the additional work; all they want is to be given the chance.

I recall an incident a few years ago, in which Tivoli Gardens striker Ricardo Fuller fouled a player and was given a red card. As he left the field, so it was alleged, he kicked the fallen player in the head. On a radio sports programme days later I heard a man call in and his words to the host were: 'I would like to discuss what happened to Ricardo Fuller.' It was clear he was not talking about Fuller's ejection from the game, but the assault on the fouled player, which was what created news in the media. Fuller, to follow the logic of the caller's wording, was a victim.

I am inclined to think that this idea of being subject to external forces is perhaps a cousin of spirit possession. Getting 'in the spirit,' or being 'mounted by a loa,' as it would be expressed in Vodun and Orisha, produces actions that are not the responsibility of the possessed but of the possessing spirit. The possessed is completely subject to the power of the deity. In a similar way our friend for whom 'notn naa gwaan' is completely subject to external controlling unspecified powers.

The second and related type of explanation draws yet again on our understanding of what Diane Austin-Broos (1997) calls the politics of moral orders. In any class/race divided society like Jamaica morality conceals a political dimension, since it affects issues of governance and the social order. Anansi's power lies in his ability to violate the established order and in so doing discover new possibilities. He is thus always a subversive, who is most effective in situations of superordination and subordination — situations essentially of politics. It is the ethos of Thomas, the newly baptised Christian, disclaiming responsibility for the debt he had contracted before his baptism when his name and old identity was Kwaashi — 'Kwaashi don't pay Thomas debt.' Same old person, but now indeed a new and different, born-again person.

All societies have political relationships of ordination, above and below, but these can be distinguished according to the quality of the relationships, for example whether the powers above share in a common understanding with those below, or whether they are antagonistic. It is relationships of antagonism and boundary maintenance that provide the most fertile ground for Anansi. Stealing becomes *taking*, and lying justifiable survival. The amorality associated with the Spider god trips in and an evasive neutrality takes over. 'The plate brok' preserves all the possibilities — spiteful revenge, simple negligence, innocent accident. Any card can play, but it depends on the quality of the relationship. If the relationship is bad, then I did not break the plate, even though 'di plate brok.' If the boss is intending to fire me because he smells alcohol on my breath, while his reeks of 'business luncheon' whisky, then I am innocent. But if the relations are good, if the boss shares the same dining room, or knows us by name, even plays on the same domino team, then at best I am negligent.

Most Jamaicans operate in two worlds, two orders, and they move the boundaries back and forth as it suits. It would be a mistake to think of the moral order I have been describing as an aberration. It is a quite wholesome and functional order based on a worldview that for all its several hundred years of evolution is neither recognized nor understood nor valued by those of us who control the maintenance of the hegemonic order.

CHAPTER EIGHT

The Values We Live By

There was a horrible incident in March 2003. Late one night a man who was allegedly caught breaking into a car on the campus of the University of Technology (UTech) was chased and cornered in a waste water pit. According to The *Sunday Gleaner* (March 16, 2003, p.A3):

> During his time in the cesspool the students rained several stones on the thief forcing him to remain under the murky waters for long periods. They also lit bush fires around the pool to prevent him from escaping. The students reported that the thief remained below overgrown lilies in the cesspool for about an hour then he popped up for air but more stones were rained down on him. They said at one point during the ordeal the thief offered to give himself up and attempted to come out of the pool but the angry mob rained down more stones on him. He eventually went below the water again and popped up a few times for air until he disappeared from the surface.

The significant points are: first, a man pays for attempted theft with his life. Leaving aside for the moment considerations of the psychology of a mob, which in moments of frenzy is susceptible to acts that each individual would abhor, the bottom line is 'tief mus dead.' So the question is 'Is theft or attempted theft worth a life?' Of course not, most of us would say, but against this has to be weighed the following: an official of the University told The *Sunday Observer* (p. 3) that they had had reports of 25 cars broken into, five of which were confirmed. Against this background, the action of the mob is reminiscent of the actions of frustrated small cultivators against praedial thieves — they chop them to death.

The second point is that the thief's offer to give himself up was ignored, refused. The bottom line is: no mercy. And the third point is that the mob was university students. Somehow, university students are supposed to be the most educated members of our society: from among them, so we hope, comes our next generation of leaders. They, because of the refinement of intellect and sensibilities that is provided by the institutions that educate our elite, should be above such acts of barbarism. But if they, in whom the society pins its future hope can sentence a man to such a horrible death-by-drowning-in-a-cesspool-for-attempted-theft, then what is to become of our civilization? What, indeed, have we become? Have we *become* anything? Weren't we always like that?

Three days after this incident three men were gunned down in a drive-by shooting in the nearby Kintyre area, an apparent reprisal for the murder of a don. They were all guilty, not by any commission but by their domicile. According to reports people have begun abandoning their homes. Why are Jamaicans so thirsty for blood? When did we *become* so? When was respect for the aged, for the child, for the pregnant woman lost? Weren't we always like that?

The call for a restoration of the values and the attitudes by which we once lived, or thought we lived, is based on the pervasiveness of these kinds of incidents. Between January and March 2003, 160 people were murdered. Civilizations flourish with the pursuit of the intellect and the human spirit in a stable social order; they decline when social instability and anarchy make the pursuit of knowledge and creativity secondary to human survival. Civilizations flourish when a stable social order allows the free flow of ideas at the crossroads of cultures; and their heights are indexed on their hospitality to strangers. They decline when fear and incivility, bred on the unpredictability of social life, become spontaneous responses in human relations. The threat we presently face as a civilization comes not from the failure to respect things intellectual and spiritual, not from a lack of creativity, not from xenophobia, but from the loss in too many of our people of the values that make us human.

A value is a worth. In economics we use the term to refer to the worth of a commodity, determined by the amount and quality of labour involved in its creation. And we distinguish its value from the price it fetches. There is thus some sense of equivalence or transference in the economic meaning of value. Something is of no value if it can be traded for nothing; or is *priceless* if its value is beyond estimate.

What we are talking about, however, is the ethical, not the economic or utilitarian use of the word. In the ethical or moral sense, a value has no equivalence as such. It is a worth in and of itself, though some values are greater than others. Values are the sentiments we attach to or associate with certain behaviours, relationships, and symbols. If culture is, as Clifford Geertz would have it, a complex system of meaning, then values are the weights of meaning we place on being human, that is, ordering life in a human way. We cannot live without meaning, therefore we cannot live without values. A handshake is a behaviour we practise as a symbol of civility. This form of physical touch is given the meaning of: 'I greet you; I respect you as a human being.' It is a value because we give it such weight that not to shake an extended hand is either a mark of incivility or a statement of hostility. Among the Japanese, the gesture of bending the upper half of the body forward in the direction of another person means respect, and there is an additional meaning that depends on the depth of the bow — the deeper the bend the higher the status of the one being greeted. We know that showing the respect due is a value in Japanese society because bowing is widely practised in day-to-day relations, and not to bow or not to bow to the appropriate depth is either a mark of incivility or a deliberate insult. The same could be said of 'Good morning' in our society. Not to say 'Good morning' or not to return the greeting is a further mark of incivility or slight. We know it is a value in the rural communities, but is not much of one in the urban areas. However, in both town and country, 'Good morning' is not merely a form of salutation: it must be used as a prelude to any request or question put to a stranger. We can tell it is a value by listening on any of the call-in programmes to the callers who always preface their contributions or questions by a greeting, sometimes quite elaborate, while the impatient time-is-money hosts would like them to get to the point. In the United States, such preliminaries whether on telephone or face to face would be unusual, but in Jamaica not to greet someone whom one is about to address is uncivil and a mark of poor upbringing.

Which brings me to consider how values are transmitted. Because many of the values that govern day-to-day behaviour come to us so instinctively and by reflex we conclude that they have been internalized and so form part of our personality. As culture is transmitted through socialization, so also are the values, the sentiments that go along with it. The main agencies of socialization are the family and the community. Some people cite the breakdown of the family as the cause of the loss of the values that used to make murder and aggression rare lapses in self-control. In examining this, a historical gloss is not without merit.

The family system we inherited was the product of a clash of cultures that remains evident even up to the present times. It is the clash of Europe and Africa here in the Americas. I call it a clash not only because of the forced circumstances of the encounter but also because of the obduracy of the enslaved, whose numbers allowed them to resist being assimilated. It is important to remember that the Africans did not come as 'Africans,' but as the unfortunate members of ethnic groups, and that their identity as 'African' was forged right here, in the realization of a common interpretation of the world against a common enemy with whom they shared the same space. African societies, whether the elaborate state systems like those of the Ashanti and the Yoruba, or stateless systems like that of the Igbo, were founded on kinship relations, on the family. One's place in a community was determined by one's lineage among many lineages. One's identity was first that of one's line, a circumstance that still obtains in many parts of the non-western world, where the individual identity as expressed in a name comes after the identity of the clan or tribe or lineage. A marriage was not merely the congress of two individuals but the forging of a relationship between lineages. Children therefore belonged not merely to a couple but to a lineage. One's rights and responsibilities were those of one's family in this wider sense, and one's debts and obligations those of one's family as well. Community order and stability were achieved through the systems of authority invested in the heads of lineages.

European slavery ruptured all this, but even before the enslaved recovered from their trauma we know from our historians that they faced the question of the kind of community they had to build with what they had at hand, in order to survive and to resist. That very survival was itself a major value, since the hope in resistance is premised on it. You cannot resist if you do not survive. It was Marcus Garvey who observed that the African peoples survived the hundreds of years of subjugation and humiliation at the hands of the whites where others had succumbed, and asked the question why. He provided his own answer: diplomacy. We survived through diplomacy. Diplomacy as I understand Garvey's use of it is saying no by saying yes, when no might hurt; is speaking without words, when 'cock mout' could very well kill cock;' [19] is getting one's way by appearing to give. It is the art of the spider deity.

In this clash, one culture says:

Speak the truth and speak it ever
cost it what it will
he who hides the wrong he does
does the wrong thing still.

Truth is a supreme value, no matter the circumstance. And so, 'Who chopped down the cherry tree?' 'Father, it is I!'

The other says: "Yu mus play fool fi ketch wise." Thus,

'Is one Mr Jones living here?'
'Who?'
'Mr Jones.'
'Jones?'
'Yes, Jones!'
'Which Jones is that? Jones? Girly, you know any Jones living here?'
'Who?'
'Who you say again sar?'
'Jones. Jones.'
'Which Jones is that?'
'Which Jones is that, Sar?'
'John Jones.'
'And who you be, sar?'
'I am from Courts Jamaica Ltd.'
'No sar, no Jones don't live here!'[20]

One of the early missionaries told of asking a woman the whereabouts of a certain slave, but before she could answer her son blurted out the answer. He later learned that the poor boy got a good whipping for telling bakra maasa the truth. This child was being socialized into the art of deception, of playing fool fi ketch wise. No doubt he would have got an even greater whipping for deceiving his mother. Thus it is not that truth is not a value, but that truth is subordinated to the necessity to survive and to the obstruction of the enemy. The art of a form of deception, camouflage, enabled the Maroons to gain the upper hand in many an encounter with detachments of soldiers, at a time when European military values considered it dishonourable and unworthy of a real soldier.

Deception in work led to the stereotyping of the males as lazy — the Kwaashi personality. What is most interesting here is that the same Kwaashi is a transformed person when on Sundays the chance came to work his own provision ground. Work is valued when it adds to the enhancement of community and of self. This contrasts with the East Indian idea of work for the sake of work, as a way of fulfilling one's purpose in life (Williams 1991), and certainly clashes with the puritanical compulsion of work as a justification for salvation. If there is no survival, no enhancement, what is the point of working?

Out of the detritus of the European transatlantic trade in human beings, the Africans reconstructed a culture and a civilization with what they had. And what did they have at hand? They had at first members of their own ethnic groups, but for the most part they had strangers, most of whom spoke different languages but who were in similar circumstances. They also had the strange-looking people who had brought them here in the first place and who now put them to work. The first attempts at community based initially on the members of one's ethnic group resulted in the Maroon communities and the Maroon wars. But for the majority, not until the ethnic boundaries could be overcome and a new ethnicity forged on the basis of a common culture did it become possible to build a sense of community. Religion was at its centre, for it was religion that gave the power to seek the overthrow of slavery, that gave meaning to the cosmos, and interpreted the place of humankind in it.

That sense of community begins with the establishment of relationships of affinity and kinship. When one sees in a work like the Thistlewood diaries (Hall 1988) the sexual license and abuse of black women by the white males in authority, it stands as a point of credit to those ancestors who set about the reconstruction of a sense of family and of family values based on old values of consanguinity and matrifocality. Barry Higman (1975) has already dispelled the stereotype that there were no stable families during slavery. In place of a unilineal descent system they established a bilineal one based on the sacredness of blood. Blood relationships are sacred and indivisible. As I mentioned in the essay 'Fatherhood in the African–Caribbean Landscape' (chapter 6) siblings are siblings: there are no half-brothers or half-sisters. Such kinship relationships are expressed by the locutions 'brother by father side,' or 'sister by mother side.' The 'former stepmother' of the car thief on the UTech campus described her 'former stepson' not as 'my former stepson,' but as 'my daughter breda.' His relationship to her came through the blood relationship of her daughter rather than through the affinal relationship of her former spouse.

Another principle is the sacredness of motherhood. Regardless of the presence and exertion of a father, it is the mother around whom the family pivots. She is the centre of affective relations. A third value is the love of children for their own sake and not because of the status of the parents. And a fourth principle is the honouring of ancestors, whom they would bury either inside or in close proximity to the houses themselves.

Out of all this, therefore, has come a system of conjugal bonding that begins in the consensual relationship of a couple, that matures in co-residence and becomes unbroken in a union recognized by church and state. (This is discussed in detail in Chapter 10). The progression from the instability of personal choices and will is towards greater and greater stability. This pattern has undergone little change over time, but what has no doubt undergone fluctuation is the incidence of the types of unions, since the movement from one stage to the next is determined not only by social maturity but by economic independence. In terms of the family, the wider network of blood relations extending beyond a nuclear unit is the understood concept.

Before attempting to trace the threads of family values into our agonizing present, I wish to emphasize the external or community-building dimension of family formation. The community I am referring to is a group of families living in face-to-face relationships. Despite the overall control of the slave owners and overseers, the enslaved Africans managed to form and sustain a sense of community that even extended beyond the confines of the slave quarters. Thistlewood had a slave called Abba, who had a son, Johnny. Johnny lived for six years before he died. Thistlewood entered in his diary on Sunday, July 7, 1771 that he gave Abba permission

> To throw water (as they called it) for her boy Johnie who died some months ago; and although I gave them strict charge to make no noise, yet they transgressed, by beating the Coombie loud, singing high, etc. Many Negroes there from all over the country (Hall 1989, 185–6).

Anyone who has been to a nine-night would see its antecedents in this very lean diary entry typical of Thistlewood. It challenges our notion of slavery as a state of being under the total control of the owner. People came 'from all over the country': that is, from all over the Westmoreland countryside. And we can imagine who they were, too: Johnny's father, perhaps, and his friends, shipmates and close co-workers; a similar group on Abba's side; people from Abba's country in Africa; people who knew her, like her former co-workers, since transferred or sold; and people who heard about the water-throwing and wanted the excitement. And all these, beside the members of her small community.

In an earlier diary entry, Saturday, February 25, 1769, Thistlewood wrote: 'A play this evening, at Egypt, made by Daniel, to throw water for his Boy, Fortune, killed by Paradise mill wheel last crop' (Hall 1989, 216). Egypt was a neighbouring estate, for which Thistlewood had been bookkeeper, and from which some of his own slaves had come. That it found its way into his diary signalled either that he was at Egypt when Fortune's water-throwing took place and had attended, or had given some of his slaves permission to attend, or both. The six months of mourning have had variations, for example the forty-day mourning that is still practised today, or the one-year tombing, but the underlying principle is the same: the processual conferral of ancestor status on the dead. The ritual of feasting, drumming and singing as the final act of mourning remains to this day the most important of our lifecycle rituals, to which people do come from all over in a display of community solidarity. Interestingly, Thistlewood also called it a 'play,' in an attempt at capturing, possibly, the drama of the event, or the joviality, the singing and storytelling, all which would have seemed to him recreational.

It takes a village to grow a child, because meaning is socially constructed. The way Geertz (1973) put it is, 'culture is public because meaning is.' There are no privately constructed meanings that are of any significance in our social relations. To be meaningful they must be understood and shared. And so it is impossible for the socialization of children to be effective without the community. Abba's Johnny, had he lived, would have been socialized by his mother, the field hands, the women, the men and other children comprising this community. He would have heard the Anansi stories from the older women in the cropover time, listened and learned from the gossip of estate life, observed and internalized the system of privilege accorded to those members of the community with a lighter complexion, especially if they worked in the Great House. He might have even been punished for failure to give deference to elders and those in authority, including Thistlewood himself, but would have, if he was a smart child, internalized and practised the art of deception on that lecher of a penkeeper, who in one year had sex with 30 of the women in his power, including once on a ladder! Who knows? Johnny's resistance might have in his mature years taken other forms, confrontational in nature, as in the case of Congo Sam, a runaway whom Thistlewood tried to recapture but who was emboldened by their being alone to try killing him. According to Thistlewood,

> 5 Negro men and 3 women, strangers, went over the bridge and would by no means assist me, neither for threats nor promises; one saying he was sick, the others that they were in a hurry. After we had stood in this manner maybe 8 or 10 minutes, London came and assisted me; tied his hands behind him with my handkerchief; but whilst I was seeking my stick in the morass, which I quitted when I seized hold of the blade of the bill, London, having a load of provisions on his head, Sam got away into the bushes, where he by some means had his hands loosed, and lost my handkerchief. Presently London called out that Sam had seized his machete and would kill him (Hall 1989, 55).

With the help of two gentlemen who rode by and London he subdued Sam. Thistlewood had him jailed and charged for attempted murder, but when the trial came up London refused to testify, so he concluded 'that London had no good intent when in the bush with Sam, if he had not heard company coming with me' (Hall 1989, 55). So, we can rewind and go back to the bush to reconstruct what probably transpired. While Thistlewood is looking for his pimento stick, London looses the knot, gives Sam his machete and signals to him to run while he, London, screams for murder — a not so clever case of Anansi playing fool fi ketch wise.

And so there is an aspect of value-formation in community life under slavery that bears relevance to our current realities. I refer to the cultivation of values that clash with those of the hegemonic order — the question again of whose truth. The Reverend Hope Masterton Waddell (147) reported the following on the eve of Emancipation:

> Some ill-disposed, disorderly people…had begun early, even a week too soon, to pervert their freedom to unworthy purposes. I had been from home for a few days, and on my return late was astonished to hear the noise of rioting and revelling in the Cornwall negro houses, which neither Mrs Waddell, nor the elders of the church, nor the constable of the estate, had been able to prevent. L— , a wild fellow, had erected a booth, proclaimed a ball, and gathered a company of loose and disorderly people from all quarters, whose singing, and drumming, and dancing, disturbed the neighbourhood. I hastened to the spot, but found all suddenly enveloped in darkness and silence. A fire-stick waved discovered some persons hiding, but none that I knew, except L — himself. He waited not to hear me, but furiously threatened, that if I should come that way again to spoil his meeting, I should not leave the negro town in whole skin. I had no right, he said to come into his yard; for he might do what he liked in his own place, and have what company he pleased. Because he had a black face and I a white one, made me do so. But when the first of August arrived, he would see who would meddle with him or his dance. He would be as good as me then, and would split my skull if I came into his yard that way again.
>
> The man was so furious he would listen to nothing I said, and the people having skulked off, I returned to my house. Immediately the place was lighted up again, and the ball resumed; and the revelry continued till morning.

Mr Waddell called the celebration a 'ball,' there being no word in his thesaurus to describe it otherwise; we would call it a dance, or a session. The whole community was out in full force, from all quarters, he told us: drumming, singing, dancing. Note the value placed on the yard, a private space in the public domain of 'a negro town.' Mr L's threat of the missionary not leaving the negro town in whole skin implied action by the community, whose values and rituals of celebration clashed with those of the Reverend Mr Waddell and the people under his sway. Mr Waddell's choice of words to describe them and their actions gives away his own value system: disorderly, loose, pervert, unworthy, rioting, revelling.

If therefore there is a breakdown in our value system and the socialization into it, we need to examine not only the family but the community also. Indeed, in the last stages of development of the child passing to adulthood the community exerts socializing pressure that is as great if not greater than that exercised by the family, even though the family has a stronger moral authority. The rural family and rural community for all their weaknesses of early conjugal instability, single parenthood, and poverty, provided the backbone and character on which the country was to develop. Right up into the 1960s this was the kind of city that Kingston grew into with an outburst of cultural creativity — the drumming, singing, dancing — that forced itself on the rest of the society and on the rest of the world, compelling the Messrs. Waddells to adopt it in their search for liturgical relevance and meaning. They bear the stamp of their rural origins, not so much from the plantation as from the hillsides of free, independent and self-motivated Mr Ls, the fathers of Paul Bogle, and grandfathers of Marcus Garvey, who, while fully aware of the status differences in race and colour, are nonetheless confident in their own blackness.

Themselves brought up on rituals of respect, they socialize their young in deference to age and authority, provided those who deserve deference also reciprocate respect. Every man and woman deserves respect, no matter how poor or downtrodden. The value placed on the cultivation of relationships demands reciprocity, hence the soliciting and giving of gifts, the establishment of fictive kinship, and

— a common one today — the announcement of one's birthday. *One han' kyaan clap* (you can't clap with one hand). The children learn that *finger rotten kyaan cut i' off* (you can't cut off a rotten finger), even though Mr Waddell tells them that *if thine hand offend thee cut it off*, and carrying this as a moral imperative into adult life find it impossible to turn their backs on sons who have gone astray. The value of the blood principle is so strong that *if yu kyãã kech Kwaaku yu kech im shut* (if you cannot catch Kwaaku his shirt will do), so that no member of a family is immune to the malice of an aggrieved, or safe from retribution.

At the same time Mr L, his wife and his community would have inspired in the young a spirit of industry aimed at moving up in society. *Ef yu waan good, yu nose hafi run* (no success without sacrifice). But at the same time you must have pride in yourself and your family, exercising a level of stoicism indicative of a will to rise above your circumstances, and so, *a no everyting good fi eat good fi talk* (private deprivation should be borne in private). As for wisdom, remember that *one time fool a fool, but two time fool a damn fool*. Therefore *if alligator come from river bottom an say it hot dung de, believe im* (he who feels it knows it). You learn the value of sharing and not to hoard, by the threat of ridicule. To be called *mean and selfish* is to reveal character flaws that according to the cosmological principles will surely be repaid. The mean and selfish will be repaid in his own currency. For, *di higher monkey climb the more im expose* (success is the source of its own downfall). One should always remember where one is coming from and thereby retain a basic humility that curbs ambition and hubris. And when we fail to take heed, the lesson accompanying the flogging is that *it is wrong for parents to spare the rod and spoil the child*, which must come from somewhere in the Bible, for it has the authority of Maasa Gad. In any case, we know for we have heard it often enough that *wha gaan bad a maanin kyaan go good a evenin* (if the head of the stream is dirty, the stream will be dirty).

Even when as children you play you learn. Boys, especially, by sneaking out to join their friends down by the river, learn the art of risk taking and escaping dangers, preparation for life. In the village square if they are lucky to be unobserved they might hear tell of the exploits of great men who by their courageous exploits and uncompromising acts in the face of injustices win the adulation of the people. And at night under granny's spinning of the Anansi stories they learn not to speak ill of the deformities and weaknesses of others, to be obedient and trustful of parents, how to turn weaknesses into strengths.

Now these are values that children grew up with, many of which are lost to the present generations, especially in the cities. Before I give an explanation for the loss, there is an important dimension that must be addressed. I have spoken about cultural patterns at the level of communities, but have not said anything about the hegemonic order. Communities are not insulated from the influences of those who exercise power or in whose name power is exercised. They maintain their rule not only by the force of arms, should it come to that — and it has many times in our history — but by ideas. As Marx would say, the ruling ideas are the ideas of the ruling class. How then has the social order been maintained if, as I have premised in this essay, the value system of the African-Jamaican majority derives from their culture-building impetus and not from the Great House?

The answer is threefold. In the first place, there are values that are universal to any community. Every community has an imperative for forms of respect between people of different rank, if not gender. And most societies give motherhood special value because of its creative power. Second, many of the hegemonic values and social forms of behaviour have been incorporated into the culture-building, a case in point being the incorporation of marriage as the end-point in the life cycle of the domestic group. The result is not assimilation into the value system of the ruling classes but an imposition of their own values on the incorporated form. Whereas in ruling circles marriage is the only recognized form of the conjugal bond and the start of a family, among the African-Jamaicans its value lies in the bestowing of social status and, as I have said before, the affirmation of stability.

Another example lies in the incorporation of some of the deities, rituals and ritual paraphernalia of the hegemon. The result is Christianity, indeed, but a Christianity infused with a somewhat different value system, as Kamau Brathwaite (1971) showed in *Creole Society* and his student Bob Stewart (1992) in *Religion and Post Emancipation Jamaica*. In a real way, therefore, both cultures touch by clashing.

But third, as I argue in 'Those Two Jamaicas' (chapter 12), the African-Jamaicans practise a code switching at the level not merely of language but of culture. Dual membership in Revival and established denominations, a practice that continued until the Jamaicanization of Pentecostalism, is one example. Another is the dual model of land tenure: the legal and customary. The legal tenure is based on the English view of the possibility of individual ownership and disposition of land at will, whereas the customary tenure, family land, is based on an African view of the corporate ownership of and identity with land and hence the impossibility of disposing of it. On the one hand the people have no problem buying and selling land, on the other hand they have no problem bequeathing land as family land. They switch as the need arises.

Thus, they develop and retain a distinct way of life while in effect subverting the hegemonic order by appearing to share in the same value system. The result is a social order that appears stable, while they gradually assert their own value system. There are in a real sense two Jamaicas, and the challenge facing the country is how to bring the main instruments of social control, namely the laws and the legal and justice system, into consonance with the culture of the ruled.

But this does not explain the fairly recent cheapening of life, the erosion of kindness and compassion, the rise of aggressive attitudes and behaviours, the loss of respect for the aged and for women. I locate the problems in the stresses and strains in the family and the breakdown of community. It is difficult to treat them separately, since, as I have been arguing, they are designed to accomplish together the socializing function. Nonetheless, I would advance the following points, some of which I admit do require substantiating.

First, the family has been declining as an effective unit, for the simple reason that for an increasingly larger number of people the economy has shrunk, while for a few it has grown. How ironic that the word *economy* is derived from the Greek which means *the running of the household*. The gap between the topmost and the bottommost has widened considerably. While this has disastrous social consequences, I focus on the strain that is imposed on the latter.

Second, the first to feel the strain is the male. This is because the male is still culturally cast in the role of provider, even though the shrinking circumstances require both male and female to work. When men cannot provide through legitimate means, they provide through illegitimate; when they choose not to pursue illegitimate routes, they lose their legitimacy in the family. The result is a female single parent bereft of financial support for children and herself, forced to neglect the children, for whose care she is still held culturally responsible, in order to make a living. If her children are male the ability to contend with the negatively socializing influences of the wider community is severely compromised.

Third, the rise of social pathologies in inner-city areas is directly linked to the difficulty in reproducing and maintaining masculinity in the normal run of things, the main criterion of which is the ability to locate and dispose of resources. On this hinge the expression of male sexuality, relations with spouse and children, social standing and reputation.

Fourth, traditional communities have been eroded by migration and neglect. Impoverishment is greater in rural than in urban Jamaica. Small farmer agriculture has declined, except for a few areas, as commodities have declined. Migration deprives the rural communities of leadership.

Fifth, urban communities, particularly inner-city, are little better off. They too are affected by the flight of intellectual capital, the deprivation of services, and by politicization, which has created monolithic dependency, giving way to armed terror. They remain communities only in the sense of being dense settlements of people living in face-to-face relationships, but lacking in the processes of civility and a social order based on morality rather than fear.

If we are to arrest the decline and cure the social pathology in addition to macroeconomic changes in favour of greater equity, we have to rebuild the family and the community. Rebuilding the family in my estimation begins with restoring the place of the male, but without undermining the gains made by women, which is to say without resorting to the patriarchy of yesteryear. To doubt that we can is to underestimate the progress men themselves have been making in more enlightened behaviour. The point is not to make the error of the past three decades by tackling the problems of women as women, leaving men completely out of the picture, and in tackling the problems of children as children, shutting out completely their male parents. Rather the plea is for a holistic approach, hence the family.

But the community issues have to be addressed too. There is no going back to the past, not with urbanization so widespread. I have no blueprint, but when I see how people are settled in housing estates like Greater Portmore it tells me that while we know how to build houses, we have yet to learn how to facilitate the creation of communities.

Finally, we do not build as if from scratch. There are values even in the worst of us that provide platforms for further building. Within young male pathogens in the very inner city communities I speak of, the value of respect remains a powerful sentiment — too powerful at times, as we well know when lethal conflicts are played out over alleged losses of respect. And close to that is the value of a person as *smadi* (somebody). If they haven't lost their humanity there is hope.

CHAPTER NINE

Cosmological Reproduction: Space and Identity

This is Grenada Corner, a captured space at the head of Cornbread Lane. Pete lives there. It began two and a half years ago when with nothing else to do he set up a little stall outside his gate, selling oranges to early morning passersby rushing out without breakfast, cheese tricks to the children, cigarettes and stout to those wishing to pause for a drink and a chat on the way home from work.

His little stall grew into a bigger one, and now, by an aperture in the fence, into a little shop from out of his yard, a space so small that it allows him only to step sideways but not back, but which he has stocked with bread, sugar, ketchup, bully beef, noodles, box drinks — fast selling commodities you would rather buy here than at the Chinese shop farther away on the main. Hot beer and Guinness are still available, but if you want them cold, it takes half a minute to get them from the fridge in the house. So over the last two to three years, a twenty-six year old young man has grown from being a beggar and race horse betting-shop hustler to sidewalk vendor to shopkeeper. Everyday developments in entrepreneurship like this one are replicated in hundreds of communities across the city of Kingston and the Jamaican countryside. Pete's is not a unique experience. But until his and similar others are carefully documented ethnographically and analysed within their wider social and economic contexts, we will continue to fail in all our predictions of doom, because we would have failed to understand the people's inventiveness and the sources of power underlying it.

But that is not what I wish to deal with at this time. With Pete's growth as an entrepreneur has come an increased identity with the captured space now watched over by this little shop. The Grenada Corner is after all a corner. Over the less than three years of this development it has become the space of other young men as well, the two Mikeys, General, Georgie, the visualization in space of the historical growth of male bonding over the time, the spatial visualization of male group identity.

We are talking here of a stretch of lane no more than 20 metres, but a 20 metres that are the result of an expansion. It did not originate in driving stakes into the ground. Rather it is the result of a complex, non-threatening relationship between a group of young males and the wider community of citizens, and of concepts about rights, property, and most importantly, the self.

The Grenada Corner envelopes no fewer than six yards on both sides of the lane, all of them fenced in with zinc to demarcate private space from the public space, yard from lane. People's fences and gateways are part of this demarcation. To break down one's fence is to violate or threaten one's privacy. Once during a recent event on the corner when some participants got carried away with the music and began pounding on the fences in salute, one of the 'Grenadians' cautioned, '*No biit dong de piipl-dem fens*' (Don't beat against the people's fence)! If the fence functions like a liminal threshold between the sacred and the profane, the gateway itself is like an extension of the private outwards. Every morning before sun up, from one end of the lane to the next, the gateways and their surroundings are sprinkled with water and swept of rubbish and dog *duudu* (excrement). For as the quality and condition of a gateway are, so also the quality and condition of those who daily pass through it. A nasty gate betokens a nasty people inside. Pride in one's gateway betokens pride in oneself. To deface or desecrate the gateway is to disregard or to show contempt for all those who enter through it.

I refer to Grenada Corner as captured space, though 'enveloped' might have been a more fitting description. The word 'capture' applied to land is an ethno-scientific term denoting the assertion of possessive or use right over space not your own. The legal term is squatting. Pete did not capture the head of the lane in this sense. What he and his peers have done is to extend themselves on to this space. It began first with the initial success of his streetside stall, a two-shelf wooden structure he brings out in the morning and takes in at night. Like any sidewalk vendor, or higgler in the market, the space where one sets about to try one's luck must be made clean, and cleansed. Clean space is not necessarily cleansed space. I do not know if Pete used lime and salt, as higglers do, to rid the space of bad luck or evil, but as an aspiring entrepreneur offering a service, and knowing that nobody bought from a vendor who kept his surrounding space 'dirty', he ritually sprinkled and swept the little space in the corner of the lane where he positioned the stall. Sometimes in the evenings, music from a tape deck provided a little entertainment for the few friends who stopped by. This was the setting one evening when a group gathered watching others play dominoes. We have to imagine the boasting and joshing and slamming that accompany this basically male activity. Domino is a game of strategy in a game of chance. It is a highly mental activity, requiring a good memory, deductive powers and some intuition, but one would not know it by the cussing and swearing that accompany it. Somewhere during that game on that evening, somebody said 'This is Grenada!' and the name stuck. I have not been able to find out why Grenada, some no longer aware of the fateful events of 1983. The name could have been propelled into consciousness not necessarily as a site of revolution and counter-revolution but perhaps as a small space where big things happen. No member of the corner could say how they came by the name. But no matter, that was their first act of identity — a name. Someone painted 'Grenada Corner' on a piece of plywood and nailed it on the light post.

Then one day, another day, Georgie got the inspiration to paint up their corner 'to make it look nice.' They asked no permission but painted the slate-coloured zinc fences white, and the curb stones and tyres yellow and blue. Then they made it into a garden, planting sunflowers, periwinkle, ten o'clock, croton, leaf of life and other green shrubs and flowers on every available inch of bare earth and in truck tyres. On both sides of the lane, the artists among them, the two Mikeys, made very interesting depictions I shall describe presently. And someone added a bench to the couple of logs that provided seating. When the sunflowers bloom and the young men 'hold their corner,' some rolling and smoking a spliff of the herbs, others playing or watching a game of the ever popular ludo, the atmosphere is that of a small recreational park.

The murals on Grenada Corner have several themes. The first theme comprises comic figures. Interestingly they were the first paintings, a large imposing picture of the green monster, the Hulk, and on the opposing fence a small picture of Fred Flintstones and one of Mickey Mouse. I believe Mikey's intention at the time was simply to make the place pretty. Though his was one of the gates on the corner, no one had known of his talent for drawing. It was a group discovery. Then there are the paintings of local heroes and personalities: Marley, his guitar strung across his shoulder, and across from him Wayne Wonder and Buju Banton. A painting of Pete himself also forms part of this type. In the mural Pete is given a title of respect, 'Mr. Mention.' Indeed the name of the shop is 'Mr. Mention Snack Shop.' Behind him in the background is a sleek Mercedes Benz sports car, because, reminisced the Mikey who drew it, 'it fit him.' The Benz is a symbol of acquired status and respect. These are big men, young fathers, articulating in representational art their respect for one of their peers. Older men who have acquired similar status and are deserving of respect are addressed as 'Faada.' This could be the revived, urban version of Taata, 'Granfaada', or an adoption of 'Godfather,' as in the influential American movie, or both, the one reinforcing the other.

At the eastern end of this captured space is a mural of Jesus, and written across the top of it, lest there should be any mistake, 'The Black Christ.' The picture is conventional: an enrobed Jesus, his arms outstretched in welcome. It was copied by one of the Mikeys from a tract left by a Jehovah's Witness passing by, 'since,' says he, 'we no have no Krais pan di kaana (we have no representation of Christ on our corner).' This is Grenada Corner's only expression of a religious theme. They did offer to paint other religious figures further down the lane if the church bought the paint, but the offer was not taken.

Nationalism is a fourth theme. Next to Christ is a painting of two black youths, with the words 'Black Power' blazoned across the chest of one of them. There are also two or three paintings titled 'Rudey,' young boys, their heads shaven around the sides but crowned with budding locks. The Rude boy was a mid-1960s rebel against society, its laws and conventions. (See Garth White, 1967). The phenomenon apparently lives on in the young men, most of whom were unborn when it traumatized society. On the other side of the lane is a portrait of Malcolm X, in his post-Mecca phase when he had grown a beard, and beneath him a small red-gold-green sketch of Africa made to look like the profile of a face, and a Rasta lion. Two weeks ago Mikey painted the Lion King in the space between the Black Christ and the Black power figures. In my interpretation this Lion falls more in the nationalist than the comic theme. Not only was the setting of the movie Africa, but the Lion King is a Rastafari theme.

But the most intriguing mural of all is one at the head of the lane on the rear wall of a building that faces the main street. It depicts Africa, with all the nations, their boundaries and names. To the left of Africa is a sketch of Jamaica. An arched bridge, reminiscent of the arched bridge on the Causeway linking Portmore with the city of Kingston, links Jamaica with Africa. There is no attempt to represent scale, for Jamaica is nearly as large as the continent. Rather, it is the symbolic identity of the two that is affirmed, and the geographic (and mental) position of Jamaica in the re-created world of young, Black Jamaican males. By extension Jamaica is a part of Africa, separated from the mainland only by the accident of water, in the same way Portmore is a part of Kingston but separated from it by the accident of a narrow strip of water. And in case one misses the symbolic representation, they imposed above it the sign: BRIDGE THE GAP TO AFRICA. As the Causeway bridge to Portmore creates the Kingston Metropolitan Area, so the imagined bridge between island and continent creates Greater Africa. This is essentially the same point made by scholars who write of the 'African Diaspora.'

Finally, one of the latest murals is that of a woman, a brown, tall–hair beauty, dressed in dance hall nudity, looking back across her shoulder at us. Her place among the murals is close to Mr. Mention's gate and across from the portrait of Buju Banton, the man who sang 'I love mi brownin.' In this inner world depicted by the murals, male sexual identity is projected on to a brown female. It is quite remarkable how subtle the distinction between brown and black is among Jamaicans, and how quickly this is recognized. The 'brownin' concept spans shades of colour from off-black to nearly red, though I suspect, judging from the tincture of the mural a light brown is preferred. The 'brownin' in the mural is no one in particular. She therefore represents an idealization of male desire.

Themes of religion, nationalism, recreation, the influence of foreign, North American culture, colour and masculinity, status, Rastafari and local culture — all these are expressions of an internal sense of selfhood. But it is their projection on to that garden space that gives them their particular identity. Who says that all that matters is who you are inside? What you are outside for others to see is just as vital a constituent part of self, for the act of creating that identity is a social act which seeks the notice if not the approval of others.

So far I have not mentioned once the word cosmology. Yet, the depiction of a people's cosmos is fundamentally a depiction of their conception of space and time, and the place of humankind in, and humankind's relations with, these two concepts. Usually a treatise on cosmology discusses first the mythological origins of the world, in the broad sense of earth, sun, moon, the planetary bodies and the forces of nature, and the merging of that world with the ethnic group.

In truth if we wanted to uncover a Caribbean cosmology, or the cosmology of the leading ethnic group in the Caribbean as a whole, namely the peoples of African descent, we could have begun with the African-Caribbean religions.

Allow me to explain how this can be done and to show some of the fruits of this pursuit. We could begin with a survey of the African religions in the Caribbean: Cuban Santeria, Haitian Vodun, Jamaican Revival and Kumina, Grenadian Big Drum, Trinidadian Orisha. Without any attempt to impose an ordered cosmological system, I think we would find first of all that the conception of the world bears the following features:

1. a high God, the creator and upholder of the universe and the ultimate source of all power; when and how the world was created is not as important an issue as the fact that it reflects the supreme power of God, Massa Gadu to the Ndyukas of Suriname, Grand Dieu to the Haitians, Jah or the Father, to the Jamaicans. This omission, however, is by no means insignificant. Myths of origin of the world are at the same time myths of origin of the tribe, of the nation. And given the known origins of the African-Caribbean peoples, there is no particular significance trying to mythologize about it. What is significant is the tradition of the people in affirming their origin, as with the Grenada corner, and in mythologizing about our destiny, as with the seven miles of Black Starliners to take us home.[21]

   It would not be accurate to describe God as a *Deus otiosus*, but we should note that his creative person is not the object of liturgical veneration. I cannot now fully develop why this is so, except to say that the religious orientation of the people requires harnessing of spiritual forces in an instrumentalist way. In a sense, these spiritual forces are neutral, neither essentially good nor essentially evil, but just powers to be deployed by humankind.

2. a population of spirits, representing various spiritual forces to be harnessed, appeased, propitiated and appropriated. Appropriated, because a fundamental feature of these religions is the possession by deities and familiars. Possession is by far the height of religious experiences.
3. a conception of the cosmos as a single entity, peopled by the visible and the invisible. Both visible and invisible may sometimes interpenetrate. Not only may certain forces and animate and inanimate objects of nature be the expressions of spiritual forces, but certain human beings, as part of the visible world, may also become part of the invisible by their acquisition of its power.
4. the mystic identity of the male principle with the powerful sun and the mystic identity of the female principle with the moon. I am certain of this cosmological system of symbols among the Jamaicans, and opine that it is probably so throughout the rest of the African-Caribbean as well. The significance of this symbolic representation is the public vs. private-domestic definition of male vs. female. Streets and roads are ruled by men, yards and homes by females.

These four points do not constitute all that could be said about the cosmology of the African- Caribbean. I have not discussed their ideas of time, of island or of water. Instead my main burden has been an essay into the daily reproduction of a cosmos. A cosmology is of little value other than to satisfy antiquarian inquisitiveness, unless we can show its relevance to daily living.

In targeting the Grenada Corner I do not wish to imply that this little world is a microcosmic replica of the wider world, such that by studying it we study the whole. I also do not believe that any one person embodies the sum total of a people's beliefs. But I do believe that by reflecting on their symbolic behaviour one can uncover order and coherence in what they do.

In this little bit of space, a street-park, a group of men have reinvented an idea much older than they, the very cosmic idea that group identity must find self expression in space and time. This idea was one that the people fought for, and that remains very much alive but in conflict with ruling conceptions about land and people's relationship to it. I refer to the institution of family land.

Family land is land bequeathed by an ancestor to all his or her future generations. It establishes the right of all those related by blood to use the fruits of the land, to live and be buried on it. Family land is perhaps the only institution throughout the Caribbean that provides a corporate identity to a lineage. This is one reason why it cannot (meaning it should not) be sold. Among the most perceptive scholarship on family land is that of Jean Besson, whose work in the Trelawny villages is well known. Besson (1979), posing the institution of family land as a peasant counter to the plantation culture, offers an answer to what she calls a paradox. The principle of inheritance by family land in theory assumes the availability of land in limitless quantity, as limitless as the number of an ancestor's progeny. But in actual fact, land is limited, not just by the size of the freehold tenure, but by the miniscule size of all the islands, from the Bahamas to Trinidad and Tobago. The only explanation to this paradox of plenty in the midst of scarcity, she proposes, is the symbolic nature of family land. Family land is a symbol of lineage identity. It binds its living inheritors to all the ancestors that have gone before and to all those yet unborn. The link with the ancestors is given expression in the family plot, the burial ground situated in the vicinity of the dwelling house. As the ancestors watch over the living, so do the living respect the ancestors. Burial is never complete until a grave is marked by a permanent structure. The value of family land, therefore, lies not so much in its use, as in its symbolic power.

To return to Grenada Corner, the projection of a group identity on to carefully cultivated space is in my view a version of the same impulse giving rise to family land. One difference lies in the primordial tie of blood which identifies those who inherit family land, as against the ties of male bonding which identify the members of a corner. But, from what I have been able to observe, ties between 'Mr. Mention' and the members of the corner are as emotive and productive as those between blood. For example, deep feelings of trust prevail between Pete and Mikey, and loyalty between Pete and Georgie. Another difference lies in the ownership of family land and its transmission by customary right. The male group does not own the corner, nor does it transmit its identity. Its identity perdures for as long as the bonds hold. These differences aside, Corner space like family land is the creative use of space by a people who, owning little or owning nothing, reproduce their own understanding of the world and their relations with it.

PART IV
Integration and Control

CHAPTER TEN

Law and the African-Caribbean Family

The Public Defender in Jamaica, Mr Howard Hamilton, in his first public statement in March 2000, declared that among the priorities of his tenure was the legitimization of the Rastafari as a religion. Even though Rastafari's beginnings were rife with clashes with the police and prison sentences, it has grown into a popular and influential religious movement, not least because of its unfashionable assertion of a Black identity and defence of Africa. So, what is one to make of the fact that the Rastafari are still not legally recognized as a religion in a 95 per cent Black country 40 years after independence from colonialism, when they are so recognized in the United Kingdom and in some parts of the United States? What of the fact that the most internationally celebrated Jamaican was a man who not only drew his inspiration from belief in the divinity of Rastafari, but also was one of the principal apostles responsible for its global spread? How does one treat the fact that the Rastafari were denied incorporation by Parliament in 1988, and the Church of Latter Day Saints, which until recently explicitly preached Black inferiority, was approved? [22]

While some cite Rastafari use of ganja as one reason the state should not officially recognize them, and some critics of the Public Defender think that there are weightier issues in need of his attention, the problem faced by the Rastafari is not one peculiar to that group. It is but one, albeit recent and topical, manifestation of a more general and deeper problem of democracy. The problem is that the laws and law-making machinery of the country do not recognize the people at their deepest and innermost level, as a people, and to that extent fall short of serving them. There is, in certain fundamental respects, a lack of congruence between the cultural practices of the people on whom Jamaican postcolonial identity and nationalism rest and the laws of the country. An examination of the family and the law shows that despite recent amendments, the law, lawmakers and jurists betray gross indifference to and lack of understanding of the relationship between law and society. The problem, I believe, is Caribbean-wide.

To say that the laws and law-making machinery do not recognize the people at their 'deepest and innermost level,' means that the laws and law-making machinery give no regard to those they were set up to govern, *at the level of their worldview.* As I said earlier in this volume, worldview comprises a cosmology, that is a philosophical understanding of the origins, order and significance of the world, and the place of humankind within it. It comprises also an understanding of what is socially good and bad, an ethics; and an understanding of the beautiful, an aesthetic. A people's worldview shapes their day-to-day living, the choices they make, the rituals they observe, and significance they attach to relationships and events.

Where the law lacks congruence with worldview, and therefore with social and cultural practice, social integration is impossible to achieve, and order is maintained mainly by force of arms.

In one important sense the Law is force: ruling force. It imposes order and behaviour to suit those who make the Law. Justice and Equity are of little moment here. As long as it serves the interests of those who rule, it is the Law. And I suppose one should not be surprised that the Law in these islands of ours was quintessentially the ruling force of law of slave owners, during the period of slavery, and of planters and Whites in the period since, backed by the ruling force of arms. But, in the period of Independence, whose law is the Law? Who rules? Whose interests does the Law serve?

The Law, in another important sense, is a codification of custom. Here, the Law is not so much an imposition as it is a definition of and a sanction against deviance. Social order is maintained not only by force of arms but as well by the social will of those who are governed. What this means is that laws that run counter to the social will in the final analysis cannot be enforced, unless through the daily use of arms. This has been the fate of ganja (cannabis) legislation in Jamaica, as already discussed in chapter 4. The eminent jurist, the late Aubrey Fraser (1975), made the point nearly 30 years ago that the Jamaican laws against ganja were unenforceable, because by then it had become clear that the social and cultural practices and beliefs surrounding this substance were culturally entrenched. The anti-ganja laws are yet to be repealed. The Jamaican laws governing family and marriage are of a similar order. They are based on a worldview different from the worldview of those the laws were instituted to govern. In this chapter I discuss the African-Caribbean family.

The family is a basic institution to every known human society. Through it children are brought into the world and socialized. How the family is formed and organized to accomplish this function, the definition and meaning society gives to it, and the roles and functions of its members, vary from society to society. They are all matters of cultural differences.

Among the Indians, demographically the second most significant cultural group in the Caribbean as a whole, the formation of a new family is not entirely, if at all, a private matter between a couple, but a social one as well, between existing families. Thus, prior to the marriage, there is an exchange of gifts between the families. Principles of caste are nowadays rarely observed, but when they were, marrying outside of one's caste was taboo. The marriage ceremony, presided over by the Pandit, takes place at the home of the bride. Thereafter, the couple goes to live in the home of the groom's father, where they and their children come under his authority. In time, a couple will go off to live by themselves, but will retain some form of recognition of the principle of jointness, for example by working together with the rest of the extended family in the rice paddy, as commonly happens in Guyana, or returning to the family home on occasion to worship together. Thus, the Indian family is an extended one, a collection of nuclear units, domiciled or bound together through the male line, under the authority of the oldest male. It comprises a man, his wife, all his sons, their wives and their children, and his unmarried daughters. When he dies, his authority passes to his eldest son, on whom falls the obligation of observing certain mortuary rites. Should a family be so unfortunate as not to have a son, a male relative is called upon to carry out this duty. The Indian family is patriarchal, male dominant and extended.

For a very long time, and up to very recent times, the peoples of African descent in the Caribbean were thought of as bereft of cultural traditions of family formation and meaning. Thanks to the work of many scholars, some of them Caribbean, it has become quite clear that they are not. And it is true that the very manner of European slavery destroyed the social foundations on which African family structures rest. In Africa, despite cultural variations among the many ethnic groups, the family, through the lineages, was the backbone of the polity. Village order rested on the organization of lineages. But it is a testimony to the inner strength and resilience of the Africans who came here that in the Caribbean they have reorganized themselves and elaborated a family structure that for all its weaknesses — and there are many — has been able to accomplish the main functions of providing a framework for conjugal bonding, for the nurturing and socialization of children, and the elaboration of a kinship structure. My decades of encounters with graduate and undergraduate students and a wider public have taught me that we social scientists should not assume that what has become for us accepted knowledge is known outside our narrow circles. And even where the African-Caribbean family structure is already known, it is rarely accepted as anything but a pathological condition, something to be ashamed of. Here then I re-engage with the family pattern life cycle.

Conjugal bonding

Any census or survey in Jamaica will show a multiplicity of union types. Some people are legally married, some live in a common-law marriage, some described as in a visiting union, and others as single.

A similar picture could be presented for Barbados, and indeed any country with an overwhelming majority of people of African descent. Viewing this synchronically, one who does not know might be inclined to look on the Caribbean as a kind of conjugal union supermarket, where people go and pick from the shelf the type of name-brand conjugal union they want. Only loose-living people would purchase common law, and irresponsible men buy the visiting brand. Christians, of course, select marriage.

This, in fact, is not far from what was earlier thought and depicted, even by social theorists, who saw the African-Caribbean people as fundamentally savage, incapable of the nobler values of civilization, except through the civilizing influence of the European's religion, education and rule of law. The multiplicity of union types was, they argued, a good example of the problem, and it even led the wife of one colonial governor in Jamaica in the 1940s to launch a mass movement to get people married.

It was not until the work of Raymond Smith (1956) among the Afro-Guyanese that an entirely new perspective began to make sense out of the apparent sexual anarchy and rank individualism. Influenced by his Cambridge teacher, Meyer Fortes, Smith applied Fortes's simple insight that family structures parallel the life cycles of the human beings within them. He found that Afro-Guyanese people entered into conjugal relationships of a visiting type early in their reproductive lives, progressed to co-residential relationships and, with greater economic stability, finally to legal marriage. Since this watershed work, virtually all scholars have found the same pattern throughout the rest of the African-Caribbean. Thanks to George Roberts, the category of visiting union was incorporated into the national censuses as a distinct form.

Visiting unions are typical of the young, although they exist in smaller frequencies among older age groups. Typically, also, the conjugal bond is established while they are still living in the homes of their parents. But it is a socially recognized form, as M.G. Smith (1965) noted. Among the folk, the term 'visiting' never gained currency, however. Nowadays in Jamaica the young people use the word 'boyfrien' and 'girlfrien,' but the meaning is the same — a relationship which includes sexual intimacy. The term visiting union may be used interchangeably with boyfriend-girlfriend relationship.

There comes a time, especially if a child is born to this union, when in the eyes of the couple or their families and the community, the young man's maturity is judged by his assumption of a co-residential household, separate and apart from that of his parents if possible, but sometimes in the domicile of his or her parents. A young man is not expected to remain for long in a visiting union. The progression is a mark of his seriousness. The typical pattern is to move to common-law union, but marriage is not unknown at this stage.

The progression is not always or even most times straight. There are zigzags. One boyfriend-girlfriend relationship may give way to another, and many common-law unions may break down, leaving the couples to establish others or return temporarily to the boyfriend-girlfriend type. For visiting unions are, almost by definition, transitory. They must lead somewhere.

This leads us to ask why. Why do people after going through courtship not enter straightaway into marriage? The answer is not at all complicated, but it requires us to descend into the subterranean recesses of the worldviews of the African-Caribbean peoples, where their attitudes to sexuality, reproduction and conjugal bonding may be understood.

Sexual initiation comes early in the Caribbean, among East Indians and Africans alike. But whereas among the former marriage provides the gateway to the typical activities of biological and social maturity, namely sexual intercourse and reproduction, among the latter it is the other way around: biological and social maturity, evidenced by sexual intercourse and reproduction, is earmarked as the gateway to marriage. Visiting unions are testing grounds on which a man and a woman will decide whether as a team they have the right combination of qualities of compatibility and outlook to bat through the entire innings of their lives. The visiting union is, in effect, a sort of trial marriage, made without any economic sanction, frail, because, formed at will, it can be broken at will, but allowing the couple the time and experience to know each other even at the deepest level of intimacy. It affords the young woman an independence from the almost inevitable subordination to male dominance, until greater certitude. George Roberts and Sonja Sinclair (1978) found that women in visiting unions guarded their independence closely.

The common-law union signals intentional commitment to a partner for life. Since it involves house and furniture, it is a step made with level-headedness, after the flush of passion. The business of managing a household is a serious business, entered into with one in whom one is reasonably confident. That a common-law union sometimes fails speaks to faulty judgment, not to the process. If it succeeds, and it often does, the couple will cement the relationship before the law, a transition that raises the couple and their children in social status and respectability. The common-law union too is a transitory type, but one in which people can get stuck, never being able to make that final grade, for any of a number of reasons: a man's inability to provide the independence of a house, the economic costs, or nagging uncertainty over one's spouse — will the ring change her? Are there weaknesses I still don't know?

Sometimes a man is pressured into getting married, often by his own children. It is possible to view marriage as a final act of concession to the hegemonic order, at which level both man and wife and their children gain in social respectability. But you could also view it as an African-Caribbean way of incorporating a Western cultural form into their cosmology but in doing so transforming its meaning. This latter perspective makes better sense to me, because the meaning of marriage arrived at in this way is different. You know it is different when the bridesmaid is the couple's daughter, the pageboy their grandson, and half the young maidens huddled together to catch the bride's bouquet after the feast have already had their 'maiden'[23] broken, for they already have their boyfriends and perhaps have borne their first child.

From the very life cycle process of the family one can interpret the social values underlying it. And here I invite you to journey into the world of values and meanings underlying the cultural practices of family formation, with which our laws are so discordant.

First is the weight given to sexuality itself, as an integral and necessary part of being adult. Sex is segmented from any form of union. This point is worth checking against the early age of first sex and of sexual activity, outside of any reference to a union. First sex varies between the genders — boys earlier than girls — and from island to island: 14 years old for boys, 16 years old for girls, in Jamaica; and two years later for boys and girls respectively, in Barbados. In this worldview, virginity is of no particular virtue, and might, indeed be regarded as a handicap. It is my opinion that the difficulty faced by the Roman Catholic Church in nurturing a truly native clergy, unlike other Christian religions, is due to the popular outlook on the place of sexual expression in the harmonious development of the human person. Countries like Dominica and St Lucia, with the overwhelming majority of their populations Catholic, still rely in great part on a foreign priesthood. It is not that sexual abstinence is understood as impossible, but rather that it is understood as unwholesome as a permanent state. The folk adage, 'Too much of one thing good for nothing,' applies as much to abstinence as to indulgences.

Second, it seems somewhat obvious that the people place greater value on stability than on form. Unions move from greater instability towards greater stability. Visiting unions do not last very long, common-law unions much longer, but when people get married — by a woman's mid-thirties — they do so for the rest of their lives. The aim is to be married, but not under any condition. Until a man is sure and economically stable, he will resist getting married.

Third, if sex is detached from unions, so too is childbearing. Children are valued in their own right. In the construction of womanhood and manhood, far greater weight is put on having a child than on getting married. Showing one's fertility is more highly rated an achievement than marrying. Children are therefore welcome additions, regardless of the type of union through which they come. In this way of thinking, it is not possible for a child to be illegitimate.

Men see in them the fulfilment of their masculinity, women the proof of their fecundity. Among the folk, parents who get justifiably angry at a too-early pregnancy will by the time of delivery receive the baby as a positive addition to the family and reincorporate the teenaged mother. But precisely because children are valued, men must attain certitude before accepting paternity. This is especially true in claims made as a result of casual sex, or in visiting relationships. They must be sure that the child is of their bloodline.

As we have already seen in chapter 6, this principle of consanguinity, or what the Jamaican people call blood, is central to the concept of family. Social scientists commonly use 'family' to mean 'household': those who live under the same roof. However, the word is also used in a wider context to mean all those related by the bloodline. To be family with someone means to be related, not by affinity, but by blood. Blood, used in this sense, is 'thicker than water,' a saying which means that the kinship bond overrides all others. It bears well to remember this principle when we come to consider the failure of the law with respect to inheritance. But for now I would like to point to three cultural practices that make sense only when we understand the principle of blood.

First is folk adoption, which is different from legal adoption. In the latter, elaborate measures are instituted to suppress the child's surname, if known, and give it the surname of its adopted parents. Here, personal identity rests on the name. But among the folk, the child is incorporated fully into a family but retains its surname. The child will grow up referring to its adopted parents as mother and father, but recognize at the same time the existence of a 'real' mother and father. The blood principle is fundamental to a child's sense of identity, which, if one follows the logic of this kind of thinking, begins to take shape in the cosmological encounter between a sperm and an egg in the womb of a woman. No change of name can erase or suppress this singular act of creation.

Second, as we have seen, the blood principle overrides all forms of conjugal bonds. While the concept of half sibling used by Europeans privileges the union status, the folk concept privileges the blood.

Third is the very basic drive on the part of the male to confirm his part in that life-creating act. In most societies, the strict enforcement of marriage as the gateway to the exclusive rights of sexual intercourse and the premium placed on female virginity, relieve the male and his kin of any doubt about his role. Among many of the African-Caribbean peoples, where, as I have said, sex precedes marriage, confirmation of paternity is required. As I have said before, in some islands confirmation is institutionalized through the practice of a visit by one of the near relatives of the putative father to search for points of resemblance. However, men do not have to resort to this or any other means, unless they have some reason to be in doubt — after all *jackets* and *ready-made* do exist — or unless they are just plain delinquent. But, statistically speaking, this is not often. Most men do in fact accept paternity.

What I am therefore arguing is that there are deeply entrenched values underlying the formation and structuring of families. You get to know what these values are by a kind of archaeology which digs beneath the surface looking for the explanations for patterns of behaviour that withstand generational and sometimes even economic changes; that defy the very strictures of religious orthodoxy preached daily and in extra measure on Sundays; but which are as common to the islands of the Caribbean as is the legacy of Africa and European slavery. This has to be the starting point.

THE LAW

More scholarly attention has been focused on the African-Caribbean family than on any other social institution, including religion, not only because it is a challenge to the hegemonic concept of family, but also because it has been seen as the source of so much that is wrong with society. With the family quite rightly seen as the foundation of society, we have been led blindly to believe that societies that have created a civilization that has influenced the world in *les belles lettres,* artistic sensibilities, political leadership, diplomacy, and sports, and without the benefit of imperial hegemony of our own, are somehow warped in their very foundations. We have been blindly led to believe that when Edith Clarke (1957) excised from George Lamming's masterpiece *In the Castle of My Skin* the title of her own masterpiece, *My Mother Who Fathered Me*, she was talking about the nature of Caribbean man and Caribbean woman. A reading of the book would have revealed that she was exposing the influence of unstable economic conditions on the ability of men to fulfil their roles as fathers. The readiness with which we berate and scourge ourselves is no doubt the very source of our unrelenting quest for excellence, but it is paradoxically at the same time the source of our own self-denial. Little attempt is made to *accept* ourselves on our own terms, because, perhaps, little attempt is made to *understand* ourselves on our own terms.

The singular exception is our writers. It was Lamming, again, who said that no region is quite as remarkable as ours for the reliance by its writers on the folk as their sources of inspiration. Whether it be Brathwaite or Brodber, Schwartz-Bart or Marshall, Lovelace or Condé, their international reputation and influence derive from that search for and embrace of a home, a Caribbean home, that crossroads of islands where *arrivants* find a burial spot.

Not so our jurists and lawyers. No search, no embrace. Home is still England. Because England's laws are our laws and her Privy Council our final court of appeal, her premises are therefore our premises. This, I suppose, could not have been otherwise, given the imperial connection, and it would be wishful thinking to call for a reinvention of our entire legal system. But it seems to me imperative that if the legal system, or parts of it, is incongruent with our cultural realities, we should be seeking to refashion our laws, not our culture. Social harmony and integration are unattainable otherwise. When the shoes do not fit you change the shoes, not the feet.

A case in point is the law as it affects marriage and the family. I wish to show that while there is fairly widespread acceptance of Jamaican social and cultural realities, and an attempt has been made to reform family laws, the effort remains short of what is required.

The place to start is with The Family Property (Rights of Spouses) Act, 1999. The Act seems to have been prompted by the celebrated case of Helga Stockert, the owner/manager of the Four Seasons Hotel in Kingston, who lived for some 20 years as the common-law spouse of Paul Geddes, the beer magnate of Red Stripe fame. They had no children between them. The relationship ended and Geddes turned Stockert out of the home. She claimed a part of his estate, or what the press dubbed 'palimony.' Geddes contested the claim and won. The laws did not support Stockert.

I quote extensively but *passim* from the Minister's Memorandum introducing the Bill. The present law, he says,

> does not provide for the equitable division of property between spouses upon the breakdown of marriage, as the basic principle governing property rights is "you own what you buy." Where there is a dispute as to the ownership of property, proof of purchase or contribution to the purchase of the property in question is required. The emphasis on financial contribution places a wife who has never worked outside the home at an obvious disadvantage. ... The present law is based on the separate property law concept, which is embodied in the Married Women's Property Act of 1887. This concept has been abolished in many countries and new statutory rules have been introduced to determine the property rights of spouses on the breakdown of marriage. ... In enacting these new provisions the Government is also aware of the social reality of men and women living together in common law unions. They build families together, they work together and they accumulate possessions together. When the union breaks down, the parties experience the same kinds of financial dislocation as if they were married. In our society legal solutions for the problems of family breakdown must address not only married couples, but also common law spouses, if they are to be effective. In enacting these new provisions cognizance is taken of the question of the division of property upon the breakdown of a common law union.

The Bill in effect seeks to give legal recognition to common-law unions, strengthening the earlier Inheritance (Provision for Family and Dependants) Act of 1993, which made a common-law widow eligible for financial provisions from the estate of her deceased common-law husband, provided the union was of a duration of not less than five years immediately preceding the date of his death.

Prior to this, the government had passed The Status of Children Act in 1976, abolishing once and for all the status of illegitimacy. This was some 20 years after George Roberts (1955) had denounced as ridiculous the status of illegitimacy applying to seventy per cent and over of live births. The change meant that an outside child was eligible for succession to property once paternity had been admitted or established.

One can thus see the incremental shifts in the law in relation to the members of the family. First, the status of all children was addressed. Then the right of a man's spouse to his estate, regardless of her common-law status. And finally the new Bill seeking to address the inequitable situation where a woman who built a family together with her common-law spouse, accumulated possessions with him, but suffered a breakdown of their union, can be left high and dry without any portion of his estate, just because they were not legally married.

A number of observations are in order. First, these developments in the law were direct results of the rise of the women's movement and its influence, and might not have been possible otherwise. Second, it is instructive that not until the upper-class adoption of the practice of common law was the deficiency of the law exposed. Which is the same as saying that we validate the cultural practices of the folk only after they have been sanctioned hegemonically, which sometimes means internationally, as happened with the music.

Third, however, the Bill seeks to exalt cultural practice, but in fact it fails to treat it on its own terms. It addresses the issue not from the point of view of the cultural practices of conjugal bonding, family formation, property and inheritance, but from the point of view of the current legal framework. It treats a common-law union as if it were a marriage, putting both of them on the same footing. What's good for the married spouse should be also good for the common-law spouse. Both are equal before the law. Marriage is therefore not understood as the end point of a process of striving but a matter of choice. Some choose common law, others choose marriage. As a result of thus tackling the issue in a less than fundamental way, the lawmakers ignore important cultural aspects of the family, which could present even greater problems.

The critical section is Section 6, subsections (1) and (2):

(1) ...[E]ach spouse shall be entitled to one-half share of the family home —
(a) on the grant of a decree of dissolution of a marriage or the termination of cohabitation;
(2) ...[W]here the termination of marriage or cohabitation is caused by the death of one spouse, the family home shall, if it is not held by both spouses as joint tenants, be deemed to have been so held during the period of the marriage or cohabitation, and accordingly the title to the family home shall pass to the surviving spouse.

It is possible under this Act for property earmarked as family land to pass out of the hands of the bloodline, and thus, while hoping to solve the problem of equity, the Act could end up creating a lot more resentment. The law is oblivious of the nature and existence of family land, and its importance to the lineage (See the discussion at the end of chapter 9).

The practice of family land is widespread in Jamaica, but how widespread we do not know with any precision. Of the 1.1 million hectares of land, 46 per cent is given to agriculture and pasture.[24] It is estimated that there must be over 650,000 parcels of land of all sizes, but less than 45 per cent of these are titled. How we know that it is widespread is from the practice of burial on the family plot. A few years ago, using newspaper death announcements I found that nearly 30 per cent of interments took place in 'family plots.' Given that a far greater number of people are buried daily than appear as notices in the newspaper, the proportion of family plot burials could be higher. The family plot is a section of family land, or land earmarked as such by oral transmission. And given also the fact that not all family lands have burial plots, one can conjecture that the practice is fairly extensive.

In the layout of a typical family land, the family house is usually the house built by the founding ancestor or ancestors. Not far from it, sometimes near the front steps, lie the tombs and vaults of those already dead, which have to be passed before one enters the house. As I have said, not all family lands have burial plots, of course, because many people choose or are forced to use the church and public cemeteries. But even without the family plot, family land retains its function.

It is this that The Family Property (Rights of Spouses) Act could, in its present draft, also divide and transfer. There is no problem with a transfer made as a result of death, or a division as a result of breakup, if the children are common to both parents. But where the children are not, there are bound to be problems.

I cite an example from a community in Kingston. A man owned a piece of property on which he and his family lived. His wife died and in time his children moved on, leaving several grandchildren. He became involved with another woman and after several years together they got married late in his life. Her children moved in to live with her. However, before he died, he had apparently let it be known that he wanted the property as a home for his grandchildren, one of whom subsequent to his death tried to acquire one of two shops on the property. After a couple of years of unsuccessful agitation, the grandchild, interpreting this as the property passing outside the bloodline, crept up on his grandfather's widow one night in the shop, shot her dead and fled the scene.

I do not know what his defence will be when caught and tried, but the case poses some of the problems likely to emerge under the law, problems deriving from disposal of family land that violate the meaning of the cultural practice. Had the law been drafted from the point of view of wanting to validate and regulate well understood cultural practices, provisions could have been made to safeguard the sanctity of family land, to honour its principles of inheritance, to institute mechanisms for resolving family disputes, and even to provide for the management of family land, which is itself a recognized weakness of the custom. This is what I mean by descent into the world of meaning underlying social practices.

Another dangerous error is in the making. In an effort to halt the incidence of teenage pregnancies and stem the tide of carnal abuse, the lawmakers have not only raised the legal age of consent from 14 years to 16 years, but are now proposing to make it mandatory for health workers, teachers, counsellors and others to report the sexual contacts of minors. If passed, this law will criminalize tens of thousands of young male adults and teenage boys, the majority of those persons in consensual sexual relationships with teenage girls — the ganja story all over again (see the following chapter). The framers of the bill ignore African-Caribbean cultural realities. Not even the falling age of menarche and sexual maturation enter their consideration. And all this in a society that sees nothing wrong in providing uncensored sexual stimulation in public advertisements and television programming 24 hours a day, in the lyrics it exposes children to on the buses and in places of entertainment. Teenage sex cannot be legislated away, not in the African-Caribbean.

Social integration is premised on one of two foundations. Either a people are completely absorbed and assimilated into the value system and culture of the hegemonic order, or the principles of good governance respect their values and culturally rooted social practices by providing them space. It is quite clear that assimilation is not the modality worked out in the Caribbean. It is the task of the intellectuals to demand and, where they are able, to fashion the congruence between the social values and cultural practices of the people, on the one hand, and the principles whereby they are governed, on the other. We should have by now emerged from the period of insecurity in ourselves, fear of what others think of us, when our models belonged to a different kind, place and era. And we should by now need no further convincing of the locus of our national identities and pride. Without the people who, as Rex Nettleford is wont to say, came from the cane-piece, the Great House would make no sense. But it is they who now occupy the Great House, as a result of the very values that allowed them to survive the ordeal of the cane-piece. For the past 60 or 70 years, with the rise of the movement for independence, the legal profession has been attracting some of the brightest men and women in our region, drawn by the prestige of the profession. However, too many have been lost in interpreting the law on behalf of clients rather than in discovery of who their clients are. They apparently fail to see the incongruity between the people they represent and the instruments with which they ply their representation. We at the University, whose task it is to educate, not just to train them, ignore this contradiction at our peril. Where is our Caribbean jurisprudence? Where is the tradition of wisdom in crafting instruments of governance and order that come out of the crossroads existence we live in these islands? We need lawyers, of course, and most of those we train have to be and will become lawyers. But we also need people versed in the profession who are dedicated to interpreting the meaning of who we are as a people, where we are coming from, where we are going or ought to go. Of all our intellectuals, it is our writers who more than any other group have taken seriously the journey of self-discovery and self-definition, and have therefore made the Caribbean home. Thus Lamming's (1997) title *Coming, Coming Home*. It is time that those of us whose particular sphere of activity is the framework of laws, jurisprudence and judicial procedures through which society is ordered and run, find the right shoes and begin that journey home.

CHAPTER ELEVEN

CRIMINALIZING CULTURAL PRACTICE: THE CASE OF GANJA IN JAMAICA

A National Commission on Ganja set up by the Prime Minister of Jamaica in 2000 recommended the decriminalization of the private use of the substance and possession of small quantities towards that end. This essay tracks the historical background leading to the enculturation of ganja, its subsequent criminalization, and the failure of the state to suppress it; reviews the work of the Commission; and explains the recommended line of approach to decriminalization without violating the United Nations Conventions on drug regulation.

The fact that in Jamaica *cannabis sativa* is known by its Hindi name is proof enough of its place of origin — India. We assume that it was brought here by Indian indentured workers, who were recruited to work on the sugar plantations vacated by the Africans following the end of slavery throughout the British empire in 1838. As there is no written or oral historical record to suggest that it was known in the island prior to that, and as the large-scale influx of Indians into Jamaica began only in the early 1850s, it is safe to conclude that the use of ganja in that country is no more than 150 years old. During that time, however, the culture contact between the two ethnic groups on the plantations and adjacent communities led to its assimilation and ownership by the African population, over what period of time we can only guess. According to an old informant long since deceased, ganja was regularly sent by ship to 'Colon' for the black Jamaican workers who migrated there to work in building the Panama Canal, an indication that by the turn of the century it was no longer identified exclusively with the Indian population. The same could not be said of the African populations of Guyana and Trinidad, countries which received the largest proportions of Indian indentured workers. And the explanation for this difference is to be found in the fact that the larger numbers taken into those two British colonies made culture contact with the Africans less of a necessity, whereas in Jamaica due to their relatively smaller numbers[25] close cultural exchange was inevitable.[26] The result is that in Jamaica ganja use became a part of the folk practices within a relatively short period of time, and not only its use but also its place in the folk pharmacopoeia, alongside other herbs, roots, barks and plants. When therefore the law was first passed in 1925 making its cultivation, possession, peddling and use a crime, the government's aim was the suppression of a practice that had already become part of the culture of the people. Seven decades later, it has to be said, this battle is as good as lost.

CHRONOLOGY OF GANJA LEGISLATION

The suppression of ganja in Jamaica has undergone three phases: (1) 1913 to 1950s; (2) 1950s to 1972; (3) 1972 to the present.

1913 – 50s

The first phase might be characterized as a period of gathering storm clouds. It began with Jamaica ratifying the International Opium Convention but adding *cannabis sativa*. There were no compelling reasons for the addition. Members of the Legislative Council were apparently satisfied that ganja produced a 'demoralizing, criminogenic influence on coolie (East Indian) laborers' and the native population (Rubin and Comitas 1975, 21), though their real reason was more probably the fear of the black population, for '[l]ocal legislatures, dominated by the plantocracy, attempted to deal with social problems mainly by repressive control' (Rubin and Comitas 1975, 23). In 1924 a Dangerous Drugs Law was passed, which increased the penalties for possession, cultivation, sale and smoking.

In the United States, ganja was already being widely smoked by African- and Mexican-Americans, who as they migrated from the southern to the northern states took the practice with them, hence the name that has achieved the greatest currency in that country, marijuana or marihuana. Outside of these minority ethnic groups, however, it was virtually unknown as a psychotropic substance, until the Bureau of Narcotics campaign against it and passage of the Marihuana Tax Act in 1937. At the time the main concern had been with alcohol, the imposition and ultimate failure of prohibition against it and repeal of the prohibition laws. The story of the campaign against this relatively unknown substance, against a background in which hemp from cannabis had been in use for industrial purposes by many states of the Union, has been interpreted by some, not without plausibility, as a conspiracy motivated by economic interests that saw hemp as a competitive alternative to pulp, but using racial hysteria to mobilize public opinion. There was certainly little scientific evidence of any credibility to support the allegations proffered in support of anti-marijuana legislation that marijuana was the source of criminal behaviour, indolence and other social pathologies. But immediately following the passage of the Act, Mayor La Guardia of New York set up a commission of experts drawn from the New York Academy of Science to study the effects of the substance.[27] After six years of painstaking work, the commission found no evidence that warranted the passage of a law to suppress its use. The Mayor La Guardia Commission became the second major Commission to have studied and exonerated cannabis, the first being the Indian Hemp Commission of 1894.[28] However, the media campaign on the evils of this substance had already produced its desired effect on the general public.

It also gave a fillip to colonial authorities in Jamaica, who intensified their attempt at suppression by amending the Dangerous Drugs Act in 1941 to include mandatory sanctions for possession with intent to traffic. Over the next 20 years, the Act would undergo three amendments, in 1947, 1954 and 1961, making the penalties stiffer. The police also tried its own version of the United States Bureau of Narcotics campaign by attempting, without much success, to link ganja smoking with the rise of crime, including rape. But it was the growing link to the Rastafari that proved decisive in marshalling public opinion in support of the harsher measures of 1961.

For most of this period, despite passage of the Dangerous Drugs Act, ganja remained easily available. An old informant attributed his ability to cope with the economic hardships of life in Kingston in the late 1930s to peddling ganja for a living, for it was available from higglers in the market. Yet the fact that one of the early preachers of Rastafari, Robert Hinds, instructed his members to refrain from using ganja within the confines of his King of Kings Mission so as not to give police any pretext to invade the premises (Chevannes 1994,131) would suggest that, notwithstanding the easy availability of ganja in this period, the law remained a tool that could be used conveniently by the police. It was so used by the police character in Roger Mais's novel *Brother Man* (discussed in 'Rastafari and Critical Tradition,' Part II), but by then the period of stepped-up police prosecution had begun.

1950s – 72

Thus by the middle of the 1950s the storm clouds began to deliver. A period of intense repression set in, lasting for nearly two decades. It was met with equally intense resistance, ending not surprisingly with a change of government in 1972. Apart from the international pressure to wipe out ganja use, developments internal to Jamaica served to polarize the society, and to pit the police against a popular democratic movement for change.

The first of these developments was the aggressive stance adopted by the Rastafari movement, which came under the influence of religious radicals who sought to create distance between the movement and the wider society. They did so by a number of means, one of which, namely the cultivation of uncombed locks, had the desired effect of making them outcasts. Another was the identification with and sacralization of ganja. Adopting ganja as a sacrament, the Rastafari invited the persecution of the state, and thereby sharpened its own critique of the society. For, so went their justification, if ganja was a known folk remedy, the prosecution of it represented a persecution of the people themselves. Further, by tracing its mythic origin to the grave of King Solomon, the Rastafari skilfully exploited Christian tradition, thereby increasing the contradiction posed for the state.

However, to the state there was no contradiction, for the Rastafari represented a marginal group to begin with. Its marginal position was exacerbated by the Claudius Henry affair in 1960 described in chapter 2. The hysteria that swept the country as a result interpreted Rastafari marginal status as having hostile intent towards the society, and so set the stage for the police to target them, with and without the pretext of prosecuting ganja. The hysteria began to abate only with the publication of the study of the movement by the three scholars from the then University College of the West Indies, M.G. Smith, Roy Augier and Rex Nettleford, and not before passage of the 1961 amendment, which increased the mandatory imprisonment for growing and trafficking to up to five years.

Two years later the Coral Gardens incident provided yet another pretext for widespread assault on the Rastafari. A dreadlocked man of unsound mind chopped to death two gas station employees at Coral Gardens before he too was killed. Many innocent members of the Rastafari movement were rounded up, beaten, and imprisoned without cause. This set the stage for yet another amendment. The 1964 amendment made five years of hard labour the mandatory minimum for 'cultivating, or selling or otherwise dealing in ganja' for a first offender, with the possibility of up to seven years. For a second or subsequent conviction, the minimum term of imprisonment was seven years, and the maximum ten. For possession, a first offence attracts a minimum mandatory sentence of 18 months, with a maximum of three years, and for subsequent offences, a minimum of three years and a maximum of five.

By this time Jamaica had just become independent (August 1962) and was being governed by the centre-right Jamaica Labour Party (JLP), founded and led by Alexander Bustamante, a popular labour leader, who was opposed in the new Parliament by his cousin Norman Manley, one of the leading barristers in the then British empire, at the head of his social democratic People's National Party (PNP). Under the JLP the years following independence were marked on the one hand by rapid economic growth, but on the other hand by widespread social dislocation and repression. Unemployment doubled, from 13 per cent in 1962 to 26 per cent in 1972, as the migration outlet to Britain was closed and the economy proved unable to absorb labour at adequate rates. On top of that, the government took a hostile, no-nonsense approach to popular movements, as the Coral Gardens incident showed and the experience of the Black Power movement of the late 1960s was to confirm. It placed a ban on books about revolution and race relations, refused the re-entry of Walter Rodney, a Guyanese national lecturing at the University and leading Black Power advocate, and withdrew the passports of several intellectuals who visited Cuba.

The targeting of the Rastafari by the State had the opposite effect to that which was intended. The movement grew — more in influence than in numbers. For one, its persistent championing of Africa and identification with the African liberation movements gave it legitimacy among important sections of the intelligentsia, so that when Jamaica gained its independence in 1962, occupied its seat in the United Nations, and began associating with independent nations from Africa, the Rastafari could no longer be seen as a lunatic fringe. The state visit of Haile Selassie in 1966 found ruling elements of the society courting the Rastafari, thereby enhancing their credibility among the popular masses. Second, Rastafari idealization of race, particularly in the form of a black God and the promotion of the black self, made it a ready-made part of the Black Power movement which swept Jamaica in the 1960s and early 1970s, the result of influences from the United States. Third, Rastafari grew when the generation that grew up during the first decade of independence took the movement at its word. It swelled the ranks of those holding and acclaiming the divinity of His Imperial Majesty, but lent the movement its own creative voice, the voice of the reggae artiste. By the end of the 1960s most artistes were dreadlocked. They became the new missionaries, spreading the message of Rastafari to the far-flung reaches of the world, while at home giving the movement the energy and defiance of youth.

The anti-ganja measures could be, and were, read by many as anti-Rastafari, and therefore anti-populist, insofar as the Rastafari were beginning to enjoy great popularity, especially in the area of popular culture. Not surprisingly, the youths played a significant role in changing the government in 1972 (Carl Stone 1974). They put words to music, joined the campaign bandwagon of the opposing party with their popular songs, and voted, believing 'better must come.'[29]

A powerful symbol of defiance was the cover picture on Bob Marley's second album with Island Records, *Burning*, which depicted him with a large ganja spliff — a popular icon defying the establishment in promoting the use of ganja. But it was left to Peter Tosh to make of himself a living icon of defiance. This rebel who, in a typical Rastafari play on words turned *system* into *shitstem*, in reference to its oppressive nature, defied the police by public smoking of his spliff in the most crowded square of the city, Half-Way-Tree, resisted arrest by fighting, and ended up badly beaten and imprisoned. Such living testimony was not to be lost on the youth, who by then could be seen smoking spliffs on the street corners in their communities, sometimes without any effort at disguising it.

Despite the draconian measures, then, ganja production increased and its use proliferated. Increased production was fuelled not so much by internal demand as by the demand in the United States. The lucre to be realised from exports to that country proved a greater attraction than the fear of the sanctions was to prove a deterrent. And any risk of running afoul of the law could be minimised by corrupting critical law enforcement agents.

1972 – present

Thus, unable to crush the popular use of ganja, the state shifted tack. In 1972 it repealed the mandatory minimum sanctions for possession, restored the discretion of the courts and ushered in the third and current phase, the phase of amelioration. The Minister of National Security justified the amendment by reference to the fact that all mandatory sentencing — the ganja offence being one of several — had had the opposite effect to that intended. Crime had increased, not abated. Opposition member Edwin Allen, in supporting the amendment, revealed that in using mandatory sentencing as a tool to suppress crime, his government, fresh into independence, was sensitive to the need to give the fledgling tourism sector a chance to develop and to attract foreign capital. Allen also made another interesting point. His government's thinking was that by removing discretion from the court, they would plug the loophole through which people of the higher social classes could escape the full force of the law. Allen's admission was most revealing: the rural and urban masses were not the only ones in violation — the middle and upper middle classes were also engaged in the traffic and/or consumption of the substance.

The Amendment also was assisted by the much-publicized study by Vera Rubin and Lambros Comitas. Under a grant from the National Institute of Mental Health these two scholars from the Research Institute for the Study of Man, in New York City, assembled a team of researchers, many of them based at the University of the West Indies, Mona, to study the effects of long-term habitual use of ganja. Their Report was serialised in The Daily Gleaner and later published in 1975 under the title *Ganja in Jamaica*. Then, in the first serious attempt at some form of decriminalisation, the Parliament, on a motion initiated by the Opposition, set up a Select Committee of the House to study the issue and to make recommendations. In 1978 the Committee recommended decriminalization for medical use and a drastic reduction in the sanctions for personal use. However, the Report was shelved as the country passed through the most divisive period in its modern political history, with the struggle for political power taking on an armed dimension. Nonetheless, both parties stood in favour of the amelioration.

The current period has been marked, then, by the introduction of measures to educate the youth and general public, by the continued spread of ganja use and, in its later stage, the adoption of an approach to drugs that treats it less as a criminal issue and more as a matter of health.

Government's main effort at education was the establishment of the National Council on Drug Abuse (NCDA) in 1983. The NCDA implements its objectives through the establishment of Community Drug Abuse Action Committees (CODACs), which are clubs of young people operating at the community level, educating their peers and others about the harmfulness of drugs. The CODACs have been very successful in increasing awareness among the youth population, but not successful in reducing ganja use. A random sample survey of 5,000 households carried out in 1990 by Carl Stone recorded a 45 per cent use of ganja, with highest incidence among males in their twenties and thirties. Four years later, Sam Wray (1994) found a use rate of 11.6 per cent, but this study, while national in scope, in the sense of covering every parish, was not based on a national sample selected at random to give it reliability. The third survey, Hope Enterprises (2001), found a lifetime use of 19 per cent and a current use of 11.5 per cent. Its sample, however, could have been compromised by the need to stratify the population of 2,380 'using the following criteria: NDCA region, urban/rural characteristics, *presence or absence of CODACs*' (Hope Enterprises 2001, 9; emphasis added). Until a survey of the type and quality of Stone's is conducted it will be difficult to establish definitively whether or not the use of ganja is contracting or proliferating. Testimony given to the National Commission on Ganja by one of the CODACs, and by members of other CODACs representing themselves, expressed the difficulty in effecting a reduction in the demand for ganja, because of the official classification, contrary to popular perception, of ganja as a drug similar to cocaine.

Latterly, since ratification of the 1988 United Nations Convention Against Illicit Traffic in Narcotic Drugs and Psychotropic Substances, the ganja offender, as also any other drug offender, appears before a Drug Court. If found guilty, and if s/he accepts the offer of the court to undergo rehabilitation, s/he is released without fine or sentence, and is discharged on receipt by the court of a positive report by the caseworkers. But if s/he refuses, or if at the end of the period of rehab the court receives a negative report, then s/he may be fined or sentenced to prison.

The use of ganja, particularly the smoking of it, has not abated. If anecdotal evidence is anything to go by, it has increased among schoolchildren, especially boys. It continues to be used openly at stage shows and on construction sites where workers find it a stimulant. Given the ethos of stage shows, the open use of ganja by artistes and their followers, as well as by the general music-loving audience, is not surprising. But the source of the belief in its stimulating qualities is the rural sugar cane workers and small cultivators. Rubin and Comitas (1975, 75) conclude from their analysis of 3,000 minutes of videotapes, over 2,000 of audiotapes, films, objective measurements of food intake and energy expenditure and laboratory studies of energy metabolism of small cultivators of a rural community, that 'ganja smoking alters the rate and organisation of movement and increases the expenditure of energy.' Actual output, however, failed to vary significantly from those of non-smokers.

In summary, for nearly 90 years the state has engaged in the suppression of the use of ganja and has failed. It spent the first four decades communicating its resolve and forcing ganja use underground, the next two in very repressive measures, and when those failed resorted to softer measures, including education and rehabilitation. The reason for that failure lies as much in the culturally entrenched nature of ganja and the practices surrounding its use as it does in the mistake of state agencies in classifying it as a drug, where the popular culture does not. So the message that ganja can be harmful encounters an impenetrable mental block.

National Commission on Ganja

In recent years the lobby for the legalization of ganja has steadily grown. The Rastafari are no longer the only section of the society campaigning for the dismantling of the laws against it. A National Committee for the Legalization of Ganja, drawing on a cross-section of people including middle-class professionals, has lent respectability to the cause, which they see as including economic considerations as well, since hemp has many industrial uses. As a result of the agitation of this Committee a motion was passed in the House calling on Government to set up a Commission to look into the issue of decriminalization. Acting on this, the Prime Minister appointed a Commission in September 2000 to consider and recommend whether Government should decriminalize ganja for personal use in private.

There were two notable points about the terms of reference of the Commission, one being the distinction between decriminalization and legalization. Legalization of ganja would encompass the repeal of all laws pertaining to the proscription of this substance, its cultivation, possession, trafficking and use, whereas decriminalization referred to a limited legalization, to wit the use of the substance under prescribed conditions. For example, so-called medical marijuana is the decriminalization under the prescribed condition of having legal medical authorization to use it.

The second point was that the remit of the Commission included consideration of its use 'for religious purposes.' What was notable here was that the terms did not specify the Rastafari, although most people would have identified the Rastafari as the intended beneficiaries should the recommendation be favourable. The wisdom of leaving the terms general rather than specific is immediately evident if one were to consider what would happen if the Commission closed the door on Rastafari use. The Commission would open itself to the charge of being anti-Rastafari in a way that could not apply were it to close the door on *religious* use.

The composition of the Commission was also carefully considered. It ensured an island-wide spread in terms of eastern, central and western Jamaica; religious representation; representation of medical expertise; youth representation; legal representation; representation of the academy; and representation from the NCDA — all within the limits of seven persons, a comfortable working group. Immediately on its being announced the composition of the Commission was attacked by the National Committee for the Legalization of Ganja, which felt that the Commission was loaded with anti-ganja people in order to guarantee a recommendation against decriminalization. The Committee felt that the medical doctor on the team, a member of the University of the West Indies community, who was also a Vice-Chairman of the NCDA, and, curiously, myself, would have been biased against decriminalization, and faulted the absence of a representative of the Rastafari movement to provide a counter-balance. They were not the only ones to lament the exclusion of the Rastafari. Rastafari themselves and others sympathetic to decriminalization were of the feeling that for all its sacrificial witness to the benefits of ganja, no Commission could be set up to consider decriminalization of ganja that did not include the Rastafari. Such persons, however, failed to take the full picture into account. Rastafari inclusion could just as easily have elicited the accusation of weighting the Committee in favour of decriminalization, especially because it could not have been assumed that the other members were not in favour. The critics also failed to see that a recommendation in favour, without a Rastafari presence, would serve to strengthen the case for decriminalization, since persons who had no known personal interest in favour of it would have taken the decision. And what if such a Commission were to recommend against decriminalization? There is little doubt, based on the precedent of the 1961 Mission to Africa, that there would have been a majority report and a minority Rastafari report.[30] In short, the membership of the Commission was one of the best possible, well balanced and including persons known for their professionalism and integrity.

Methods of Work

It took two months after the announcement and meeting with the Prime Minister before we were able to begin our work. Despite being able to obtain a majority should the Commission be deadlocked, we took the decision to work by consensus. However, decisions on issues were a long way off, since our first task was to gather data. This we would do by ensuring the widest coverage of the island and representation of views of all the important sectors and stakeholders of society. We interpreted our mandate not as a polling of opinion, which could be done scientifically and possibly more cost-effectively by random sampling, but rather as an uncovering of and deliberation on the issues involved. Decisions were to be based not on majority opinions but on consideration of all the legal, scientific, ethical, cultural, political and international issues as they were identified.

Hearings were to be of two sorts: *in camera* and in public. It was felt that this balance would allow those who might have felt intimidated or compromised by the presence of others to make their depositions in confidence, while affording as many people as possible the opportunity of being heard. In addition, the Commission invited representation from a wide range of private sector and professional organizations, and organizations of civil society, as well as commissioning briefs on the legal and international treaty dimensions. A web page and email address opened up the Commission to views from interested persons overseas. Finally, the Commission took advantage of a business trip of one of its members to gain firsthand information on the controlled decriminalization of *cannabis* use that has been a feature of the drug policy of The Netherlands.

Not long into the hearings the Commission had to adjust its method, since the staging of the public hearings failed to bring forth much response; it decided to take the hearings to the people in targeted communities and urban centres. Thus, the combination of hearings held *in camera* and in town squares and markets characterized our visits to every parish of the island. With these adjustments, it found that people, male and female, of all ages and walks of life were generally forthcoming and willing to share their views. As most of these were extolling the virtues of ganja, the Commission made a deliberate attempt to seek out sources it thought might be *contra*. Thus were visits made to one church and two seminaries, and comments invited from the leadership of several Christian denominations.

The Issues

What then were the issues identified which formed the substance of the Commission's deliberations? The most salient ones may be summarized. The first in logical priority was whether *cannabis* was harmful, sufficiently so to warrant the sanctions imposed against it. A review of available medical and scientific evidence established that ganja could produce acute but temporary disorders such as anxiety, paranoia, and psychosis, not to mention impairment of certain cognitive functions. This was not surprising. Ganja is, after all, a psychoactive substance. Against these effects the Commission had to place many well-known benefits, some of them already part of Jamaican folklore for generations, and providing important clues for medical scientific investigation. The Commission took note of the rise of 'medical marijuana,' which an increasing number of states had begun taking on board. It had to place in its deliberation the fact that virtually all ingested substances, including prescribed medicinal treatments, often produced unwelcome, even harmful, side effects, leaving open the issues of over-use, tolerance and personal psychic disposition to explain differences in effects. One effect that was of concern to the Commission was the *amotivational syndrome*, a condition to which adolescents were reported to be especially vulnerable, leading to lower educational achievement and dysfunction.

A second issue was the matter of the perceived inequity in the treatment of substances, such that alcohol and tobacco, which were known causes of incapacitation and death across the world, were legal, but *cannabis*, far less debilitating and not known in its history of use for causing a single death, was not. To many people, especially those influenced by Rastafari beliefs, this created a sense of victimization, ultimately serving to undermine the rule of law. Others, however, while conceding the inequity, felt that the decriminalization of *cannabis* would make an already bad situation worse.

Third was a cosmological argument, which by distinguishing natural from man-made substances, reasoned that the natural form in which ganja was consumed and banned in Jamaica not only precluded its classification as a 'drug' with other artificial substances like cocaine and alcohol, but placed it in the same category as any other vegetable matter or herb. The sanction against this plant flew in the face of the natural order and was therefore tantamount to hubris. According to the leader of the influential Roman Catholic Church, because sin lay in abuse rather than in use *per se*, the use of ganja was not of itself sinful or immoral, but the abuse of it was.

A fourth issue was the extent to which ganja contributed to the proliferation of a drug culture, whether by association due to its criminal status or by inducing the use of harder substances. Although the charge of its being addictive has been dismissed, and its inducement of predisposition to other substances is unproven, there was still the argument that since the criminal drug network was the same for ganja as for cocaine and crack, the passage from ganja to cocaine was made easier. This argument was used by both those for and those against decriminalization. For the former, decriminalization would serve to isolate crack/cocaine and other hard drugs; for the latter, by removing the cover of illegality it would expose more people to the hard substances. Those against also feared that decriminalization would lead to more widespread use of ganja itself, while those in favour believed that ganja being so widely available with impunity, whatever increase in use decriminalization would cause would be minimal and insignificant.

Fifth was the extent to which ganja use and its cultural significance in Jamaica posed problems for law enforcement. The Commission received evidence from a wide cross-section of people, including some law enforcement officers, claiming that the inability of the police to suppress the criminal activity of ganja use was serving to undermine respect for the police and the rule of law. Indeed, there were allegations that some law enforcers were not above using it themselves, which was not surprising, given the evidence of its endemic nature.

Deliberating on these and other issues, taking account of the opinions for and against, the Commission came:

> to the unanimous conclusion that ganja should be decriminalised for adult personal private use. Its criminal status cannot be morally justified, notwithstanding the known ill effects it causes in some people. It contravenes natural justice, seeing that it has been, like other natural substances, a part of the folk culture in Jamaica for decades prior to its criminalisation, a part of recognised medical practice for centuries, and a part of herbal lore for millennia in other parts of the world. Nor was its criminal status first recommended by scientific evidence in any way remotely resembling the proliferation of research, some of it of questionable value, now being called on to justify its current status.

In reaching that conclusion, the Commission basically left the *status quo* untouched, except in one singular respect. By *status quo* was meant the stand-off between the existing sanctions and enforcement, on the one hand, and the widespread, uncontrollable use of it, on the other hand. Ganja, though retaining its illegal status, was nonetheless available for use with relatively little or no penalty. The exceptional change would be in the great relief decriminalization would give to the five or six thousand Jamaicans of all ages who annually run afoul of the law, whose careers were often wrecked as a result.

DIFFICULTIES OF IMPLEMENTING RECOMMENDATIONS

Once the decision had been taken the immediate consideration was how it might be acted upon. The preamble to the Commission's terms of reference drew attention to the existence of 'international treaties, conventions and regulations to which Jamaica subscribes that must be respected.' The pertinent international conventions were: (1) the 1961 Single Convention on Narcotic Drugs, (2) the 1971 Convention on Psychotropic Substances, and (3) the 1988 Convention Against Illicit Traffic in Narcotic Drugs and Psychotropic Substances. None of these Conventions requires the prohibition of the consumption or use of *cannabis*, but they do require the prohibition of possession. Although the Secretary-General's Commentary and the interpretation given by the International Narcotics Control Board explained that the intent of the 1961 Convention was to criminalize possession for the purpose of trafficking and not for personal use, the 1988 Convention made explicit the requirement to criminalize 'possession, purchase or cultivation...for personal consumption.'

How then would it be possible to decriminalize personal use but not purchase or possession for personal use? To the legal mind, this is unworkable. And this was the conclusion reached by Professor Stephen Vasciannie of the University of the West Indies in the very detailed brief he prepared for the Commission. The Conventions would require subjecting to criminal law 'all important stages preceding consumption, but not consumption itself.' Thus, the possibility of decriminalizing consumption was but a formal one, 'implausible in practice.'

An important rider limitation to the Conventions is their subjection to the constitutional principles and basic concepts of the legal system of each country which is party to the Conventions, and this is set out in the pertinent articles. For example Article 3, paragraph 2 of the 1961 Single Convention reads:

> Subject to its constitutional principles and the basic concepts of its legal system, each Party shall adopt such measures as may be necessary to establish as a criminal offence under its domestic law, when committed intentionally, the possession, purchase or cultivation of narcotic drugs or psychotropic substances for personal consumption....

This limitation, the Commission was of the view, opened the way for Jamaica to decriminalize possession for personal use and use itself, if the Charter of Rights made the right to privacy and to freedom of religious belief and expression inviolate. At the present time a saving clause in Jamaica's Constitution allows all laws in force prior to the Day when the Constitution came into effect (the 6th of August 1962) to supersede the Human Rights provisions in the Constitution, where they conflict. However, both Government and Opposition have tabled draft amendments to the Constitution that would effectively remove the saving clause and allow Jamaica to take advantage of the limitation clause. The intention of both drafts is to make the human rights of the citizens subordinate only to the requirements of public emergencies, public disasters, and not to any other laws. Thus, the Commission's recommendation would first require an amendment to the Constitution that entrenched a Charter of Rights.

But is the decriminalization of use unworkable? The Commission thought of the possibility of allowing the growing of a limited number of the plants in the private space of one's home, but felt that such a concession would be open to abuse. Given the still flourishing export trade, and the difficulty of policing the tens of thousands of householders who would now become legitimate growers of a small number of plants, what would prevent these private user/growers from selling their crops to the exporters? Decriminalization is unworkable only in an abstract sense. In the real world of twenty-first century Jamaica it is quite feasible, since as things now stand the overwhelming majority of users evidently do procure the substance with impunity. The Commission's proposal would make procurement still subject to sanction, but, under the constitutionally guaranteed right of privacy, possession of small quantities for use in private not so subject.

Conclusion

Decriminalization represents an initial and necessary step in correcting a grave ill. Clearly, what is called for is the complete legalization of ganja, which is possible only by amending the UN Conventions to remove *cannabis* from the list of banned substances. But the imposition of the law in the first place and the failure of its prosecution over the years raise an important issue concerning the rule of law, or, more generally, the relationship between the State and society. Does the fact that behaviour is culturally meaningful mean that it cannot be sanctioned? What makes cockfighting illegal but boxing not? What is the meaning of Independence if the postcolonial people are still subject to the colonial laws?

From an anthropological point of view, law is the codification of customary manners and behaviour. It works in synchrony with morality, protecting society against deviance. Laws that depend solely on the naked power of the State for their enforcement are repressive, and they succeed only to the extent that the balance is tipped in favour of the State. But as the history of colonialism shows, such victories are only temporary, unless the hegemonic classes succeed also in bringing about moral conformity to the law. The rule of law is never secure unless it is sanctioned by the moral order.

Jamaica's dilemma lies in maintaining a colonial order in a postcolonial State, a task that demands repression and must undermine the moral foundation of the independent State. During the colonial times, Rastafari opposition to the rule of law, particularly where ganja was concerned, sought to undermine the moral authority of the colonial State. This was in effect the thrust of their defiance, for which they were willing to pay the price of marginalization and imprisonment. The failure of the postcolonial State to remedy this contradiction has contributed in no small measure to the rise of open defiance of the law, such that now ganja is smoked openly on the streets and at public gatherings such as football matches and popular music concerts. Indeed, many of those who oppose decriminalization oppose it because of its association with what they see as a breakdown of the moral (read *colonial*) order, such that people can publicly flout the law at will.

The sooner the State is able to harmonize the law with social morality, the better for the rule of law. The longer it vacillates, the worse. Already in at least one other area, the public use of 'bad words,' or Jamaican expletives, enforcement of an obsolete law has led to its defiant violation, so that enforcement depends on the power of the State rather than on repulsion and ostracism by the general public. The lesson from *cannabis* is that the State may criminalize cultural practice at its peril.

CHAPTER TWELVE

Those Two Jamaicas: The Problem of Social Integration

Social integration has been a central problematic of Caribbean social sciences ever since M.G. Smith. To be more precise, the question concerns the place of the Africans/Blacks in the post-Emancipation societies of the Anglophone Caribbean, and the place of Indians in Guyana and Trinidad and Tobago, where they once formed a significant, and now a majority, ethnic grouping.

Smith's (1965) social and cultural pluralism was based on two premises. One was a formulation of culture as institutions. Thus cultural differences are differences in institutional patterns: marriage, family, religion, education, sports and recreation, and so on. The other was that only state power held culturally diverse groups together.

Pluralism was vigorously attacked from beginning to end. At the beginning Lloyd Braithwaite (1953), basing his attack on the premise that no society can exist without a shared value system, maintained that even in culturally diverse Trinidad, values such as education and colour preferences transcended class and ethnicity. Towards the end in a bitter debate with Smith (1983), Don Robotham (1980; 1983) exposed pluralism as a cover-up for the failure of the brown middle class to acculturate the Black populace, and concluded that it was premised on a pessimistic post-Independence future. In between, many of us had difficulty with the idea of race and colour as some sort of social glue, and not one serious Caribbean scholar was won to pluralism, with the exception of a few who used the model to explain the bitter cleavages between Africans and Indians in Guyana. No school of cultural pluralism developed among Caribbean intellectuals.

Why not? Most scholars I believe sensed in pluralism an extremism, which, except for Guyana, except also for a very brief period around the time of Emancipation, did not reflect the lived reality of the Caribbean. The withdrawal of the colonial power did not result in the disintegration of the social order, as premised on the nature of a plural society. And yet, most had to agree, there were indeed differences in the institutional life of the peoples. That these differences also paralleled class differentiation allowed some to offer a short-lived Marxist paradigm,[31] which, by reducing cultural differences to differences of class, explained social disintegration as an inherent feature of class-divided society, and social integration, wherever it existed, as based on hegemonic control. The failure of Marxist praxis to achieve working class hegemony,[32] and therefore a social integration based on a new paradigm in the Caribbean, was quickly followed by the demise of Marxism as an explanatory tool. It had been quite weak on the cultural question, and was never at home with the culture of the folk, African or Indian.

We are still faced with the task of explaining the basis of social integration among societies that are internally culturally differentiated, and of identifying the threats to it. Using the Jamaican experience, I propose an angle from which I believe light can be shed on the problem.

CODE SWITCHING

Our scholars in linguistics use the concept of code switching to identify a sort of bilingualism among Caribbean creole speakers. The 'creoles,' or patois, are, it is generally agreed, languages with a largely anglophone, francophone or hispanic lexicographical base, but with underlying structures that are closer to African than to European languages. That creole speakers are also fluent in European languages makes them bilingual. However, linguists speak not of bilingualism but of code switching. Creole and European languages are, among creole speakers, not merely languages, but social and cultural codes. They are not just media for the expression of thoughts, but their uses are codes for class positioning, orientation and meaning, or for personal advantage and power. Code switching is an expression of inequality between languages. Speakers who know the codes, know when to and when not to communicate in the particular language.

In Jamaica, it is this ability to switch from patois to English that misleads both those who are arguing for some sort of official recognition of patois, and those who believe that people do not out of some sort of perverse nationalism speak English. The unfortunate result of the latter tendency is to assume that English need not be taught as the foreign language it is.

Code switching as a paradigm can, I believe, explain how it is that two Jamaicas have not just merely coexisted, but have together formed an apparent status quo which gives the appearance of social integration through a common value system. Nothing could be further from the truth. Two Jamaicas do exist, but because the Jamaica of creole speakers knows how, where and when to code switch, both Jamaicas appear to exist on the same plane. The people take advantage of both worlds, seeking to maximize opportunities.

I would argue that there are three prerequisites to code switching. First there must be inequality. If the languages are equal, then it matters little which is used when, if simple communication is the objective. However, I know of no island of the region where the creole has equal status, not even in Curaçao where *papiamentu* is used freely by political and religious leaders, or in St Lucia, where the same may be observed about *kweyol*. In all the islands of the Caribbean the creole is accorded lower social status relative to the European language. But, secondly, at the same time there must be some value to the subordinate language, other than sheer ignorance of the European languages, to explain its persistence. A sense of identity may provide ample reason for the persistence, but where, as in the Jamaican patois, new words are constantly being invented, it would appear that the language is also valued for its aptness. Third, there must be a discernment of advantage, which would cause a speaker to switch codes.

Let me now give three examples of cultural practices which I believe may be understood by using the device of code switching.

The first pertains to land tenure. An enterprising couple worked their way up and managed to buy an eleven-acre property of coffee, cocoa and timber, which they put to commercial use. They bought a smaller property of four acres, on which they set up their home. After the death of her husband, the now head of the family, in her old age, subdivided the first property into as many equal plots as she and her husband had children, together and separately, with new titles, but the second she willed as family land.

As we saw in 'Law and the African-Caribbean Family,' family land, found all over the Caribbean, is land bequeathed by an ancestor, male or female, to his/her descendants in perpetuity. It functions as a source of identity, security and unity for members of the lineage group: the living, their ancestors, and those yet to be born. All lineage members have usufruct and burial rights on family land.

Here we have side by side, in one and the same family, two different uses of land, two different meanings to tenure. In one, land can be owned, as you would a horse or pig or a house. In the other, land can only be used. The legal system recognizes the former, but not the latter. A person or corporation may acquire a legal title over land, but there is no system that allows title to a lineage. And yet there is a significantly large number of parcels of land in Jamaica that are either family land or earmarked as such. The process begins when persons with legal tenure bequeath land as family land. It may revert to legal tenure after a few generations, but usually not without conflict within the lineage. The point I am making is that quietly, without making any big fuss, the African-Jamaican peasants, living in a world structured by others, take advantage of it, while retaining an understanding and use of land all their own, but with a different function. In the language of pluralism, they practise the same institution but in two culturally different ways.

My second example is marriage and the family, subjects I dealt with in chapter 6. It is astonishing that with all of the studies on the Black family in the Caribbean, so little is understood of the value system underlying it — but not really astonishing, because it has largely been diagnosed as pathological. For a pathology it is extraordinarily persistent. Even in the most Roman Catholic of countries, where the majority of people are Black, and where sex before marriage is a mortal sin, the overwhelming majority of births are to unwed mothers, many not yet separated from their families of orientation. As we saw in chapter 6, conjugal relations pass from greater instability to greater and greater stability, from casual to visiting to common-law unions, to legal marriage. It is not that people do not get legally married, but they understand legal marriage not as the legitimizing of sexuality, but as the bestowing of social respectability. With legal marriage come other things than the mere joining of a couple as man and wife. Both increase their standing in the eyes of the community and are expected to behave in a manner befitting this status. Men, particularly, do not rush, but grow into marriage. When they do, they seldom divorce. Both Church and State, on the other hand, see marriage as the gateway to sexual cohabitation. As for the concept of family itself, we have seen that it is understood not as the nuclear unit but an extended network connected by blood. Thus, again in the language of pluralism, the same people practise two culturally different institutions, though in this case not synchronically but diachronically over the period of their life-cycle.

A third example is drawn from religious practice. Observers used to talk of 'dual membership' to describe the adherence in one and the same people to two different, almost opposing, religious orientations. People used to claim nominal membership in the establishment churches — Anglican, Baptist, Methodist, Moravian, and so on — but at the same time practise a spirituality that was unmistakably African: belief in and possession by the powers. They attended church on Sunday morning and the Revival or balm yard on Sunday night. The church, with all its respectability, gave them access to social mobility; the Revival yard, for all its low social standing, gave them spiritual fulfilment. Culturally speaking, these are two different traditions, although Revival borrowed extensively from Christianity. Their belief systems are different, their rituals are different, and their underlying worldviews are different.

Dual membership has disappeared now, because by making internal adjustments and by making external linkages with North American Pentecostalism, Revival has gained in respectability. Only now is it possible for the people Rex Nettleford likes to refer to as 'ladies of quality' to fall in the aisles, writhing in the spirit. Pentecostalism has grown by leaps and bounds since these developments. In 1960 it accounted for no more than 13 per cent of the nominal church membership, with the Anglican and Baptist denominations accounting for nearly 40 per cent between them. Forty years later, Pentecostalism accounts for nearly 30 per cent, while the Anglican and Baptist churches together barely account for 20 per cent. Now it enjoys equal status with the establishment churches.

As with these examples in the institutional life of the Jamaican people, so with other areas. They operate, or know how to operate, in two worlds at the same time, switching from one to the other, as it suits. Fundamentally, as I suggested in the essay, 'Forward to the Past,' they retain a world outlook that has been derived from African world outlooks brought here and renewed over the centuries by incoming Africans, but reconfiguring and incorporating elements from the new social and physical environment.

What are the implications of all this? Where Jamaica appears as a socially integrated society, it is because the people code switch. I repeat with sadness the observation that in 40 years of independence there has not developed a jurisprudence capable of reflecting our Caribbean realities. Lawyers, politicians (most of whom are lawyers) and jurists who value the people as a resource cannot but be concerned at the deficiency of the legal system and become advocates for its reform in the direction of reflecting the culture of the people. It is remarkable that the things we highlight and value as markers of our national identities as Caribbean peoples are the things which for the most part derive from the people: music, the performing arts, food ways, language, even the people we salute as heroes. Social integration is not possible without social recognition.

Which is also to say that the social disintegration which some see taking place in Jamaica, to the extent that one can classify the murders as such, is a function of our failure to recognize by legitimization the *other* Jamaica. After 160 years, Jamaica remains not one but *two* Jamaicas, divided not even so much by social class as by thinking.

Notes

1. Following an appeal for reparations made by the Public Prosecutor representing a group of Rastafari on the grounds that slavery constituted a crime against humanity, Her Majesty Queen Elizabeth II, the self-styled *Defensor Fidei*, wrote back to say that slavery was perfectly legal according to the laws *in opere* at the time. The formula for absolution pronounced by the priest at confession was *Ego te absolvo* — I absolve you. If the priest himself sinned, he had to seek absolution from another priest. Nobody pronounces his own absolution. 'But Prospero is... dangerously poised between his doing and his doubt. He is not beyond Caliban's pardon; but he dares not ask it. To ask a favour of Caliban is to enter too fully into what is not known' (Lamming 1992, 15).
2. Europeans developed a system of privileges and social status based on the nuances of racial colour, premised on the assumption, natural of course, of the purity of racial whiteness. It still reigns in the Caribbean, but in the United States it had the perverse effect of valorising the strength of the black gene pool since anything touched by blacks became black. There is no reason why the offspring of a black and white couple should be black instead of white.
3. The 'John Crow' is a vulture, completely black but for its bald neck and head.
4. I am grateful to Professor Rupert Lewis for referring me to this source.
5. This could have been a case of mutually reinforcing systems of thought. The BaKoongo conceived of the ancestors as white, and regarded those who had been taken away across the Atlantic as gone to the land of

the ancestors (MacGaffey 1983). Bedward's well-publicised flight has been generally used to discredit him as insane and the Revival movement as a ridiculously deluded religion. My interpretation accords with that of the playwright Stafford Ashani who several years ago linked Bedward's flight with the well known tradition among the slaves of flying back to Africa. The playwright had Bedward abstaining from salt prior to his flight. As already mentioned in Chapter 2 above (pp. 75–76), the salt taboo survives among the Rastafari.

With regards to Revival's adoption of the white Jesus, in contrast to the later Rastafari, the case can be made that the incorporation of European deities and saints without alteration reflected an attempt by Myal and its later developments to strengthen itself, rather than to indigenise Christianity. In contemporary Revival cosmology Jesus and all the saints are powers. So also is the Indian spirit, who, when he possesses, transforms his agent into an Indian with a wig of soft hair, speech that is said to be Hindi, and a dance style reminiscent of Indian female dancers on the balls of the feet and with the gestures of the hands and arms.

6. Monsignor Dr Gladstone Wilson, a renowned man of letters, with a doctorate in Psychology, dismissed the sympathetic *Report on the Rastafari Movement in Kingston, Jamaica* by M.G. Smith, Roy Augier and Rex Nettleford, all scholars of the University College of the West Indies, on grounds that the movement was made up of demented people. A similar analysis was made by a well known psychiatrist at a symposium organised by the late Vera Rubin (See Rubin and Comitas, 1975).

7. Bedward was declared insane in 1895 and sentenced to the Bellevue mental asylum. He was released a month later. He was again interned there in 1921, following the ambush of his march on Kingston, his arrest and trial. He died at Bellevue on November 2, 1930, the same day Haile Selassie was crowned Emperor.

8. The person who led the delegation was Mortimo Planno and the person they went to was the young black scholar, not long returned from Oxford, Rex Nettleford. Sir Arthur Lewis, the Principal of the College, at the time a college of the University of London, appointed the anthropologist M.G. Smith to lead the team of researchers, which included the historian Roy Augier and Nettleford. The three undertook what decades later development experts were to call a brief but intense 'rapid appraisal', an exercise in allowing people to describe as fully as

possible their condition. Lewis, whose father had been a Garveyite, took a personal interest in the study, and would sometimes accompany one of the researchers to observe. On receiving their Report he sent it with a disarmingly simple cover letter to Premier Norman Manley, and the rest, as they say, is history. Manley authorised the much publicised Mission to Africa, which included Planno and two other Rastafari. A Technical Mission followed but was aborted when Manley's party lost the referendum to the opposition which campaigned against Jamaica remaining in the Federation.

9. See Maureen Warner-Lewis (2003) for a discussion of evidence that the water pipe might have been known among Jamaicans through a Central African diffusion.

10. One should not lose sight of the ambiguity in this statement: it is after all a song — a song that cannot be sung. Ted Chamberlin (2000 [1993]) treats with it from the point of view of the poetic reappropriation of the African heritage in the language of a West Indian identity. See Chapter 1.

11. The Twelve Tribes of Israel is one of the three main Rastafari organizations, the others being the Nyabinghi and the Bobo. Twelve Tribes grew out of a chapter of the Ethiopia World Federation under the leadership of Prophet Gad.

12. On October 16, 1968, University of the West Indies students at Mona took to the streets to protest the exclusion of Guyanese history lecturer Walter Rodney from his return from a conference in Montréal. The protest, which was joined by thousands of the urban youth population, erupted into a riot, when police fired tear gas into the demonstration. Damage from the fires and the looting was put at eight million pounds. The reasons given for Dr Rodney's exclusion was his subversive activities among the Rastafari and his visits to the Reverend Claudius Henry who had not long before returned from prison. In actual fact Rodney taught them African history.

13. See note 5 above.

14. This is the title of the last chapter of his book, where he reminds us that modernity itself was born out of the disorder of violence.

15. In this calypso, a father advises his son that he can't marry the girl he likes, for 'di girl is yu sista, but yu mama don't know'. In distress, he tells this to his mother, who encourages him to marry the girl, for 'yu daddy ain't yu daddy, but yu daddy don't know!'

16. A member of Fathers Incorporated, a group whose aim is to project a positive image of fatherhood, married with two boys, one eleven, the other seven, and unable to find a steady job for the past three years, revealed recently that only now did he understand why some men ran away from their responsibility. Without a penny to his name, his son unable to bear the pangs of hunger any longer, and with a single tin of sardines the only food in the house, for the first time in his life as a father, he was seriously tempted to leave his family.
17. A caller on a radio talk show, asked to say why hers was a good father, gave the example that he always left a little of his dinner on the edge of his plate for her.
18. There are exceptions. Texaco, an informant in a study by Chevannes and Mitchell-Kiernan (1995) maintained two women, but on the condition that they had to know and be prepared to get along with each other.
19. 'Cock mout' kill cock' is a proverb which warns against boastfulness. By crowing the cock identifies his roost to the fowl thief.
20. In this imagined dialogue Jones does in fact live where the encounter takes place but the residents feel justified in hiding the truth from the company come to repossess his furniture.
21. The Black Star was the name of Garvey's Shipping Line. Many Rastafari held the belief that Repatriation will be by a fleet of Black Star Liners stretching seven miles.
22. Incorporation allows a religious group to own property and exempts them from taxes. It is tantamount to official recognition.
23. The 'maiden' is the hymen.
24. This and the following estimates are taken from Government of Jamaica 1996, pp. 3 & 29.
25. According to Roberts (1979) Jamaica received only 8 per cent of the immigrants over the entire period of indentureship.
26. Ganja use was not the only practice assimilated by the Africans. Indian influences can be seen in the food ways, particularly in the use of curry, and in the Jamaican folk religion, Revival, in the presence of the Indian spirit.
27. Mayor's Committee on Marihuana (1944), *The Marihuana Problem in the city of New York: Sociological, Medical, Psychological and Pharmacological Studies*. Lancaster, Pennsylvania: Jaques Cattell Press.
28. Great Britain. 1969. *India Hemp Drugs Commission, 1893–1894*. Silver Springs, Maryland: Thomas Jefferson.

29. *Better mus' come* was a hit song of Delroy Wilson.
30. The Government accepted the recommendation of Smith et al. (1961) to send a Mission to Africa to investigate the possibilities for migration there. The nine-man Mission included three members of the Rastafari movement, who, unable to agree with the majority, submitted their own minority report. Despite this, however, the majority report was accepted.
31. See Munroe and Robotham (1977); William Riviere (1982).
32. The collapse in 1983 of the four-year old Grenada Revolution signalled the end of Marxism as political praxis. Within five years, the Workers Party of Jamaica, the Working People's Alliance (Guyana) and various other groups throughout the region were no more.

References

Adewale, S.A. 1988. *The African Church (Inc.): a synthesis of religions and culture*. Ibadan: Oluseyi Press.

Akama, E.S. 1987. 'The Emergence of the Igbe Cult in Isokoland.' In *New Religious Movements in Nigeria, African Studies* vol. 5, ed. Rosalind I.J. Hackett. Queenston, Ontario and Lewiston, NY: Edwin Mellen Press.

Alleyne, Mervyn. 1988. *Roots of Jamaican Culture*. London: Pluto and Karia Press.

Amadi, Gabriel I.S. 1987. 'Continuities and Adaptations in the Aladura Movement: The example of Prophet Wobo and his clientele in south-eastern Nigeria.' In *New Religious Movements in Nigeria, African Studies* vol. 5, ed. Rosalind I.J. Hackett. Queenston, Ontario and Lewiston, NY: Edwin Mellen Press.

Apter, Andrew. 1987. 'Ritual Powers: The Politics of Orisa Worship in Yoruba Society.' PhD diss. Yale University.

Apter, Andrew. 1991. Herskovits Heritage: Rethinking Syncretism in the African Diaspora. *Diaspora* 3, 235–60.

Asante, Molefi Kete. 1980. *Afrocentricity : The Theory of Social Change*. Buffalo, NY : Amulefi Publishing.

Asante, Molefi Kete. 1990. *Kemet, Afrocentricity and Knowledge*. Trenton, N.J.: Africa World Press.

Asante, Molefi Kete. 2002. Afrocentricity and the Decline of Western Hegemonic Thought : A Critique of Eurocentric Theory and Practice. In *Black Identity in the 20th Cenury : Expressions of the US and UK African Diaspora*. Ed. Mark Christian. London : Hansib Books, 101–18.

Austin-Broos, Diane. 1997. *Jamaica Genesis: Religion and the Politics of Moral Orders.* Chicago. University of Chicago Press.
Baeta, C.G. 1962. *Prophetism in Ghana.* London: SCM Press.
Balandier, Georges. 1988. *Le désordre :Éloge du mouvement.* Paris : Librairie Arthème Fayard.
Berger, Peter, and Thomas Luckman. 1967. *The Social Construction of Reality: a Treatise in the Sociology of Knowledge.* Garden City, NY: Doubleday.
Besson, Jean. 1979. Symbolic Aspects of Land in the Caribbean: The Tenure and Transmission of Land Rights among Caribbean Peasantries. In *Peasants, Plantations and Rural Communities in the Caribbean,* eds. Malcolm Cross and Arnaud Mark. Guildford: University of Surrey and Leiden: Royal Institute of Linguistics and Anthropology.
Besson, Jean. 1984. Family Land and Caribbean Society: Toward an Ethnography of Afro-Caribbean Peasantries. In *Perspectives on Caribbean Regional Identity,* ed. Elizabeth M. Thomas-Hope. Monograph Series No. 11. Centre for Latin American Studies, University of Liverpool: Liverpool University Press.
Besson, Jean, and Barry Chevannes. 1996. The Continuity-Creativity Debate: The Case of Revival. *New West Indies Guide* 70, nos. 4 & 5.
Bilby, Kenneth, and Elliott Lieb. 1986. Kumina, the Howellite Church and Rastafarian Music. *Jamaica Journal* 19, no. 3: 22–8.
Bockie, Simon. 1993. *Death and the Invisible Powers: the world of Kongo Belief.* Bloomington: Indiana University Press.
Braithwaite, Lloyd. 1953. Social Stratification in Trinidad: A Preliminary Analysis. *Social and Economic Studies* 2, nos. 2 & 3 (October).
Brathwaite, Kamau. 1973. *The Arrivants: A New World Trilogy.* Oxford: Oxford University Press.
Brathwaite, Edward Kamau. 1971. *The Development of Creole Society in Jamaica: 1770–1820.* Oxford: Clarendon Press.
Brathwaite, Edward Kamau. 1986. *Roots.* Havana: Ediciones Casa de las Américas.
Brown, Anderson and Barry Chevannes. 1993. 'The Contribution of Caribbean Men to the Family.' Unpublished Study, Caribbean Child Development Centre, University of the West Indies, Mona.
Carroll, John B, ed. 1956. *Language, Thought, and Reality: Selected Writings of Benjamin Lee Whorf.* Cambridge, MA: MIT Press.
Chamberlin, J. Edward. 1999. *The Idea of a University.* Ontario: Council of Ontario Universities.
———. 1993. 2000. *Come Back To Me My Language: Poetry and the West Indies.* Kingston: Ian Randle Publishers.

Charsley, Simon. 1992. Dreams in African Churches. In *Dreaming, Religion and Society in Africa*, eds. M.C. Jedrej and Rosalind Shaw. Leiden, New York and Koln: E.J. Brill.

Chevannes, Barry. 1976. The Repairer of the Breach: Rev. Claudius Henry and Jamaican Society. In *Ethnicity in the Americas*, ed. Frances Henry. The Hague: Mouton.

Chevannes, Barry. 1985. *Jamaican Male Sexual Beliefs and Attitudes*. Kingston: National Family Planning Board.

Chevannes, Barry. 1989. Drop Pan and Folk Consciousness in Jamaica. *Jamaica Journal* 22, no. 2.

Chevannes, Barry. 1994. *Rastafari: Roots and Ideology*. New York: Syracuse University Press.

Chevannes, Barry. 1995. The Phallus and the Outcast. In *Rastafari and Other African-Caribbean Worldviews*, ed. Barry Chevannes. Basingstoke: Macmillan and New Jersey:Rutgers University Press.

Chevannes Barry. 2001. *Learning To Be A Man: Culture, Socialization and Gender in Five Caribbean Communities*. Jamaica, Barbados, Trinidad and Tobago: University of the West Indies Press.

Chevannes, Barry. 2002. Gender and Adult Sexuality. In *Gendered Realities in Caribbean Feminist Thought*, ed. Patricia Mohammed. Barbados, Jamaica, Trinidad and Tobago, The University of the West Indies Press and the Centre for Gender and Development Studies.

Chevannes Barry, and Claudia Mitchell-Kiernan. 1995. "How We Were Grown:" Cultural Aspects of High Risk Sexual Behaviour in Jamaica. Unpublished Paper, UCLA-UWI: Sexual Decision-making Project. University of the West Indies, Mona.

———. 1995. Focus Group Discussions. Unpublished Paper, UCLA-UWI Sexual Decision-Making Project. University of the West Indies, Mona.

Chivallon, Christine. 2005. Can one Diaspora hide Another? : Differing Interpretations of Black Culture in the Americas. Social and Economic Studies 54, no. 1, Maison des Sciences de l'Homme, University of Bordeaux III, Bordeaux.

Clarke, Edith. 1953. Land Tenure and the Family in Four Communities in Jamaica. *Social and Economic Studies* 1, no. 4.

Clarke, Edith. 1966. [1957]. *My Mother Who Fathered Me: A Study of the Family in Three Selected Communities in Jamaica*. London: Allen and Unwin.

Comaroff, John and Jean Comaroff. 1992. *Ethnography and the Historical Imagination*. Boulder, San Francisco and Oxford: Westview.

Curtin, Philip. 1969. *The Atlantic Slave Trade: A Census*. Madison, Milwaukee and London: University of Wisconsin Press.

DeLisser, H.G. 1913. *Twentieth Century Jamaica*. Kingston: Jamaica Times.

Devisch, René. 1993. *Weaving the Threads of Life: The Khita Gyn-Ecological Healing Cult Among the Yaka*. Chicago: The University of Chicago Press.

Durrant-Gonzalez, V. 1976. 'Role and status of rural Jamaican women: Higglering and Mothering.' PhD diss. University of California, Berkeley.

Edwards, Bryan. 1793. 1819. 1966. *The History, Civil and Commercial, of the British West Indies, with a Continuation to the Present Time*. 5th edition. New York: AMS Press.

Erskine, Noel. 1978. *Black Religion and Identity*. DD diss. Emory University.

Equiano, Olaudah. 1789. 1995. *The Interesting Narrative and Other Writings*. New York : Penguin Books.

Fanon, Franz. 1967. *Black Skin, White Masks*. New York : Grove Press.

Fernandez, James W. 1982. *Bwiti: An ethnography of the religious imagination in Africa*. Princeton, NJ: Princeton University Press.

Fernandez, James W. 1990. Tolerance in a Repugnant World and Other Dilemmas in the Cultural Relativism of Melville J. Herskovits. *Ethos* 18, no. 2 (June): 140–64.

Forsythe, Dennis. 1983. *Rastafari For the Healing of the Nation*. Kingston: Zaika Publishing.

Fraser, H. Aubrey. 1974. The Law and Cannabis in the West Indies. *Social and Economic Studies* 23, no. 3: 361–85.

Geertz, Clifford. 1957. Ethos, Worldview and the Analysis of Sacred Symbols: *The Antiop Review* 74.

Geertz, Clifford. 1973. *The Interpretation of Cultures: Selected Essays*. London: Hutchinson.

Gilroy, Paul. 1993. *The Black Atlantic: Modernity and Double Consciousness*. Cambridge: Cambridge University Press.

Goodison, Lorna. 2001. *Travelling Mercies*. Kingston: Ian Randle Publishers.

Hackett, Rosalind I. 1989. *Religion in Calabar: the Religious Life and History of a Nigerian Town*. Berlin, New York: Mouton de Gruyter.

Hall, Douglas. 1989. *In Miserable Slavery: Thomas Thistlewood in Jamaica*. London: Macmillan.

Hallgren, Roland. 1988. *The Good Things in Life: A Study of the Traditional Religious Culture of the Yoruba People*. Loberod, Sweden: Plus Ultra.

Herskovits, Melville. 1958. *The Myth of the Negro Past*. Boston: Beacon.

Higman, B.W. 1975. The Slave Family and Household in the British West Indies, 1800-1834. *Journal of Interdisciplinary History* VI, no. 2: 261–87.

Horton, Robin. 1971. African Conversion. *Africa* XLI, no. 2 (April): 85–108.
Horton, Robin. 1975. On the Rationality of Conversion. *Africa* 45, no. 3: 219–35 and no. 4: 373–99.
Jedrej, M.C. and Rosalind Shaw (editors). 1992. *Dreaming, Religion and Society in Africa*. Leiden, New York and Koln: E.J. Brill.
Lamming, George. 1960. *The Pleasures of Exile*. London: M. Joseph.
———. 2000 [1995]. *Coming, Coming Home: Conversations II*. St. Martin: House of Nehesi Publishers.
Littlewood, Roland. 1995. History, Memory and Appropriation. In *Rastafari and Other African-Caribbean Worldviews*, ed. Barry Chevannes. Basingstoke: Macmillan; New Jersey: Rutgers University Press.
Long, Edward. 1774 [1970]. *The History of Jamaica, or General Survey of the ancient and modern state of that island with reflections on its situations, settlements, inhabitants, climate products*. London: Cass.
MacGaffey, Wyatt. 1983. *Modern Kongo Prophets: Religion in a Plural Society*. Bloomington: Indiana University Press.
Mais, Roger. 1966. *The Three Novels of Roger Mais*. London: Jonathan Cape.
Mansingh, Ajai and Laxmi Mansingh. 1999. *Home away from Home: 150 Years of Indian Presence in Jamaica, 1845–1995*. Kingston: Ian Randle Publishers.
Marshall, Paul A., Sander Griffioen and Richard Mouw. 1989. Introduction. In *Stained Glass: Worldviews and Social Science,* eds. Paul A. Marshall, Sander Griffioen and Richard Mouw. Lanham (Maryland), New York and London: University Press of America.
Mbiti, John. 1969. *African Religions and Philosophy*. London: Heinemann.
McClelland, E.M. 1982. *The Cult of Ifa among the Yoruba, Volume 1: Folk Practice and the Art*. London: Ethnographica.
Meeks, Brian. 2000. *Narratives of Resistance: Jamaica, Trinidad, the Caribbean*. Barbados, Jamaica, Trinidad and Tobago: University of the West Indies Press.
Mintz, Sidney and Richard Price. 1992. *The Birth of African-American Culture: an Anthropological Perspective*. Boston: Beacon Press.
Moore, Joseph Graessle. 1953. Religions of Jamaican Negroes; A Study of Afro-Jamaican Acculturation. Northwestern University, PhD diss. Northwestern University.
Mudimbe, V.Y. 1988. *The Invention of Africa: Gnosis, Philosophy and the Order of Knowledge*. Bloomington: Indiana University Press.

Mullings, Leith. 1979. Religious Change and Social Stratification in Labadi, Ghana. In *African Christianity: Patterns of Religious Continuity*, eds. George Bond, Walton Johnson and Sheila S. Walker. New York: Academic Press.

Munroe, Trevor, and Don Robotham. 1977. *Struggles of the Jamaican People*. Kingston: Workers Liberation League.

Naipaul, Vidia. 1962. *The Middle Passage: Impressions of Five Societies, British, French and Dutch, in the West Indies and South America*. London: Andre Deutsch.

National Commission on Ganja. 2001. *Report of the National Commission on the Decriminalisation of Ganja*. Kingston: Jamaica Information Service.

Nettleford, Rex. 1970. 1998. *Mirror Mirror: Identity, Race and Protest in Jamaica*. London: William Collins and Kingston, Jamaica: Sangster.

Nettleford, Rex. 1993. *Inward Stretch, Outward Reach: A Voice from the Caribbean*. London: Macmillan.

Norris, Katrin. 1962. *Jamaica: The Search for an Identity*. London: Oxford University Press.

Nugent, Maria. 1839. 1966. *Lady Nugent's Journal of her Residence in Jamaica from 1801 to 1805*. 4th Edition. Kingston: Institute of Jamaica.

Ojo, Matthews A. 1988. The Contextual Significance of the Charismatic Movements in Independent Nigeria. *Africa* 58, no. 2: 175–92.

Olthuis, James H. 1989. On Worldviews. In *Stained Glass: Worldviews and Social Science*, eds. Paul A. Marshall, Sander Griffioen and Richard Mouw Lanham. (Maryland), New York and London: University Press of America.

Olupona, Jacob O.K. 1983. A Phenomelogical/Anthropological Analysis of the Religion of the Ondo-Yoruba. PhD diss. Boston University.

Oudemans, Th. C.W., and A.P.M.H. Lardinois. 1987. *Tragic Ambiguity: Anthropology, Philosophy and Sophocles' Antigone*. Leiden, New York, Copenhagen, Koln: EJ Brill.

Peel, J.D.Y. 1968. *Aladura: A Religious Movement Among the Yoruba*. London: Oxford University Press.

Peel, J.D.Y. 1977. Conversion and tradition in two African Societies: Ijebu and Buganda. *Past and Present* 77: 108–141.

Peel, J.D.Y. 1990. The Pastor and the Babalawo: The Interaction of Religions in nineteenth-century Yorubaland. *Africa* 60, no. 3: 338–69.

Pelton, Robert. 1980. *The Trickster in West Africa: A Study of Mythic Irony and Sacred*. Berkeley: University of California Press.

Phillippo, James Mursell. 1843. 1969. *Jamaica: Its Past and Present State*. London: Dawsons.

Riviere, William. 1982. Contemporary Class Struggles and the Revolutionary Potential of Social Classes in Dominica. In *Contemporary Caribbean: A Sociological Reader*, volume 2, ed. Susan Craig. Maracas, Trinidad and Tobago.

Roberts, George. 1955. Some Aspects of Mating and Fertility in the West Indies. *Population Studies* 8, no. 3.

Roberts, George, and Sonja Sinclair. 1978. *Women in Jamaica*. New York: KTO Press.

Robotham, D. 1980. Pluralism as an Ideology. *Social and Economic Studies* 29, no.1 (March).

Robotham, D. 1985. The Why of the Cockatoo. *Social and Economic Studies* 34, no. 2 (June).

Robotham, Donald. 1988. Emergence of a Black Ethnicity in Jamaica. In *Marcus Garvey: His work and Impact*, eds. Rupert Lewis and Patrick Bryan. Kingston: Institute of Social and Economic Research and School of Continuing Studies, University of the West Indies.

Rubin, Vera, and Lambros Comitas. 1975. *Ganja in Jamaica*. The Hague: Mouton.

Schuler, Monica. 1979. Myalism and the African Religious Tradition in Jamaica. In *Africa and the Caribbean: The Legacies of a Link*, eds. Margaret Crahan and Franklin W. Knight. Baltimore: Johns Hopkins University Press.

———. 1980. "*Alas, Alas, Kongo*": *A Social History of Indentured African Immigration into Jamaica, 1841-1865*. Baltimore: Johns Hopkins University Press.

Schwarz-Bart, Simone. 1992. *Between Two Worlds*. Oxford: Heinemann.

Scott, David. 1991. That Event, This Memory: Notes on the Anthropology of African Diaspora in the New World. *Diaspora* 1, no. 3: 261–284.

Seaga, Edward P.G. Revival Cults in Jamaica: Notes Towards a Sociology of Religion. *Jamaica Journal* 3, no. 2.

Senior, Olive. 1973. *The Message is Change: A Perspective on the 1972 General Elections*. Kingston: Kingston Publishers.

Simpson, George E. 1980. *Yoruba Religion and Medicine in Ibadan*. Ibadan: Ibadan University Press.

Smith, M.G. 1965. *The Plural Society in the British Caribbean*. Berkeley: University of Washington Press.

Smith. M.G. 1983. Robotham's Ideology and Pluralism: A Reply. *Social and Economic Studies* 32, no. 2 (June).

Smith, Raymond T. 1956. *The Negro Family in British Guiana*. London: Routledge and Kegan Paul.
Smith, Raymond T. 1970. Caribbean Kinship and Family Structure. Paper presented at Conference on Continuities and Discontinuities in Afro-American Societies and Culture, April 2–4.
Smith, Raymond T. 1988. *Kinship and Class in the West Indies: A Genealogical Study of Jamaica and Guyana*. Cambridge: Cambridge University Press.
Stakeman, Randolf. 1986. The Cultural Politics of Religious Change: a Study of the Sanoyea Kpelle in Liberia. *Africa Studies* 3. Lewiston, Queenston, Canada: The Edwin Mellen Press.
Stewart, Robert. 1992. *Religion and Society in Post-Emancipation Jamaica*. University of Tennessee Press.
Stone, Carl. 1974. *Electoral Behaviour and Public Opinion in Jamaica*. Mona, Jamaica: Institute of Social and Economic Research, University of the West Indies.
Thompson, Robert Farris. 1984. *Flash of Spirit: African and Afro-American Art and Philosophy*. New York: Random House.
Waddell, Hope Masterton. 1970. 1863. *Twenty-nine Years in the West Indies and Central Africa, 1829-1858*. Second Edition. London: Frank Cass.
Walcott, Derek. 1992. *Omeros*. New York: Noonday Press.
Walker, Sheila S. 1979. The Message as the Medium: The Harrist Churches of the Ivory Coast and Ghana. In *African Christianity: Patterns of Religious Continuity*, eds. George Bond, Walton Johnson and Sheila S. Walker. New York: Academic Press.
Walker, Sheila S. 1983. *The Religious Revolution in the Ivory Coast: The Prophet Harris and the Harrist Church*. Chapel Hill: University of North Carolina Press.
Warner-Lewis, Maureen. 1992. *Guinea's other Suns: The African Dynamic in Trinidad Culture*. Dover, MA: Majority Press.
Warner-Lewis, Maureen. 2003. *Central Africa in the Caribbean: Transcending Time, Transforming Cultures*. Barbados, Jamaica, Trinidad and Tobago: University of the West Indies Press.
Wedenoja, William. 1978. *Religion and Adaptation in Rural* Jamaica. PhD diss. University of the West Indies.
White, Garth. 1967. Rudie, Oh Rudie! *Caribbean Quarterly* 13, no. 3.
Williams, Brackette. 1991. *Stains on my Name, War in my Veins: Guyana and the Politics of Cultural Struggle*. Durham: Duke University Press.
Williams, Eric. 1964. *Capitalism and Slavery*. London: Andre Deutsch.

Wolters, Albert M. 1989. On the Idea of Worldview and its relation to Philosophy. In *Stained Glass: Worldviews and Social Science*, eds. Paul A. Marshall, Sander Griffioen and Richard Mouw. Lanham, (Maryland), New York and London: University Press of America.

Wray, S.R. 1994. Prevalence and Patterns of Substance Abusers' Neurobehavioural and social dimensions: a 1994 National Survey Report on Substance Abuse in Jamaica. Kingston: The University of the West Indies Neuroscience, Adolescent Development and Drug Research Programme, Faculty of Medical Sciences.

Wyllie, Robert. 1980. *The Spirit Seekers: New Religious Movements in Southern Ghana*. Massoula, Montana: Scholars Press.

Index

Abstractive reduction: in European cosmology, 73–74
Abyssinians: and Jamaican popular music 103
Accompong: of the Maroons, 84
Africa: in Jamaican cosmology, 170–171; Rastafari and, 31–33, 57–59, 120; in West Indian heritage, 16
'Africa and the Caribbean', xv
African identity, 152–153. *See also* Black identity
African-American rhythm and blues: and reggae, 14–15
African-Caribbean cosmology, 171–175
African-Caribbean family: and the law, 179–194
African-Caribbean linkages: and Caribbean identity, 3–4, 5–6
African heritage: in the Caribbean, 27–30
African-Jamaican worldview, xvi
African retentions: in the Caribbean, xi, xii, xv, 27–30; in Caribbean literature, 22; in Kumina, 57; in Rastafari, 31–33, 57–59, 120
Afro-Guyanese family, 183
Afrocentricity: concept of, 11–15
After the Beginning Again (ABA), 12
Agbara: power of, 50, 51, 52, 53
Age: respect for, 55, 160, 174
Aladura movement: and Christian conversion, 49–53; similarities to Revivalism, xvi, 28
Allen, Edwin: on class, crime and punishment, 203
Ambiguity: and Caribbean identity, 75
'Ambiguity and the Search for Knowledge', xvi

'Amnesiac blow': of slavery, 10, 15
Amotivational syndrome: and ganja, 209
An Absence of Ruins: and the 'amnesiac blow', 15
Anansi, 136; amorality of, 147–148; and the art of deception, 154; in folk tradition, 83; and Rastafari, 95, 112; symbolism, 66
Ancestors: defining, 38; honouring of, 156, 160; respect for, 174; in Yoruba religion, 46
Angels: in Christian cosmology, 37–38
Anthropological Approach to the Afro-American Past to the Birth of the African-American Culture: an anthropological perspective, xii
Anus: symbolism in Jamaican culture, 24–25
Apter, Andrew: critique of Herskovits, 32–33
Asante, Molefi: and the concept of Afrocentricity, 11
Ase, 47
Augier, Roy: study on Rastafari, 200
Autsin-Broos, Diane: on Jamaican Pentecostalism, 136

Babalawos: and the power of knowledge, 47, 52, 54
Bakoonga cult: and salt, 57, 58
Balandier, Georges: and disorder in Jamaican society, 82–83
Baldwin, James: and colour, 7
Beckwith, Martha: on Bedward, 87
Bedward, Alexander, 84–85, 87, 91, 119; influence of, 36–37
Before the Beginning Again (BBA), 12

Belly: symbolism in African worldview, 23–24
Besson, Jean: on family land, 174
Between Two Worlds: African theme in, 20
Betwixt and Between, xi
Bible: and knowledge, 39–40, 55, in Yoruba religion, 52
Black Atlantic: defining the, 13
Black identity, 7–8
Black inferiority: religion and, 87
Black Power Movement, 201
Blackness: demonization of, 118
Blood relationships: significance of, 155–156, 187
Bobo: similarities to Revivalism, xi
Bogle, Paul: and the Morant Bay rebellion, 84, 88
Bongo: fire ritual, 26
Boukman, 119
Brathwaite, Lloyd: critique of cultural pluralism, 216
Braithwaite, Kamau, 105; and Africa, 15–18
Brodber, Erna: on language, 5
Brother Man, 92; folk wisdom and Rastafari in Mais's, 113–116
Brown, James: African retention in music of, 14
'Browning': and idealization of male desire, 171
Burning Spear: and Jamaican popular music, 103
Bustamante, Alexander, 201
'But, Every John Crow Tink Him Pickney White: identity theme in Nettleford's, 69

Cannabis sativa. See Ganja
Cannes brules: T&T carnival and symbolism of, 25–26
Capitalism: Williams and slavery and, 86–87
'Capture': concept of land, 168
Caribbean heritage: Africa in, 15–22, 27–30
Caribbean identity: search for a, 67–77

Caribbean intellectuals: and Africa, 15–17, 28
Cartesian cosmology: interconnectedness theory in, 75
Castro, Fidel: Leonard Howell and, 93
Casual relationships: defining, 127; outside child in, 134–135, 136, 137. See also Common-law unions, Conjugal bonding, Family, Marriage and Visiting relationships
Central Africa in the Caribbean, xv–xvi, 4
Christianity: culture clash in Jamaican, 163; spiritual in, 37
Circulation of cultural forms: between Africa and African Diaspora, 14
Chamberlin, Professor Ted: and Caribbean storytelling, 62–63; and the search for Africa through language, 16–18
Charisma: and prophecy, 43–45; and Rastafari, 43; in Yoruba religion, 52
Charter of Rights: and freedom of religion, 213
Children: law and status of, 191; love of, 156; value of, 186–187
Christ Apostolic Church (CAC): in Nigeria, 49–52
Christian conversion: among the Yoruba, 48, 58–61
Christianity: development in the WI, 45
Church: and ganja, 210
Church of England: in colonial Jamaica, 88–89
Class: colour and, 6
Claudius Henry Affair. See Henry, Claudius
Code switching: defining, 217–219
Colour: and class, 6; and identity, 6, 7–8; and self-esteem, 88–89
Come Back to Me My Language, 16
Coming; Coming Home: Conversations II: on the role of the Caribbean intellectual, 107–123
Comitas, Lambros: study on ganja, 202
Common-law unions, 131, 183, 184, 185; and *Family Property (Rights of*

Spouses) Act, 191–193. *See also* Casual relationships, Conjugal bonding, Family, Marriage and Visiting relationships
Community: slavery and, 155; socialization by the, 157–159
Community Drug Abuse Action Committee (CODAC): and ganja, 204
Community order: in African society worldview, 153
Communication: with the spirit world, 44–45
Conjugal bonding: types of, 182–188. *See also* Casual relationships, Common-law unions, Family, Marriage and Visiting relationships
Constitution: and human rights, 213
Convention Against Illicit Traffic in Narcotic Drugs and Psychotropic Substances (1988): and the decriminalization of ganja, 212
Convention on Psychotropic Substances (1971): and the decriminalization of ganja, 212
Coral Gardens incident, 200–201
Cosmological system: features of a, 172–174
Cosmology: concept of, xiv
Cotton tree: magic and the silk, 58
Creativity: in the Jamaican ghetto, 82–83; Negro, 72;
Creativity vs Continuity debate, xi–xii, 11–12
'Cross-over Griot': African theme in Goodison's, 21–22
Cross roads: symbolism of, 64–67, 75–77
Cuba: Elián González and relations between US and, 66–67
'Cultural nakedness': slavery and the concept of, 4
Cultural pluralism: in Caribbean society, xviii; and the problem of social integration, 216–222
Cultural transfer: process, xii
Culture: defining, xii, 4

Dance Jamaica: governance and politics in Nettleford's, 72
Dancehall: violence in, 82
Dangerous Drugs Act, 199; and ganja, 94–95
Dangerous Drugs law, 198
Dead: Jamaican folk tradition and the, 38, 44; power of the, 54
Death: rituals in slave society, 157–158; in Jamaican folk tradition, 65; in Yoruba mythology, 46
Deception: the art of, 153–155
Decriminalization: of ganja, 206, 210–214
Destiny: in Jamaican worldview, 145–146
Development of Creole Society in Jamaica, 17
Differentiation: identity and, 73
Diop, Chiekh Anta: and emergence of Afrocentricity, 11
Diplomacy: and survival in slavery, 153
Disease: Yoruba treatment of, 50–51
Disorder: in Jamaican society, 75, 82–83
Dogon worldview, xv
Dopi (duppy): defining, 38
'Double Consciousness': West and the concept of, 13
Dread talk: and the Jamaican identity crisis, 96–98
Dreadlocks, 199; symbolism of, 42, 92, 95–96, 100, 113, 118, 120
Dreams: and the spirit world, 38, 44; in Yoruba religion, 50
Drug culture: ganja and the, 210

Eccles, Clancy: and Jamaican popular music, 102
Education: Church of England and, 89
Enlightenment: and modernity, 13
Entepreneurship: rise of, 166
Esu: in Yoruba mythology, 46
Ethiopia: Rastafari and symbolism of, 86, 87
Europe: and African identity, 153

European cosmology: abstractive reduction in, 73; separation in, 73–75
Europeans: and Caribbean history, 107–110
External forces: individual as victim of, 146–147
Extra-union affairs: women and, 126
Eyre, Governor: and the Morant Bay Rebellion, 93

Fallen angels: in Christian cosmology, 38
Family: and breakdown of values, 163; Caribbean concept of, 155; cultural pluralism and, 220; defining, 181, 187; socialization and role of, 152. *See also* African-Caribbean family
Family Court: and paternity tests, 124–125
Family formation: in slave society, 156–157
Family land: concept of, 174–175; inheritance of, 128, 192–194
Family Propeity (Rights of Spouses) Act, 1999, 190–195
Fatherhood: and the African-Caribbean family, 189; bonding in, 133; proof of paternity and, 129
Female sexuality, 136
Fernandez, James W.: critique of Herskovits, 33–34
Fire: and power, 25–26: symbolism in T&T carnival, 25–26
First Time: critique of Price's, 34
Folk adoption: defining, 187
Folk philosopher: role of the, 112
Folk traditions: African retentions in Caribbean, 8–9
Freedom of religion: Charter of Rights and the, 213

Gateway: symbolism of the, 167
Ganja: criminalization of, 91, 196–197; history of, 196–197; and the law, 179,181, 197–215; Rastafari and, 179, 199–200, 207; sacralization of, 94, 113, 200; in the US, 197–199
Ganja in Jamaica: study by Rubin and Comitas, 203
Ganja legislation: chronology, 197–215
Garvey, Marcus, 84–86, 88, 90, 102; and Africa, 32, 36; Black consciousness of, 12; and colour in Jamaica, 8
Geddes, Paul: *Family Property (Rights of Spouses) Act,* 1999, 190
Gender: and power, 127–128; and socialization, 132
Ghetto: violence and creativity in the Jamaican, 82
Gilroy, Paul: and the Black Atlantic, 12–13
Grammatical principles (worldview): of slaves, xiii–xiv
Grenada corner: and male bonding, 167–174
Group identity: Jamaican, 174
God: in the Jamaican spirit world, 37; in Rastafari, 90, 113; in the Yoruba spirit world, 47
González, Elián: symbolism in US–Cuba relations, 66–67
Goodison, Lorna: Africa in the work of, 17, 19–22; and the role of the poet, 22
Gordon, George William: and the Morant Bay Rebellion, 93

Hair: symbolism in Rastafari, 42. *See also* Dreadlocks
Healing: in Revivalism, 43; in Yoruba, 51
Henry, Rev. Claudius, 200; and Rastafari, 31–33, 92–96
Henry, Ronald: and Rastafari, 93
Herskovitz, Melville: on African retentions in the Caribbean, 3; critique of, 32–34
Hibbert, Joseph: and Rastafari, 54
Holy Spirit: power of the, 54
Homophobia: symbolism of anus and, 24–25

Homosexuality: Caribbean attitude to, 24–25
Howell, Leonard, 89; and Rastafari, 57–58
Human rights: and the Constitution, 213

Identity: African-Caribbean linkages and Caribbean, 3–4; in Caribbean scholarship, xvi; colour and, 6, 7–8; Jamaican male, 169–171; search for a Caribbean, 67–77
Identity crisis: Rastafari and Jamaican, 96
Ideology: concept of, xiv
Independence, 201
Illegitimacy: law and, 191
Indian Hemp Commission (1894), 198
Indians: and family, 181–182
Inner cities: and breakdown of values, 164
Intellectual theory: and Christian conversion, 59
Intellectuals: Africa and Caribbean, 15–17; defining, 109–110; Lamming and the role of Caribbean, 29, 107–123; and the search for a Caribbean identity, 67–77
Interconnectedness: theory of, 75
International Narcotics Control Board: and the criminalization of ganja, 212
International Opium Convention, 197
Inward Stretch, Outward Reach, 29

'Jacket': and African-Caribbean culture, xvii; and paternity, 12–129, 135–137
Jamaica: Christian conversion in, 58–61; historical background, 84–89; spirit world of, 36–45; loss of values in, 151; violence and disorder in, 81–83
Jamaica Labour Party (JLP), 201
Jamaican cosmology: features of, 170–175
Jamaican identity, 67–77

Jamaican worldview: similarities between Yoruba and, 55–61
Jamaicans: comparison between Yoruba Nigerians and, 35, 36
Jazz: in South Africa, 14
Journey: symbolism, 64–67

Kalanuga: and loss of tradition, 9; and the role of the Caribbean intellectual, 28–30
Kambule: in T&T carnival, 25–26
Kinship: community and, 155
Knowledge: Babalawos and the power of, 47, 52, 54; Bible and, 39–40; of spiritual power, 39–40
Kojo: of the Maroons, 84
Kumina: African retention in, 25, 26, 57
Kumina, A Kongo-based Tradition in the New World, 17
Kuti: Tela Pansome, 14
Kuyiper, Abraham; definition of worldview, xv
Kwashi personality: and the art of deception, 155

Lamming, George: and African-Caribbean family, 189; and colour in the Caribbean, 8; and the role of the Caribbean intellectual, 29, 107–123
Land tenure: cultural pluralism and, 219. *See also* Family land and Property
Language: African retention in, 3, 4, 30; code switching and, 217–219; disorder of, 96–98; philosophy of, 5; search for Africa through, 16–22
Language structure, xiv–xv
Law: and the African-Caribbean family, 179–195; defining, 180–181; and family, 189–191; and ganja, 181
Legalization: of ganja, 206, 207, 210–214
Legislation: anti-ganja, 199, 203, 210–214; property, 219
Lifecycle process: family and the, 183, 185

Lion: symbolism in Rastafari, 100
Literature: Africa in Caribbean, 15–22; Rastafari in, 92,
'Literature of African expression' 18
'Literature of reconnection', 18, 21
'Literature of survival, 18
Livity: defining, 41
Louisiana: philosophy of language in, 5

Madness: Rastafari association with, 91
Mais, Roger, 92; and Rastafari as prophet, 117
Male bonding, 167–175
Male group identity. *See* Male bonding
Male marginalization: and breakdown of values, 164–165
Manhood: paternity and, 128–129, 131
Manley, Edna: and Rastafari, 89–90, 113
Manley, Norman, 201
Marihuana Tax Act, 1937, 198
Marley, Bob, 102–105; and ganja, 202; and Jamaican popular music, 82
Maroons: ethnicity and, 155; resistance by, 84
Marriage, 133, 135; African-Caribbean, 182–183, 185; cultural pluralism and, 220; and family, 162; Indian, 181–182; and the law, 189–195; and property rights, 190–191, 192
Married Women's Property Act, 1887, 191
Mayor LaGuardia Commission: on effects of ganja (marihuana), 198
Mediation: defining, 110
'Medical marihuana', 209
Medicine: Yoruba and, 50–51
'Melody of Europe, Rhythm of Africa': identity theme in Nettleford's, 69–77
Mento: and Jamaican music, 101
Migration: and breakdown of values, 164
Mintz, Sidney: and the Creativity vs Continuity debate, xii, xiii, 27–29

Mirror, Mirror: identity theme in Nettleford's, 68–70
Modernity: and enlightenment, 13
Moral responsibility: erosion of, 141–148
Morant Bay Rebellion, 84, 93
Morgan, Derrick: and Jamaican popular music, 101
'Morning sport': African retention in, 58
Motherhood: sacredness of, 156
Multiple partnerships: in African-Caribbean society, 135. *See also* Casual relationships, Common-law unions, Conjugal bonding, Family, Marriage and Visiting relationships
Music: ganja and popular, 202; ghetto and Jamaican popular, 82; history of Jamaican popular, 101–104; Rastafari and, 103; similarities between African and African Diaspora, 14
Myal: emergence of, 84, 87
Myth of the Negro Past, 8–9, 10

Naipaul, Vidia: and the 'amnesiac blow' of slavery, 15
Nammo: concept of, 17
Nanny: of the Maroons, 84, 119
'Natal Song': African theme in, 19–21
Nation language; defining, 18
National Commission to decriminalize the private and religious use of ganja, 95
National Commission on Ganja, 196, 204, 206–213
National Commission for Legislation of Ganja, 206
National Council on Drug Abuse (NCDA), 204; and ganja, 207
Negritude: and Afrocentricity, 11–12
Negro: identity, 72–73. *See also* African identity, Black identity, Caribbean identity and Jamaican identity
Nettleford, Rex: and the Jamaican identity, 67–77; study on Rastafari, 200

Nigeria: comparison between Jamaica and, 35, 36; Yoruba Christianity in, 45
Nine night: ritual in Revivalism, 43–44, 64
Njia: ritual, 121
'Non-traditional tradition': Gilroy's concept of, 14
Nurturing role: baby father and the, 131, 132
Nyabinghi: similarities between Revivalism and, xi

Obya: defining, 40
Orisa, 46
Outside child: fathers' relationship with the, 134–135, 136, 137

Pan-Africanism: and Afrocentricity, 12, 32; race and, 12, 36
Paternity, 187, 188; and teenage pregnancy, 130–134
Paternity tests: and proof of fatherhood, 124–125
Patterson, Orlando: and the 'amnesiac blow' of slavery, 15
Pentecostalism: Jamaica, 136; cultural pluralism and, 221; Jamaicanization of, 163
People's National Party (PNP), 201
Planno, Mortima: and Rastafari, 104
Poet: Goodison on the role of the, 22
Power: African religion and, 118–119; fire and, 25–26; gender and, 127–128. *See also* Knowledge and Spiritual power
Price, Richard: and the Creativity vs Continuity debate, xii, xiii, 27–29; critique of, 34
Private space: concept of, 167–169
Process: in development of an African-American culture, xii
Property: concept of, 167–169, 175
Property rights: marriage and, 190–191, 192
Providers: babyfathers as, 131, 132
Pukumina: African retention in, 25

'Quest fever': theme in Goodison's poetry, 10, 19–20, 21

Race: and identity, 68–70
Rastafari: and Africa, 29, 31–33, 57–59, 120; in African Jamaican culture, xvi–xvii; beliefs, 35; charisma and, 43; and disorder, 83, 89–95; dreadlocks in, 42; and fire, 26; and folk intellectuals, 112–113; and ganja, 179, 199–200, 207; legitimization of, 179; and music, 103–106; religion, 37–39; and salt, 57, 58; and self-actualization, 120; similarities to Revivalism, xi; spiritual in, 37, 39–40, 41–42; subversion of English, 96–98; in Zimbabwe, 14
Rastafari philosophy: source of, 118–123
'Ready-Made': and paternity, 125–129, 135–136; phenomena, xvii
Rebel Destiny: critique of Herskovits's, 34
Rebellions: slave, 84
Reggae: emergence of, 102; evolution of, 14–15
Religion: African retention in Caribbean, 25, 58–59; cultural pluralism and, 220–221; Myal, 84; and slave resistance, 155
Repatriation: movement, 85; Rastafari and, 31–32
Report on the Rastafari Movement in Kingston, Jamaica, 29, 200
Revivalism, 87; beliefs, 35; cultural pluralism and practise of, 221; Holy Spirit in, 54; and Jamaican music, 101; similarities with Aladura Movement, xvi, 28; similarities to Rastafari, xi; spiritual in, 37–38, 43–45
Rights of Passage: and Africa, 16
Ritual: death, 157–158; power of, 40–41, 46–47, 65

Roberts, George: and legitimization of visiting unions, 183–184
Robotham, Don: critique of cultural pluralism theory, 216
Rodney, Walter, 111, 201
Rubin, Vera: study on ganja, 202

Salt: symbolism in African worldview, 17, 26, 57, 58, 146
Santeria: spirit possession in, 42
Satan: in Christian cosmology, 38
Savage: defining, 123
Schwartz-Bart, Simone: African theme in work of, 20; and the search for a Caribbean identity, 75–77
'Scientist': defining, 40; DeLaurence, 56
Scott, David: critique of Herskovits, 34
Seaga, Edward: on Pukumina, 25
Season of Adventure: and concept of a pre-modern past, 15
Selassie, Emperor Haile: crowning of, 86; and Rastafari, 33, 37, 99, 103
Self-actualization: religion and Rastafari, 118
Separation: in European cosmology, 73–75. *See also* Differentiation
Sexual initiation: among adolescents, 184–185
Sexuality: adolescent, 186, 194
Sharpe, Sam, 84, 119
Single Convention on Narcotic Drugs (1961): and the decriminalization of ganja, 212
Ska: growth of, 101–102
Slave society: family formation in, 156–157
Slavery: and the 'amnesiac blow', 10, 15; and the concept of 'cultural nakedness', 4; and the loss of tradition, 9
Smith, M.G.: and cultural pluralism, 216; and the cultural process, xii; study on Rastafari, 200
Smith, Raymond: and the Afro-Guyanese family, 183
Social mores: and order, 151–152

Social order: Anansi's subversion of, 147
Social integration: Jamaica and the problem of, 216–217
Social relations: defining, xii–xiii
Socialization: agencies of, 152–153
Sons of Negus: and Jamaican popular music, 103
Spider god. *See* Anansi
Spirit: as extreme force, 146
Spirit possession, 42–43
Spirit world: Jamaican, 36–45; Yoruba, 45–53
Spiritual: defining, 37
Spiritual power: acquisition of, 54–56; Jamaicans and, 53; Yoruba and, 47, 53
St Georges College: class divisions at, 7
Stability, in conjugal unions, 186
Status of children: legal, 191
Stockert, Helga: and *Family Property (Rights of Spouses) Act*, 1999, 190
Stone, Carl: study on ganja, 204
Storytelling: Caribbean, 62–67

Taki, 119
Teachings of Njia, 12
Teenage pregnancy: and paternity, 130–134
'The African Presence in Caribbean Literature', 17
Thistlewood diaries: portrayal of slave community in, 155–158
Ti-Jean: symbolic ambiguity of, 75–77
Tosh, Peter: and Jamaican popular music, 98, 103; and ganja, 202
Tradition: Gilroy's definition of, 4; role of, 35
Transcending Time, Transforming Cultures, 3
Treason Felony Act: Claudius Henry and the, 93
Trickster deity. See Trickster hero
Trickster hero: in African-Caribbean folk culture, xvi–xvii, 65–67; and ambiguity, 75; Rastafari as, 83, 95, 100

Trinidad and Tobago (T&T): race in, 88
Turner, Victor: on West African culture, xiii
Twelve Tribes of Israel, 99
Two Jamaicas: and the African-Jamaican worldview, xvi; and cultural pluralism, 216–222

United Negro Improvement Association (UNIA), 85
United States of America: Cuba relations, 66–67; ganja in the, 198
United States Bureau of Narcotics: and ganja, 198–199
University of the West Indies: study on Rastafari, 200
Urbanization: and breakdown of values, 164–165

Value systems: breakdown of, 163–165; slavery and formation of, 159–162
Values: loss of, 151–152; transmission of, 152–153
Violence: in Jamaica, 81–83, 149–150
Virginity: value of, 187, 186
Visiting relationships, 131, 143, 144; defining, 183, 184–185. *See also* Casual relationships, Common-law unions, Conjugal bonding, Family, Marriage and Visiting relationships
Visiting unions. *See* Visiting relationships

Walcott, Derek: and Africa in West Indian heritage, 16
Warner-Lewis, Maureen: and the Creativity vs Continuity debate, 27–28; research on African retentions in the Caribbean, 2–3, 22–26; on salt in African tradition, 17
Water: symbolism, 146
West: and racism, 13
West Africa: similarities between worldview of Jamaicans and, xvi

Western hegemony: and Caribbean history, 107–110
White identity, 9
White supremacy: in colonial Jamaica, 87–88
Whites. *See* Europeans
Williams, Eric: and capitalism, 86
Witches: in Yoruba worldview, 51
Womb: in African worldview, 23–24
Word: power of the, 18. *See also* Language
Worldview: concept of, xiv–xvi; defining, 180

Yoruba language: Lewis' analysis of the, 5
Yoruba Christianity, 45–53, 58–61
Yoruba Nigerians: comparison between Jamaicans and, 35, 36; spirit world of, 45–53
Yoruba worldview: similarities between Jamaican and, 55–61
Yemoja festival, 46

Zimbabwe: Rastafari in, 14